BEYOND the COURTROOM

By the Same Author

India's Legal System: Can It Be Saved?

Before Memory Fades: An Autobiography

The State of the Nation

God Save the Hon'ble Supreme Court

Harmony amidst Disharmony: The Indian Framework
(The Arbitration Series—Volume 1)

Harmony amidst Disharmony: The International Framework
(The Arbitration Series—Volume 2)

You Must Know Your Constitution

Legally Speaking

BEYOND the COURTROOM

Reflections on Law, Constitution, and Nationhood

FALI S. NARIMAN

Compiled by
Subhash Sharma

HAY HOUSE INDIA
New Delhi • London • Sydney
Carlsbad, California • New York City

Hay House Publishers (India) Pvt Ltd
Muskaan Complex, Plot No. 3, B-2, Vasant Kunj, New Delhi – 110070, India

Hay House LLC, P.O. Box 5100, Carlsbad, CA 92018-5100, USA
Hay House UK Ltd, 1st Floor, Crawford Corner, 91-93 Baker Street, London W1U 6QQ, UK
Hay House Australia Publishing Pty Ltd, 18/36 Ralph St., Alexandria NSW 2015, Australia

Email: contact@hayhouse.co.in
Website: www.hayhouse.co.in

First published by Hay House India, 2025
Reprint, 2026
14 13 12 11 10 9 8 7 6 5

ISBN 978-93-6611-429-3
ISBN 978-93-66118-45-1 (eBook)

Printed at Thomson Press India Private Limited

FSC www.fsc.org MIX Paper | Supporting responsible forestry FSC® C010615

Hay House is committed to a sustainable future for our business, our readers and our planet. This book is made from Forest Stewardship Council® certified paper.

Contents

Section IV
Law

Section V
Arbitration

Section I
NATION

1

The State of the Nation[1]

The managing director of the International Monetary Fund, Christine Lagarde, once said that there are three types of countries in the world:

1. Those that are growing
2. Those that are not growing, and
3. Those that are shirking (i.e., not working)

The trouble about India is that we presently have all three types located at different places in this vast subcontinent, so which part of it should I mention? If one has to generalise and say something about the nation as a whole and its present condition, I cannot do better than quote the famous Irish playwright and critic George Bernard Shaw. Being a playwright, he once went to see a Shakespearean play at a theatre. When he came out, he was asked how he enjoyed it, and this was his reaction: "The play was a great success. But the audience was a failure."

Applying this typically Shavian sentence to current affairs, I would say: "The nation is a great success, but it is the people (in some parts of it) that are a bit of a failure." This is reminiscent of the apocryphal story of the Great Lord Brahma. The nations of the world made representations to him, protesting against giving to this vast subcontinent the longest of rivers, the highest of mountains, the deepest of oceans, and the densest of forests and thus discriminating against all other countries of the world. And Lord Brahma smiled and said: “Yes, you are right. But to balance everything, see the people that I have put there!”

A nation is not merely about geography or history but about the people that inhabit it. And there are simply far too many—far too many disparate people. There were only 330 million people when India gained independence and when the Constitution of India was drafted. It was far more manageable then. We are now 1.3 billion-plus and it is expected that the growth of the population will not stop till the year 2030. This, then, is the mother of all problems. Our infrastructure—never great at the best of times—has simply not kept pace with our exploding population. And along with all this, there is so much hypocrisy as well, illustrated by the barber’s story. Most of you must have heard the barber’s story, which is already doing the rounds on the internet.

While cutting a cabinet minister’s hair, the official barber asks: “Sir, what’s this Swiss Bank issue?”

The minister shouts: “You are cutting my hair or conducting an inquiry? Stop asking!”

Barber: “Sorry sir, I just asked.”

The next day, while giving a haircut to another minister, the barber once again asks: “Sir, what’s this black money issue?”

This minister also shouted at him: “Why have you asked me this question?”

Barber said: “Sorry sir, I just asked.”

The following day, the CBI (Central Bureau of Investigation) sends a team to interrogate the barber.

CBI: “Are you an agent of Baba Ramdev?”

Barber: “No, sir.”

CBI: “Are you the agent of Anna Hazare?”

Barber: “No sir.”

CBI: “Then while cutting hair, why do you ask these VIPs about Swiss Bank and black money issues?”

Barber: “Sir, I don’t know why, but when I ask about Swiss Bank or black money, their hair stands up straight and that helps me to cut the hair easily. That’s why I keep asking.”

On a serious note, as I see it, Prime Minister Jawaharlal Nehru's vision of democracy for our nation as an experiment of unity amidst diversity has been only partially successful. You will remember what he wrote in his book *The Discovery of India,* which inspired many students of my generation when we were in college or university. Writing in the quiet seclusion of a British prison in 1944 (during Nehru's ninth term of imprisonment for revolting against the British), he contemplated "the variety and unity" of India.

> "In ancient and medieval times, the idea of the modern nation was non-existent, and feudal, religious, racial, and cultural bonds had more importance. Yet I think that at almost any time in recorded history, an Indian would have felt more or less at home in any part of India and would have felt as a stranger and alien in any other country. He would certainly have felt less of a stranger in countries, which had partly adopted his culture or religion. Those, such as Christians, Jews, Parsees, or Moslems, who professed a religion of non-Indian origin or, coming to India, settled down there, became distinctively Indian in the course of a few generations. Indian converts to some of these religions never ceased to be Indians on account of a change of their faith. They were looked upon in other countries as Indians and foreigners, even though there might have been a community of faith between them."[2]

This was Nehru's vision of our nation. It approximated to that of his friend, the British author E. M. Forster, who had visited the subcontinent. But he was a bit critical of Indian democracy and gave it only two cheers, not the customary three: "So, two cheers for Indian democracy: one because it admits variety and two because it permits criticism. Two cheers are quite enough: there is no occasion to give it three."[3] This is why Nehru's vision of democracy in this great nation has only partially succeeded.

It was with the promulgation of India's Constitution on 26 January 1950 that the Indian *nation* was truly born, bringing, for the first time in over 2,000 years, geographical and political unity in a vast subcontinent. Not since the time of Chandragupta Maurya and his immediate successors[4] had Hindustan been under one ruler or government.

A contemporary assessment of the record of the first sixty-five years in the life of a nation is bound to be faulty. It lacks perspective. It does not have the historical advantage of time and distance. Yet, over the past six-and-a-half decades, the Indian experiment with unity amidst diversity has been continuing—a major plus point during a period when the country has witnessed much economic, political, and social upheaval, but during which it has also experienced material progress with remarkable achievements in the fields of medicine, science, and technology. However, we have not yet resolved the complexities that lie buried in the great but elusive doctrine of equality spelt out in Article 14, which provides that: "The State shall not deny to any person equality before the law or the equal protection of the laws within the territory of India."

The tension between the commitment to non-discrimination as well as to equality was poignantly expressed by Prime Minister Nehru during the debate in Parliament at the time of the Constitution First Amendment Bill (in May 1951):

> "We cannot have equality because in trying to attain equality, we come up against some principles of equality . . . We cannot have equality because we cannot have non-discrimination because if you think in terms of giving a lift up to those who are down, and out, you are somehow affecting the present status quo undoubtedly. Therefore, you are said to be discriminating because you are affecting the present status quo. Therefore, if this argument is correct, then we cannot make any major change in that respect because every change means a change in the status quo, whether economic or in any sphere of public or private activity. Whatever law you may make, you have to make some change somewhere. Therefore, we have to come to grips with this subject in some other way."[5]

Over the past sixty-plus years, we have not yet "come to grips with this subject." To what extent should the claim based on merit and on the fundamental right to equality be ignored? How far does our document of governance, truly interpreted, direct us to go? How soon are we to atone for the oppression of the lower castes for centuries? Should we go on equalising under a regime of enforced downward uniformity? And for how long? These questions keep surfacing periodically, but the answers given are never quite satisfactory or convincing.

Some time ago, one of America's youngest college presidents, Anthony Marx, was on a visit to India and he provided some home truths about the elusive doctrine of equality. He was then president of the Amherst College, which was established in the United States way back in the year 1821. In an interview with a national newspaper in Delhi, he said that his college Amherst, supports 64 per cent of its students with financial aid—the highest number in any US college, and that colleges like Yale, Princeton, and Harvard, which have been traditionally catering to white privileged students, have now been realising the social need to reach out to the blacks, browns, and the less privileged.

Anthony Marx then spoke about talent and said that those who have had privileged backgrounds are often visibly talented, but that is only because they have had exposure. The obsession about merit is really only one facet of better exposure, and the truly meritorious are often the ones who are better exposed! Young people, who are poor, are not talented because they are not exposed in an obvious way, and competition, by itself, simply does not necessarily bring the best results.

Anthony Marx also spoke about the history of inequality in America, about how in the United States neighbourhoods have poor schools and bad teaching, whilst rich neighbourhoods have very good schools, and the divide is sharp. There is a history of inequality in America, and he emphasised the need for higher education to be an equaliser: "No society, not American or Indian, can progress with inequality. If you have affirmative action in education, it is a win-win situation for everyone, for the underprivileged and the economy."

Anthony Marx had spent some years in South Africa where black students had been subjected to apartheid education, designed to keep them down. And he says that when these young people were given high-quality courses for a year, the same students who were kept down started doing well. Nelson Mandela, the wisest of all living statesmen, once said: "We need to make sure that the doors of learning are always kept open." Wise words. Words that need retelling.

We in this country also "need to make sure that the doors of learning are always kept open." Because even in the year 2012-13, the representation of the underprivileged in public employment has continued to remain grossly disproportionate when compared to those belonging to the more privileged classes. As academic Ralph Bunche[6] once said: "Inalienable rights can never be enjoyed posthumously!"

However, on the other side of the argument, there is the spectre of agitated public opinion, which cannot be ignored: The judges, who have the final say in all constitutional matters, have interpreted compensatory discrimination clauses in our Constitution differently at different times. A perceptive commentator has said that (in this area) "the law does not evolve—it meanders!"[7] On occasions, the courts have prodded and energised governments to live up to their constitutional commitment to alleviate the lot of the downtrodden, but the ground rules have kept changing. A sympathetic critic Prof. Marc Galanter who visits India often, explains why:

> "In an area of law founded on the constitutional embrace of conflicting principles, it should not be expected that courts would provide an enduring synthesis that transcends and encompasses them and settles disputed issues with finality. Rather, we would expect—if the courts are at all representatives of the larger society—some ambiguity and vacillation. And the courts have vacillated, sometimes emphasising compensatory discrimination; other times, formal equity; sometimes, rectification of communal disparities, at other times, non-

> recognition of communal units . . . a number of factors operate to relax the pressure for consistency and economy of doctrines, not all of them reconcilable, which reflect the tensions between antagonistic principles."[8]

Amidst "the tensions between antagonistic principles," one thing is certain: so long as poverty, dire poverty, continues to stalk the land and so long as gross disparities between the very rich and the very poor get accentuated (as they have in recent years), the ideal of an egalitarian society envisaged in our basic document of governance remains an evanescent dream. Whatever the nation's karma, our founding fathers cannot be faulted for a lack of idealism, nor can providence. It is not in our stars but in ourselves that we are thus. It is not because of our Constitution, but despite its provisions, that as a nation, we have failed to fulfil what were naïvely assumed to be achievable goals. We the people of India boldly abolished untouchability in our Constitution, but after more than sixty years of its working, we have not been able to eliminate it from our hearts!

There is another problem. When members of India's Constituent Assembly first resolved to dedicate themselves, in all humility, to the service of the country and its people, Dr S. Radhakrishnan (later president of India), who had seconded the resolution, warned that "when power outstrips ability, we will fall on evil days." Power has overtaken ability. We have fallen on evil days. There is a crisis of competence along with a conspicuous lack of integrity in almost all fields of activity, more markedly in the political. And the entire country is submerged in a tidal wave of corruption. The public is fed up with politicians as a class, not only in India but in other parts of the world as well. In that delightful British television series, *Yes Minister*, there is an opinion expressed, which, if it had been recorded in a serious programme, would have rung alarm bells. It said:

> "When civil servants will remove politicians on grounds of incompetence, it would empty the House of Commons and

> remove the Cabinet, and that would be the end of democracy, but it would be the beginning of responsible government!"[9]

I believe that what has sustained the freedom enjoyed by our people has been basic horse sense, which has been defined as the good sense that horses have in not betting on people! But, in a democracy, we have to bet on people, set store by them, and take to heart the decisions they make.

The most recent example has been the response of the government of the day to the growing pressure of public opinion stirred up by social activist Anna Hazare over the inordinate delay in the introduction of an effective Lokpal Bill in Parliament. In a government gazette notification issued on 9 April 2011, members of Hazare's team (or "Team Anna" as it is called) were officially associated with the drafting of the bill! That all this has so far come to naught is of little consequence; what is noteworthy and significant is the realisation that members of Parliament (once elected) can no longer be unresponsive to the views and protests of large sections of *We the People*.

Mercifully, despite tremendous odds, we have so far managed to pull through with our written Constitution, and we are still one nation. What we appear to have lost over the last sixty-plus years is the fine art of conserving the political freedom we had won and the spirit in which the Constitution itself was drafted—a spirit of accommodation and consensus, so wanting now in all fields of activity.

In the days of the Roman Empire (106-43 BC), Senator Cicero expounded his philosophy in ten short bullet points.

1. The poor: work and work.
2. The rich: exploit the poor.
3. The soldier: protects both.
4. The taxpayer: pays for all three.
5. The wanderer: rests for all four.

6. The drunk: drinks for all five.
7. The banker: robs all six.
8. The doctor: kills all seven.
9. The undertaker: buries all eight.
10. The lawyer (9) and politician (10): prosper happily on account of all the above.

This is not far from the truth in India, even today!

2

Roots of a Nation[10]

Louis Brandeis[11]—judge and jurist—used to say that "it is only when a nation has lawyers who understand the public interest and the changing needs of society that a country will have judges to provide social as well as legal justice." To support this statement, he used to tell the following story: At the end of the nineteenth century, when the nation of Montenegro (in the continent of Europe) had secured its independence, its ruler wanted his country to have a code of laws like other civilised nations. He requested a great scholar of the law (Bogigish, a professor at the University of Odessa) to prepare a code. The professor agreed, and he undertook the task, not by relying on law books or his own phenomenal legal knowledge, but he went out to live with the people of Montenegro for two long years, studying their customs and practices, familiarising himself with the "roots" of the nation. He then drafted a constitution for Montenegro and (as Brandeis put it): "The people respected it because it expressed the will of the people."[12]

This is how Mahatma Gandhi wanted India's Constitution to be written. But economist Shriman Narayan had already published a book in 1946 titled, *The Gandhian Constitution for Free India,* which had introduced, for the first time, the complete draft of an *indigenous* "Indian Constitution" with decentralised legislative, executive, and judicial bodies based on village panchayats. It also laid out a set of fundamental duties to go along with fundamental rights. The Mahatma then endorsed the author's proposal by contributing a foreword to the book.

However, this was *not* the way India's Constitution was fashioned—neither in the Brandeis way nor in the Shriman Narayan way! India's Constitution was fashioned in the manner in which ordinary laws are made. 296 members of India's Constituent Assembly[13]—a body elected on the basis of a very limited franchise—debated for nearly three years a draft Constitution, the text of which was prepared by India's Constitutional adviser, B. N. Rau.

Shortly after it was adopted, the Constitution First Amendment Act was steamrolled through India's Provisional Parliament in June 1951 by a then super-majoritarian Congress government amidst much opposition. An avowedly liberal Constitution had been transformed into a staid, pragmatic one. Tripurdaman Singh's book, *Sixteen Stormy Days*[14], contains a fascinating critique of this first amendment of India's Constitution which exposes the perils of having majoritarian national governments at the centre. [15]

In the Indian subcontinent, one unforgettable lesson about written constitutions has been that they *do not work on their own*. A special effort has to be made by those entrusted to work them, so that they do not collapse and flounder. Pakistan, an independent state, had been brought into existence by Britain's Parliament at the same time and in the same manner as independent India.[16] It also had its own Constituent Assembly, but before that body could produce a written constitution, it was summarily dissolved by Pakistan's governor-general. Then, six years later, a constitution of the "Islamic Republic of Pakistan" was pieced together in 1956, heralding a parliamentary system of government. However, shortly thereafter, it was abrogated by Pakistan's president without having the constitutional authority to do so. As a consequence, Pakistan (unlike India) had to undergo prolonged periods of martial law.

When India's Constituent Assembly was about to complete its task of finalising a Constitution in November 1949, the chairman of its Drafting Committee (Dr B. R. Ambedkar) addressed members saying that since the working of a written Constitution did not depend solely upon its text, he would refrain from discussing the merits "because I feel however good a Constitution may be, it may turn out to be bad because those who are called upon to work it happen to be a bad lot, and however bad a Constitution may be, it may turn out to be good if those who are called upon to work it happen to be a good lot.[17]"

The Constitution of India (1950) is one of the longest ever framed for an independent country. It contained 395 articles and eight schedules, occupying as many as 251 printed pages in the official edition. It has been added to and amended on 105 separate occasions[18] and yet it remains a highly centralised document. "Unity of the nation" has been mentioned up front in the Preamble[19], and the very first article described its structure: "INDIA (that is BHARAT) shall be a Union of States."

The length of the Constitution was not only due to the size of the country but also the problems of accommodating the points of view of representatives of people speaking different languages, observing different faiths, and at the same time, striving to transform a rigid, hierarchical social order into an egalitarian society. The chapter on Fundamental Rights (Part III) owed much to the standard-setting charter of the United Nations and the almost contemporaneous Universal Declaration of Human Rights, 1948.

The Constitution was (and remains even after 105 amendments) divided into twenty-two parts dealing with various aspects of the country's governance. In some places, it suffers from an excessive emphasis on detail, which could have been left to ordinary legislation. And it often also displays a *hybrid mixture of different, sometimes conflicting, concepts*. With more than thirty main indigenous languages and dialects from which to choose, the Constitution recognised English as one of the only two official languages. Among the fourteen regional languages then listed in the Eighth Schedule was Sanskrit, which, like Latin, is a dead language, spoken only in prayer.

The Preamble to the Constitution (by amendment) proclaimed India to be a *secular* republic, yet the chapter on Fundamental Rights continued to recognise and protect India's six main religions and nearly 200 "religious persuasions."

The Right to Equality was guaranteed (Article 14), and the state was prohibited from discriminating against any citizen on grounds of race, religion, caste, or place of birth. Yet the Constitution recognised and encouraged *compensatory discrimination* in favour of socially and educationally backward classes of citizens (Articles 15, 16, and 335); however, economic backwardness arising from dire poverty was not recognised as a basis for preferential treatment in educational institutions or public employment.

Whilst adopting adult suffrage as the basis for periodic elections to Parliament and state assemblies (Article 326) and abolishing special electoral rolls based on race, religion, caste, or sex, the Constitution also provided for the *reservation of seats* (in the House of the People and in the legislative assembly of every state) for Scheduled Castes and Scheduled Tribes (outcastes of Hindu society for centuries) (Article 326, 330, 332). Such reservation, though initially for ten years, has been extended indefinitely from time to time and remains in place.

Despite these seemingly disparate and contradictory provisions necessitated by social, historical, and political considerations, if there is one overriding concept discernible in India's Constitution, it is a concern for the *unity of the nation*.

The framers, in 1950, had undertaken an ambitious and noble enterprise, and their product pleased nearly everyone. There were, however, a few who were not impressed. A former chief minister of Karnataka, a down-to-earth politician, K. Hanumanthaiya, was disappointed with the work of the Constituent Assembly, and he complained: "We wanted the sweet notes of the veena, but we were given the music of an English band."

The parliamentary system of government set up under India's Constitution—"the music of an English band"—as Hanumanthaiya irreverently (though accurately) put it, is based on a clear-cut division of governmental functions: *executive, legislative,* and *judicial*—though not in watertight compartments.

At the centre, the union executive consisted (and consists) of the president of India (along with a vice-president, who presides over the Council of States), and a council of ministers with the prime minister at its head to "aid and advise" the president in the exercise of his functions. (There is, of course, a similar division of functions in the states.)[20]

The union legislature (Parliament) consisted (and consists) of the president at the head, with two houses of Parliament known as the Council of States and the House of the People. The Council of States (the Rajya Sabha) having 238 representatives of the states in India, elected by the elected members of the legislative assemblies of each state as well as representatives of union territories that are not fully-fledged states. (In addition, there are twelve members nominated by the president.) The House of the People (the Lok Sabha) consists of not more than 550 members, chosen by direct election from territorial constituencies in the states and union territories—the entire country being a Union of States.[21]

Importantly, the words "president" and "governor"—words that frequently occur in the Constitution—are euphemistic. They do not, in fact, mean the president acting on his own or the governor acting on his own. They mean the council of ministers at the centre, with the prime minister at its head, acting in the name of the president, and the council of ministers in each state, with a chief minister at its head, acting in the name of the governor.

The third part of the union—the *Union Judiciary*—consists of the Supreme Court of India, the final interpreter of the Constitution and the laws, and the final appellate authority from all decisions of high courts and tribunals (Articles 132, 134, 135, and 136). It is also the exclusive forum for deciding all federal disputes between the union and the states (Article 131).

Under India's Constitution, the power to promulgate ordinances (a law-making power) has been (designedly) conferred additionally on the executive, but only to be exercised when Parliament or state legislatures are not in session (which is for several months every year). In England, where the parliamentary system of government originated, the executive has no such power to legislate by ordinance except when a state of emergency is declared. The ordinance-making provisions in the Constitution (Articles 123 and 213) establish—at the very start—a tilt in the balance of powers and functions in India's Constitution: *they emphasise that it is the executive branch that is in the driving seat of government.* And, as if to stress the dominance of the executive, there is no period prescribed in India's Constitution for the duration of each session of Parliament and of state legislatures. It is left entirely to the governments (both at the centre and in the states) to decide as to when the houses of Parliament and state legislatures are to be summoned and for how long.

The Constitution thus envisages, both at the centre and in the states, an *all-powerful executive* with the prime minister and his council of ministers (at the centre) and the chief minister and his council of ministers in the states. It is the executive that sets the agenda for all legislative business. When the elected bodies are not in session, it is the executive that is empowered to make laws (under the ordinance-making power), and it is the executive that takes all action pertaining to subjects within the legislative competence of the legislatures.[22]

Under India's Constitution, the executive is dependent for its continuance on the confidence of the elected members of the legislatures, i.e., the House of the People (Lok Sabha) at the centre and state legislative assemblies in the states. The executive remains omnipotent only as long as the council of ministers retain the confidence of the elected representatives. Once that confidence is lost, the government in office has to resign, and fresh elections have to be called. This is the essence of what is known as *ministerial responsibility*—a doctrine at the heart of the parliamentary system of government.

Subject to ministerial responsibility to the elected legislative bodies, the executive can do all that the legislatures can do: an aspect that was highlighted within a few years of the Constitution being promulgated. In 1955, it was held by the Supreme Court of India that the Constitution of India—unlike other Westminster-type constitutions elsewhere—*did not recognise the doctrine of separation of powers "in its absolute rigidity."*[23] Howsoever powerful the executive may be, *the purse strings are controlled by the legislatures (Parliament and state legislatures), and not by the executive.* All revenues of the Government of India and all other monies received by and on behalf of the Government of India have to be credited to the Consolidated Fund of India (Article 266), as is the case in the states. No monies can be withdrawn from the Consolidated Fund of India (or the consolidated fund of a state) except under appropriation made by enacted law. Importantly, this cannot be done by the executive in the exercise of its ordinance-making power (Article 114). Expenses of governments can only be met by means of a bill introduced in the elected House of the People (Lok Sabha) in Parliament (as well as in the elected legislative assembly in the states). Such a bill has to provide for appropriation out of the Consolidated Fund of the union (or of the consolidated fund of the state) and has to be passed by the people's elected representatives.

The constitutional authority that supervises all financial matters is the comptroller and auditor general of India—a personage who exercises a restraining influence on the all-powerful executive. The CAG is appointed by the president by warrant under his hand and seal and can be removed from office only in like manner and on like grounds as a judge of the Supreme Court, i.e., on a motion passed by a two-thirds majority of members present and voting in Parliament, not otherwise. In the Constituent Assembly, the comptroller and auditor general of India was described by Dr Ambedkar as "the most important officer in the Constitution." He still is.

The most significant feature of the Constitution of India is the area, extent, and nature of the jurisdiction of India's Supreme Court; it is all-pervasive. Laws enacted by India's Parliament and by state legislatures, as well as all executive actions taken in the name of the president at the centre and in the name of the governor in the states, are finally and authoritatively interpreted (and corrected) by the courts—the high courts, and ultimately by the Supreme Court of India. The law declared by the Supreme Court of India is binding on all courts and authorities in the country (Article 141), though not on the Supreme Court itself (larger benches of the Supreme Court can review and revisit its prior decisions). It is the ultimate court of appeal in all civil and criminal cases. Its writ extends to the two million square miles of Indian territory and over its (now) 1.4 billion inhabitants (India was far more governable in 1950 when there were only 330 million people!).

There is virtually no area of legislative, executive, and administrative activity that is beyond the highest court's scrutiny. But ever since 1950, in the process of adjudication of centre-state disputes under Article 131 (by India's Supreme Court), there has been a lurking fear of a Balkanised and fragmented India. And it is for this reason that a centrist bias has dominated judicial thinking, as well as decision-making, to uphold and preserve the union.

Under the Constitution, courts are empowered to invalidate not only executive orders but also laws that violate any one or more of the fundamental rights guaranteed in Part III of the Constitution (Part III is India's Bill of Rights). *But are they also empowered to adjudicate on the validity of constitutional amendments passed with the requisite special majority and following the procedure prescribed in Article 368* (the article that authorises amendments to the Constitution)? On that great question, the Constitution is silent. With one single political party almost consistently returned to power at each election since 1952—and often returned with an overwhelming majority—the judges had plumbed the depths of silence in one of the world's longest constitutions, looking for some limitations on the amending power. After a prolonged and tortuous quest,[24] they found it (by a majority of 7:6) in a case decided only in April 1973, where one of the justices delivering judgement in that case had said: "The largest bench sat for the longest time to decide issues of grave moment not only to the future of this country but to the future of democracy itself." The case was titled *His Holiness Kesavananda Bharati* vs. *State of Kerala*[25] though it is better known as *Kesavananda* or as the *Fundamental Rights Case*.

The power to declare the law, a great American judge once said, carries with it the power, and within limits, the duty to make law where none exists. In reading implied limitations in the amending power, the majority in the Supreme Court (7:6) had certainly made new law; it had been criticised as an assertion of naked political power in the guise of judicial interpretation. Frankly, it was. By propounding the basic structure theory, the guardians of the Constitution had, at one bound, become guardians over the Constitution. Constitutional adjudicators had assumed the role of constitutional governors—a merited criticism. With one single political party (the Congress) having an overwhelming majority of members in Parliament, India would have moved into a state of grave constitutional crisis. But then, fate intervened; at times, fate helps to preserve a Constitution. In June 1975, Mrs Indira Gandhi (then prime minister) lost an election petition filed against her in the Allahabad High Court, and her election was as a member of Parliament. The extraordinary had happened—a serving prime minister had been unseated in Parliament. Whilst her appeal in the Supreme Court was pending, the Constitution 39th Amendment Act, 1975 was hastily drafted and even more hastily passed.

The Constitution 39th Amendment Act provided that, notwithstanding any order of any court, the election of a prime minister could never and would never be deemed to be invalid or void. The judgement of Justice Jagmohan Lal Sinha of the Allahabad High Court unseating Mrs Gandhi as a member of Parliament was attempted to be reversed by a constitutional amendment! Fortunately, India's highest court resisted this crude attempt, relying for the first time after *Keshavananda* (1973) on the basic structure theory of the Constitution.[26]

In *Indira Gandhi* vs. *Raj Narain* (1975), a Constitution bench of the Supreme Court held, under compulsions of what could only be characterised as a monstrous law, that *free and fair elections* were a fundamental part of the Constitution—so fundamental as to be beyond the reach of the amending power. This decision constitutes the high-water mark in the assertion of the court's judicial power in the presence of a very determined majoritarian regime. If the pernicious clauses of the 39th Constitution Amendment Act had been upheld, Indian democracy would not have long survived. The basic structure theory was the response of an anxious and activist court to the experience of the working of India's Constitution during the nation's first twenty-five years.

Fortunately, Parliament itself then endorsed and recognised the validity of the basic structure theory! By the Constitution 44th Amendment Act, 1978, Parliament (acting in its constituent capacity) declared that the fundamental right to life and liberty guaranteed by Article 21 of the Constitution could never be suspended, even during a period of emergency, because the right to life and liberty (safeguarded under Article 21) was *basic* to the constitutional framework. The basic structure theory is now an indissoluble part of the constitutional framework.

There is yet another aspect. The Constitution provided (and continues to provide) that appointments of high court judges and judges of the Supreme Court are to be made by the "president of India," which, under our Constitution, means the president of India acting on the advice of the prime minister and his council of ministers (in practice, on the advice of the law minister). In addition, the Constitution provided (and continues to provide) that appointments of judges (to the Supreme Court and high courts) can only be made "after consultation with the chief justice of India and such other judges of the Supreme Court or high courts" as the president (i.e., the government of the day) may determine (Articles 124 and 217 of the Constitution).

In the past, as a matter of convention (though not as a matter of constitutional compulsion), the advice of the chief justice of India had been invariably accepted by the government then in office. However, in 1981, a bench of seven judges of the Supreme Court (by a majority of 4:3) in a case that came to be later known as the *First Judge's case*[27] held that even after constitutional consultation, the last word in appointments would remain with the executive, i.e., with the Government of India. This was held on a textual reading of Article 217. But power grows by what it feeds on. No sooner had it been so held by the Constitution bench of the Supreme Court in the *First Judge's case* (1981) than the central government began to ignore the advice and recommendations of the chief justice of India as to the selection of judges to be appointed in the higher judiciary (i.e., in the high courts and in the Supreme Court of India). The Government of India then proceeded to appoint judges to the high courts in a manner as though they were effectively on probation, their tenure being extended from three to six months at a time. Although Article 222 of the Constitution enabled the Government of India to transfer a judge from one high court to another ("after consultation with the Chief Justice of India"), it had been a settled practice that this could be done only for administrative exigencies. But after the majority decision of 1981 (4:3), transfers of judges were affected for punitive reasons as well, where, for instance, a particular judge had rendered a decision unfavourable to the government of the day.

These aberrations were challenged before the Supreme Court of India. Fortunately, the challenges were all upheld by successive benches of nine judges in the years 1993 and 1998.[28] The 1981 decision was overruled. The judges now said that a Constitution was not to be interpreted literally and a purposive construction was to be preferred. All of this recalls the same old adage (suitably adapted) that "power (wheresoever it resides) grows by what it feeds on!"

What of the Future?

In India's Constitution, as enacted after considerable debate and also with much acrimony, it was decided that both Hindi as well as English should be national languages in India—not in an attempt to anglicise the people of India but only to keep the north and south together. In other words, to preserve the identity of "One Nation." Besides, India's entire legal system was originally an English transplant with Anglo-Saxon roots. Introduced by the British in India, it had grown over the years, being nourished in Indian soil. What was intended by the British to be a solid English oak had, over the years, turned into a large banyan tree whose serial roots descended to become new trunks. India's Constitution, along with the entire legal system, is now *rooted* in Indian soil.

On the eve of the day that we now annually celebrate as Constitution Day, Dr B. R. Ambedkar (regarded as the father of the Constitution) expressed very serious misgivings. On 25 November 1949, he said in India's Constituent Assembly (he also went on to make a prediction that has since proved prophetic):

> "We must begin by acknowledging the fact that there is complete absence of two things in Indian society. One of these is equality. On the social plane, we have in India a society based on the principle of graded inequality which means elevation for some and degradation for others. On the economic plane, we have a society in which there are some who have immense wealth as against many who live in abject poverty.
>
> On the 26th of January, we are going to enter into a life of contradictions. In politics, we will have equality and in social and economic life we will have inequality.
>
> How long shall we continue to deny equality in our social and economic life?"[29]

For the past seventy-five years, the troubling question remains unanswered.

Besides, a constitution is all about politics. And the real problem with politics in India, as in other truly democratic countries of the world, is its unpredictability. James Reston, the doyen of twentieth-century American journalists, started his newspaper career as a sports writer. Some years before he died, he told the *Washington Post* that he preferred sports to politics because: "at the end of the day, you know who has won; in politics, you have to wait sixty years to see how it all comes out."

The 1.4 billion people of India have waited, not sixty but seventy-five years and it is still not clear how it will all come out! Only one thing is predictable, only one thing is certain: India's Constitution as adopted in 1950 (and as amended from time to time) has survived.

God willing (and humans equally willing), it will continue, but only if we keep working it the way Dr Ambedkar had prescribed.[30] In other words, only if those who are called upon to work the Constitution continue to remain *a good lot!*

Democracy in India: Strengths and Weaknesses[31]

I cannot think of democracy in India without recalling Pandit Jawaharlal, its founder. My first darshan of Panditji was more than seventy years ago when I heard him speak at an open-air function in faraway Rangoon (now Yangon), the place where I was born. I was in college in Bombay then and was visiting my parents. Panditji spoke (I cannot remember the subject) with such intensity and such disarming frankness that it became for me a memorable event. I felt instinctively drawn towards him. Over the years, after listening to and reading what Panditji's detractors have said about him, especially after his death, I am still drawn towards the great man, principally because he truly believed in the dicey concept of democracy. To believe in Indian democracy today requires tremendous faith and unbounded enthusiasm, and Panditji had these qualities in ample measure. Though he never wavered in his conception of political democracy, which was freedom for all individuals under the rule of law, his ideas about economic democracy underwent a sea change over the years.

The great Harold Laski was Panditji's professor when he was studying in England, and Laski's perception of Nehru was that he was a *thinker*. Panditji's colleague (or his political rival, if you will), Sardar Vallabhbhai Patel, whose 125th birth anniversary was celebrated with much aplomb a few years ago, was a doer, and it is a stark fact of modern Indian history that the establishment and survival of our nascent democracy in the 1940s and 1950s—critical years after independence—owes as much to the thinker as to the doer.

Lord Meghnad Desai (also a product of Gujarat), a professor emeritus of economics and a keen student of political history, in his book *Divided by Democracy*[32], has contrasted India and Pakistan by one single fortuitous divider: living long.

Nehru and Patel nursed and brought India's democracy to fruition by just remaining alive for the first sixteen years after independence. Unfortunately for Pakistan's democracy, its great leaders Muhammad Ali Jinnah and Liaquat Ali Khan (who also believed in democratic ideals) died soon after Pakistan's independence. But what Nehru and Patel had was more than mere longevity; they both had a deep personal commitment to democracy. If India did not go the way of Burma (now Myanmar), Pakistan, Nigeria, Ghana, or Zimbabwe, it was due to the happy accident that Prime Minister Nehru saw to it that elections—the first requirement for democracy—were periodically held every five years. Nehru was the first post-colonial leader who not only led a large country but who stayed a constant democrat. With nearly two decades of democratic leadership at its start, India has become addicted to democracy. And for this reason alone, I believe our democracy has come to stay.

It is sometimes said that the system of parliamentary democracy we have adopted is an alien one and it does not suit our Indian ethos. This is not true. Each country must live out its own history, and India's history has been one of domination from outside forces—first the Mughal Empire for 250 years and then the British occupation and conquest which lasted a couple of centuries more. Yet from the earliest stages of discussion on the form of self-government, Indian opinion was overwhelmingly in favour of adopting a system in which the executive was responsible to an elected legislature.

The first non-official attempt at drafting an Indian Constitution was made way back in the year 1895 under the inspiration of Lokmanya Balgangadhar Tilak. It was known as the Constitution of India Bill, 1895. In its first chapter, it envisaged a Parliament of India and an electoral system in which every citizen had one vote.

Thirty years later came another attempt at Constitution-making. Under the chairmanship of Sir Tej Bahadur Sapru, India's political leaders prepared a bill providing for self-government and sent it to England. The Labour Party, which was then in power in the UK, was responsive. Its leaders introduced the Commonwealth of India Bill, 1925, in Britain's Parliament, which also provided for a parliamentary system of government. The bill passed its first reading in the House of Commons and was ordered to be printed. But the Labour Party lost its majority in the House of Commons soon after, and Indian aspirations were set back for nearly twenty more years.

It is not true that the Westminster model was foisted on us by the British. Traditionally, the goal of all Indian leaders of the past had always been for a parliamentary system of government. The importance of an elected Parliament, elected by the people, lies not only in how it functions (it does not function at all well today), but simply in the fact that it exists. The great constitutional historian of the Commonwealth, Sir Ivor Jennings, used to say that "dogs might bark in Parliament, but if there were no Parliament to which the government is responsible, the people might bite." This emphasises the importance of a parliamentary system of democracy.

But then why has our parliamentary system of democracy not worked? I think this is not the right question. The question should be: "Why have we failed to work a system that guarantees (as no other system) a free and democratic way of life?

It worked, and it worked well for the first nineteen years after independence. What changed since then? I think the answer lies in the fact that it ceased to work well the moment politics in this country became immoral and unprincipled. We have not been able to work the system, and we cannot work any system unless we reinject some degree of morality into politics.

We Indians are brilliant. We have great talent, but we also have one super-failing which is that we do not have the will to recognise our failings. We must always have a scapegoat for our failures. If we cannot run a system, it must be because there is something wrong with the system, never anything wrong with ourselves.

In our part of the Indian subcontinent, our parliamentary democracy has come of age, and I believe that it has come to stay. Democracy as a concept means different things to different people in different parts of the world. It is a variable concept. But do remember that democracy corrodes very fast, and it corrodes because most people don't care very much about it—neither in India nor elsewhere.

The European Parliament, which has the largest transnational democratic electorate in the world (375 million voters), has been directly elected every five years since 1979 by universal suffrage. In the very first election of 1979, they had a turnout of well over 60 per cent, but the turnout at all successive elections has kept declining. It was 40 per cent at the last election held a couple of years ago. This is even though the European Parliament matters more now than it ever did and has far more powers than when it first started.

Whilst speaking of democracy in the United States of America, Ralph Waldo Emerson compared it to an unsophisticated raft that is put out into angry seas. "This is a raft," he said, "which would never sink, but then your feet are always in water." Democracy is a messy business—unpredictable occasionally tragic, often frustrating, and sometimes plainly ludicrous. It is incompetent but fortunately, the sort of tolerable incompetence which is not threatening. Nobody quite knows how democracy works. The most readable historian of the twentieth century, Will Durant, described it as the best of all forms of government "because it requires the widest spread of intelligence," but then he perceptively added, "it is deficient because we forgot to make ourselves intelligent when we made ourselves sovereign!" Former prime minister of the United Kingdom, Winston Churchill, called it "the worst system of government in the world," but added the rider, "except all those other systems."

"The worst of all systems" was what our neighbour in Pakistan, Zulfikar Ali Bhutto, always used to say but without Churchill's rider. I had the good fortune to know the late Piloo Mody, one of the founding members of the Swatantra Party. He had gone to visit Zulfikar Bhutto (who was his friend) when he was in prison in Pakistan, awaiting a death sentence for murder—a crime which many believed he was innocent of. When Piloo came back, he told me that in his conversation with Bhutto, the Pakistan leader nostalgically recalled "the noise and chaos of Indian democracy," regretting that he had made fun of it in the heyday of his political power. The noise and chaos of parliamentary democracy, he told Piloo, had a certain vitality; it had the strength and more importantly, the safety of numbers. No citizen's fate depended on the whims or dispensation of one man. Bhutto was right.

Look around you and you will see those who would cavil at the system of democracy we in India have. Or as some like to say, the "functioning anarchy" that is our government of the day. Look around the entire continent of Asia and beyond and then (I beseech you) count your blessings. But do remember that democracy is not enough, because democracy does not simply mean majority rule, but majority rule that is fair[33]—otherwise described as the rule of law.

What is the rule of law? Again, it was Jawaharlal Nehru who defined it when he inaugurated the Congress of the International Commission of Jurists in New Delhi in 1955. It was the most famous Congress of the International Court of Justice because it adopted what is now known as the Delhi Declaration of the Rule of Law. Speaking of the changes in society, Nehru said that the rule of law was not a static concept, but that it had to run closely to the "rule of life." And he gave the following example of the close interrelation of law and life as it is lived:

> "If the distinguished lawyers and jurists of Plato's day had met together—and they were very able men—they would have taken slavery for granted, human slavery. When they accepted slavery, no one challenged it. And yet later, it was not only challenged and condemned but uprooted practically all over the world because the social mind would not accept it."

This last bit of the quote, "the social mind would not accept it," reveals one of the other major challenges to Indian democracy and let me illustrate this challenge with an example.

In China, they have conceived and implemented the ambitious Three Gorges Project to tame the mighty and turbulent Yangtze River. It is already in operation and set to expand. It is already the largest hydropower plant in the world in terms of total installed capacity and annual power generation. It is also the world's largest water conservation facility. But it has inundated 653 square kilometres of densely populated area—the world's largest area inundated by a single project. The resettlement effort and the area to be inundated have been unprecedented in Chinese history. The inundation has affected more than 365 townships in 21 counties, cities, or districts and over one million people have been resettled. The reservoir, when expanded, will also inundate 31,000 hectares of farmland and require the relocation of 1,500 industrial and mining enterprises. An official reportedly said, "In spite of preliminary success, more difficulties are involved in the resettlement drive, but we are optimistic about its final success."

Some years ago, in an international arbitration, I asked a leading Swiss expert on dams who was visiting New Delhi what he thought of the Three Gorges Project. The Swiss expert thought for a while and said that it was a laudable venture because, after just two decades that it would take to build, commission, and operate it, fifty million people downstream would be able to cultivate their land without flooding and be assured of regular releases.

I asked him, "What about the over one million people who have been deprived of their homes and have to be resettled elsewhere on account of this mega project?"

He replied, "That is the price we must pay for future progress!" But what a price! I told the Swiss expert that the Three Gorges Project—beneficial as it is in the long run—would be an impossibility in India under our democracy based on individual rights and freedoms.

The Chinese believe in the Benthamite principle of the "greatest good for the greatest number" (a worthy principle in itself). They believe in rule *by* law, not rule *of* law, whereas we who cherish individual freedoms have to undergo the constraints and pangs of personal liberty—constraints that do not exist in the People's

Republic of China. It is no use saying that China is not democratic. Every country that prides itself as independent stresses in its name or in its Constitution that it is democratic. The most undemocratic of countries today is North Korea, but its official name is the Democratic People's Republic of Korea.

One of the great challenges to our democracy is that we could not possibly undertake in the future anything so grandiloquent or useful as the Three Gorges Project, or any other large beneficial irrigation and power project, because it would involve enormous sacrifices for a small group of people in the present and infringe on their rights. This is because of our emphasis on individual citizens' rights—an emphasis that has transformed into an obsession in recent years. We live in an age of an all-pervading *rights* culture. We claim a right to this and a right to that. Experience shows that a rights culture generates greater dissatisfaction amongst persons propounding different sets of rights. Too much emphasis on *rights* only serves to divide and fragment society and spread discontent. In India today, we find ourselves in a stage of profound discontent simply because we have forgotten our responsibilities to one another.

Decades ago, soon after the end of the Second World War, the Human Rights Commission of the United Nations carried out an inquiry into the theoretical problems raised by the then-proposed Universal Declaration of Human Rights. A questionnaire was circulated to various thinkers and writers living in the member states of UNESCO. They were asked, as individual experts, to give their views. One of them was Mahatma Gandhi. He responded in a brief but now almost forgotten letter to Dr Julian Huxley (then director of UNESCO). The letter was written in May 1947, in a moving train (those were troubled times, just before India's Independence when Gandhi was constantly on the move). This is what he wrote:

> "I learnt from my illiterate but wise mother that all rights to be deserved and preserved came from duty well done. The very right to live accrues to us only when we do the duty of citizenship of the world. From this one fundamental statement,

> perhaps it is easy enough to define the duties of men and women and correlate every right to some corresponding duty to be first performed. Every other right can be shown to be an usurpation hardly worth fighting for."

How true. How profound. How simply put. A sense of collective responsibility engenders a regard for societal or group rights, not just individual rights.

Nehru's vision of Indian democracy was definitely not "the greatest good of the greatest number." And that has had its advantages. Just think of it: if he had subscribed to the Benthamite view of the greatest good for the greatest number, he would have gone in for a Hindu state (as some of his compatriots wanted him to do) because the largest number of people in India profess the Hindu faith. But Nehru's vision was not a constricted one. Hinduism, to him, was a civilisation, not some dogma. It was unthinkable to him that the majesty of a great religion could be confined to some narrow definition of Hindutva.

Nehru's vision of Indian democracy encompassed the vastness and diversity of the country and the diversity and plurality of its people. Diversity in India began with its geography. The geographical diversity of India greatly impressed Pandit Nehru, and it also shaped his vision which one can find in his book, *The Discovery of India*. It greatly inspired students of my generation when we were in college. You all must read it. It was written in the quiet seclusion of a British prison in 1944 (during Nehru's ninth term of imprisonment for revolting against the British). It is here that Nehru contemplated "the variety and unity" of India.

> "The diversity of India is tremendous. It is obvious it lies on the surface, and anybody can see it. It concerns itself with physical appearances as well as with certain mental habits and traits . . ."

> "In ancient and medieval times, the idea of the modern nation was non-existent, and feudal, religious, racial, and cultural

> bonds had more importance. Yet I think that at almost any time in recorded history, an Indian would have felt more or less at home in any part of India and would have felt as a stranger and alien in any other country. He would certainly have felt less of a stranger in countries, which had partly adopted his culture or religion. Those, such as Christians, Jews, Parsees, or Moslems, who professed a religion of non-Indian origin or, coming to India, settled down there, became distinctively Indian in the course of a few generations. Indian converts to some of these religions never ceased to be Indians on account of a change of their faith. They were looked upon in other countries as Indians and foreigners, even though there might have been a community of faith between them."[34]

This was Nehru's vision of Indian democracy, and I suggest that it should be your vision as well. Should we then say three cheers for Indian democracy? No, I don't think so. It was Pandit Nehru's friend, E. M. Forster (author of *A Passage to India*[35]), who, always a bit critical of democracy after a visit to India, quite truthfully said, "I would say two cheers for Indian democracy. One because it admits variety and two because it permits criticism. Very important for freedom. But two cheers are quite enough. There is no occasion to give it three."[36]

So don't get too enthusiastic about "government of the people, by the people, for the people," but above all, don't get too disheartened either!

3

JAMMU AND KASHMIR: FALLOUT OF THE SUPREME COURT JUDGEMENT

Politically, it is a good thing that a temporary provision in India's Constitution (Article 370) has ceased to be operative and was upheld on 11 December 2023 in three judgements (one main and two concurring) of the Constitution bench of five judges of the Supreme Court. This has facilitated the complete integration of the state of Jammu and Kashmir into the Union of India. If that was all that had happened, the unanimous judgement would have been, and should have been, welcomed. But this is not all that happened.

What was actually done by the centre was (in my view) not according to the provisions of the Constitution, nor in accordance with well-settled principles of federalism (a basic feature of the Constitution, as was held in a 1994 judgement of a Constitution bench of nine judges). Under Article 370 of the Constitution of India, 1950, read with Presidential Order No. 48 of 1954 passed there under, for the state of Jammu and Kashmir an important safeguard was introduced, namely Article 3 was applied to the state with the condition that the area of the state of Jammu and Kashmir (which in 1950 was 39,145 square miles—something not mentioned in any of the three judgements) would not be diminished by the executive or by Parliament without the consent of the State Assembly of Jammu and Kashmir. However, contrary to this assurance a very substantial diminution of the area of the state (viz. of 22,836 square miles—not again mentioned in any of the three judgements) was effected by the centre in August 2019, admittedly without the consent and without even the knowledge of the inhabitants of Jammu and Kashmir. As for the consent of their representatives in the elected legislative assembly, this was avoided by the assembly itself having been dissolved by the centre (a few months earlier) on 19 December 2018, when, under Article 356 of the Constitution, "President's Rule" (a euphemism for central government rule) was imposed in the state.

What is also not mentioned in any of the three judgements is that not only was the area of the state of Jammu and Kashmir substantially diminished (from 39,145 square miles in January 1950 to just 16,304 square miles in August 2019), but even the status of Jammu and Kashmir was unilaterally altered from a state to a union territory (with the much diminished area)—a situation neither warranted nor justified by any provision in the Constitution.

Another important safeguard for the state had been set out in Article 370(3) itself, as enacted in 1950, which reads as follows:

> "(3) Notwithstanding anything in the foregoing provisions of this Article, the President may, by public notification, declare that this Article shall cease to be operative or shall be operative only with such exceptions and modifications and from such date as he may specify: Provided that the recommendation of the Constituent Assembly of the State referred to in clause (2) shall be necessary before the President issues such a notification."

Hence, the power of the president under Article 370 (which is in fact the power of the centre) to declare the entire Article 370 inoperative was to come into effect only if the precondition mentioned in the proviso to Article 370(3) was fulfilled, viz. the recommendation of the Constituent Assembly of the state, which was a precondition to the exercise of the power to declare that Article 370 ceased to be operative. Disregarding this, and also disregarding the true function of a proviso to a section, the court in the main judgement stated:

> "Since the Constituent Assembly of Jammu and Kashmir had not yet been constituted when the Constitution of India was adopted, the proviso to Article 370(3) merely encapsulated the ratification process as decided by the Ministry of States. The words 'recommendation of the Constituent Assembly referred to in Clause (2) shall be necessary before the President issues such a notification' as it appears in the proviso to Article 370(3) must be read in this context. Thus, the recommendation of the Constituent Assembly was not binding on the President to begin with."
> (paragraph 346(a) on page 244 of the main judgement)

The conclusion of the court that the recommendation of the Constituent Assembly is not binding on the president was based on the court's erroneous interpretation of Article 370(3) as being in two separate parts. This is what the main judgement says to support its finding that Article 370(3) is in two separate parts:

> "The power under Article 370(3) did not cease to exist upon the dissolution of the Constituent Assembly of Jammu and Kashmir. When the Constituent Assembly was dissolved, only the transitional power recognised in the proviso to Article 370(3) which empowered the Constituent Assembly to make its recommendations ceased to exist. *It did not affect the power held by the President under Article 370(3).*"
> (paragraph 514 (f) at page 349 of the main judgement)

What the main judgement has said is not only directly contrary to Article 370(3) but is also in the teeth of a prior decision of a Constitution bench of five judges reported in AIR 1961 SC 1596, which stated that: "a proviso is added to an enactment to qualify or create an exception to what is in the enactment, and ordinarily, a proviso is not interpreted as stating a general rule."

Therefore, I feel that the present decision of the court, even if politically acceptable, is not constitutionally correct.

4

Campaign Against Corruption: Has It Succeeded?[37]

The interrogation mark in the heading of this chapter is intentional. In fact, it is the most vital part of the subject: Has the campaign against corruption succeeded? (Question mark)

Answer: I am not at all sure it has. Let me tell you why.

When talking about corruption, we always make a common mistake: to use the number of laws enacted or convictions obtained as an index of the fight against corruption. Wrong. The only real index is the visible degree of tolerance of corruption amongst people who individually abhor it, or at least say that they abhor it.

Over the years, it seems to me that we have come to tolerate it more and more, not less and less. For instance, in the general elections, I don't think any political party in the country, major or minor, national or regional, has raised the issue of corruption in public life in a big way.

My dear friend Ram Tahiliani never just talked about corruption. He actively fought against it. He was the thirteenth chief of the naval staff from December 1984 to November 1987, and then from 1990 to 1994, he was governor of Sikkim, when we came much closer, since we were invited to Gangtok every year as guests of the Tahlianis, in that rambling but beautifully ancient Raj Bhawan, from where on a clear morning you could see Mount Kangchenjunga, almost next to you. The world's second-highest peak, covered in snow, stood towering over us, and we felt we could almost reach out and touch it!

Ram took all his achievements in his stride, but I could see that in the latter part of his life, his sole aim was to seek the end of corruption. He was president of the Indian chapter of Transparency International. He helped initiate a series of measures to control corruption. But I am afraid he did not see the end of it. I doubt if any of us here, howsoever young, will ever see the end of corruption.

His was the experience of all great and good men living in the former colonies—colonies that emerged as independent developing nations after the end of the Second World War, in which Ram had also bravely fought. The message that had dawned on all these good men was the same: "Freedom brings in its wake corruption." This was the same theme to which the Polish Nobel Laureate, Czeslaw Milosz, gave eloquent expression:

> "Ill at ease in the tyranny, Ill at ease in the republic.
> In the one I longed for freedom, in the other the end of corruption."

In our part of the world, people's expectations were, and unfortunately still are, that whatever be the form of government, be sure that corruption will ultimately corrode it. I am convinced that we have to fight the menace of corruption, i.e., not ordinary day-to-day corruption, but what I call tidal-wave corruption. We have to fight tidal-wave corruption, which is becoming more and more a tsunami, and we have to fight it with whatever weapons we can call in aid—with laws, with education, with persuasion, and by instilling in the dishonest and fraudulent the fear of God, i.e., if anyone genuinely believes in God anymore!

The fear of God, or the fear of the wrath of God, used to be a deterrent, but in this scientific and technological age, it is no longer. Only recently, a publisher sent me a magazine in which there was an article that gave the good news that in February, the Australian Government had at last set up a Commonwealth Anti-Corruption Commission. The article borrowed and published a chart from the

Association of Democratic Reforms in India to show the number of Lok Sabha MPs in India's three elections of 2004, 2009, and 2014, with serious criminal cases filed against them, all of which were pending.

The number at each of these three elections has gone higher and higher in each five-year period. It does not matter by how many or by how much. In any case, there is a growing concern that under official auspices, statistical data on almost everything is being "doctored." To put it more bluntly, "being fudged!" The Australian author Benjamin Disraeli's famous words have come to mean something in India: "There are three kinds of lies: lies, damned lies, and statistics." He then criticises an earlier proposal of the then Australian government to establish what was then called the Commonwealth Integrity Group, and he quotes one appellate judge in Australia saying: "This kind of integrity commission is one you would have when you don't want to have an integrity commission . . . it creates a wall behind which corrupt public officials can hide . . . (it was and is) . . . like a colander, it would be really good to make rice in it as it's got so many holes."

The same goes for our vigilance commissions, the CBI (Central Bureau of Investigation), and the lot. They are all like colanders in which you can boil your rice as they too have many holes in them. Recent events, too close, too embarrassing to recall, have proved it.

I have a fat book in my library of about 800 pages, *Bribes*, authored by an American called Noonan, who believes that the fight against corruption will ultimately succeed because "the nature of bribes is antithetical to the nature of human power in its full development." He ventures a prediction: "Just as slavery was once a way of life and now has become obsolete and incomprehensible, so the practice of bribery in the form of the exchange of payment for official action will become obsolete."

However, then let me be the devil's advocate and tell you the true story of how "slavery" did "become obsolete" in the USA with the passing of the 13th Amendment (to the US Constitution). It was accomplished by means that were far from praiseworthy! Did you know that what has been described as the greatest single ameliorative measure of the nineteenth century was passed only because of corruption? And it was aided and abetted by reputedly the purest man in American history: President Abraham Lincoln. Here is the story, though only "in capsule form."

In the elections held in the US back in the year 1864, the Democrats in Congress (the House of Representatives) were reduced in strength, from sixty-four to thirty-five members. The newly elected Republican members could not take office until March 1865, when the new Congress would first meet.

Meanwhile, the old Congress, where the Democrats were still in a majority, assembled in a traditional last session—known as a lame-duck session—that ran from December 1864 to March 1865. In his presidential message to this session, Lincoln (a Republican) asked the members to pass the 13th Constitution Amendment (for the abolition of slavery). But under the US Constitution (like in ours), the passage of a constitutional amendment required two-thirds majority of members present and voting. There were two votes lacking to make up the requisite majority, and Lincoln had said that *these votes must be procured*. Mark the word "procured."

Two "trusted" members of the House were sent for, and Lincoln again told them that those two votes *must* be procured. When asked how, all he (reportedly) said was: "I am president of the United States, clothed with immense power. The abolition of slavery by constitutional provision settles the fate, for all coming time, not only of the millions now in bondage but unborn millions to come—a measure of such importance that those two votes must be procured. I leave it to you to determine how it shall be done but remember that I am president of the United States clothed with great power, and I expect you to procure those votes."

According to the recorded and printed recollection of a fellow called Albert Riddle, a Republican Congressman from Ohio, twenty-eight years after the event, the task of procuring the needed two-thirds majority was entrusted to another Congressman, called James Ashley, also from Ohio. The Republicans were told in confidence that

Ashley could report "the acquisition" of the needed Democrats. One Democrat wanted "a place" for his brother in New York. Another was told that an election contest in the next Congress "would depend entirely on his vote on the impending 13th Amendment." The third was a lawyer representing a railroad in Pennsylvania, threatened by pending legislation in the Senate: all three were "satisfied" (satisfied in inverted commas).

Every hostile member who stayed away at voting time helped, as their absence reduced the number required to constitute two-thirds of those present and voting! Ultimately, on the day of voting (31 January 1865), the lawyer and seven other Democrats stayed away (having been "bought"). 175 members voted, and the amendment was carried by a two-thirds majority, 119-56—a margin of just two votes!

If Lincoln had lived longer, and if the Democrats who controlled the House in 1874 had investigated the circumstances surrounding the passage of the Constitution 13th Amendment, it is possible that a price would have been exacted in political terms and to the detriment of the reputation of the great Abraham Lincoln. But the investigation did not occur, simply because Lincoln did not live that long. He was assassinated on Good Friday in 1865 (on 15 April), and his death overshadowed everything. It also sealed the emancipation of the slaves forever (thank God!). Good and bad, God and the devil, all mixed up—rare in the history of politics—played a major part in the constitutional abolition of slavery in the US. A noble end was achieved but by entirely ignoble means!

Some time ago, in a revealing article in a national newspaper, my lawyer friend K. N. Bhat related a story about Thomas Edison. It is topical and worth reading.

Edison was a great inventor. He invented, amongst other things, a tamper-proof voting machine, and he presented it to the US Senate, hoping that its members would appreciate and applaud his efforts. But they were silent. In exasperation, Edison wrote to the Senate chairman: "Sir, my machine is tamper-proof. Do you have any doubt?"

The chairman did not reply but invited Edison to his chamber and privately told him: "Yes, we have no doubt, but that is *the problem . . . the problem is that the machine you have invented is tamper-proof!*" The story is probably apocryphal, but it nearly accurately reflects the current realities in India—about EVMs and the like.

There is another difficulty in India: that of tardy implementation. The anti-corruption laws that have been brought on the statute book have so far exhibited a marked tendency to grind slowly. Too slowly for the likes of the great former Chief Vigilance Commissioner (CVC) N. Vittal (1998-2002). Who among us can forget him? When in office, he had publicly "named" ninety-four civil servants who were under investigation (i.e., who were accused of corruption on the basis of documentary evidence but not yet charged in any court of law). It was on his instructions that their names were posted on the internet! "Sue me if you dare," Vittal appeared to say, but no one sued him. His bravado struck a sympathetic chord with many people, myself included.

Vittal retired from government service decades ago and was succeeded by CVCs who have not been half as effective as he was. In January 2012, Vittal was at last remembered by an otherwise forgetful government and was awarded the Padma Bhushan for his "more-than-significant role in public affairs!"

They say that corruption in politics is as old as the hills! But never forget that in India, it is even older. Older even than the hills. In a comprehensive treatise on public administration and statecraft in ancient India, *Arthashastra* (the first copy was discovered only in the last century), it is believed that Kautilya (also known as Chanakya) had perceptively written (circa fourth century BC): "Just as it is impossible not to taste honey or poison that one may find at the tip of one's tongue, so it is impossible for one dealing with government funds not to taste a little bit of the king's revenue. Just as it is impossible to know whether a fish moving in the water is drinking it, so it is impossible to find out when government servants employed in government work are taking money for themselves!" Beautiful imagery!

The Nehru era had produced great bureaucrats who believed in, and practiced, honour, integrity, and self-denial. One of them was Dharma Vira, ICS. We came to know him when we moved from Bombay to Delhi in May 1972. His life spanned almost a century. He rose from a humble recruit to the highest rank that of cabinet secretary of the Government of India. After retirement, he wrote *Memoirs of a Civil Servant* in which he spoke of Percy Marsh, district magistrate of Aligarh (now in Uttar Pradesh), who had taken a keen interest in Dharma Vira then as a young service officer. One day, Marsh told Dharma Vira:

> "Now listen carefully. Two things you must always do. One is to take a decision and take it quickly, right or wrong. Most often you are likely to be right in your decision. But even if you are wrong, less damage will be done than by not taking a decision.
>
> And the second thing is that you are an executive officer. You should keep your mouth shut as far as possible. The less you speak the less trouble you will get into . . . Talking is the task of politicians. You will be judged by your actions and not by your talks. So, you better speak less and act more."

Dharma Vira greatly valued this advice.

One evening, at a mutual friend's place, he told us a fascinating story. As cabinet secretary, he had headed a government delegation that went abroad to purchase some aircraft (no, not Rafales, but older stuff). After the agreement was signed, the sellers' representative asked Dharma Vira as to in whose name the cheque for the customary discount should be made out. Dharma Vira's reply was: "Excellency, make out the cheque in the name of the Government of India."

When he came back to India and handed over the cheque to Prime Minister Pandit Jawaharlal Nehru, Pandit Nehru was aghast. "What have you done?" he asked. "You have accepted a bribe from the sellers? The reduction in price was a bribe for you to clinch the deal."

"Yes sir," responded Dharma Vira, "but would you have preferred it if I had asked the sellers to open an account in my name in Switzerland and deposit the money there?"

Panditji, still smouldering with rage, did not reply. The moralist in Nehru was quietened by the realist in Dharma Vira.

In his lifetime, Dharma Vira was typical of many generations of noble, upright public servants. After his passing (and the passing of those like him), there has been a steep decline in standards of public life. So deep that a cartoon by R. K. Laxman, which I have reproduced (with permission) in one of my books, *The State of the Nation*, says it all. Let me describe it.

All this is not in India alone. A Harvard professor, Lawrence Lessig, recounts a somewhat similar story of Senator John Stennis from Mississippi. Like Dharma Vira, the senator belonged to the old school. When Stennis retired from the Senate in 1989, after forty-one years, he was the most senior member in the Senate's history. He thought and acted differently from other senators. When asked by a colleague to hold a fundraiser with defence contractors, Stennis recoiled and remarked, "Would that be proper? I hold life and death over those companies. I don't think it would be *proper* for me to take money from them."

It is a story (Lessig writes) about a *change of norms*. Stennis wasn't concerned whether holding a fundraiser with defence contractors would break the law. Probably it would not. He was worried that it *wasn't proper*!

He was worried about breaking prevailing *norms* on Capitol Hill. Lessig says that it is this that has changed over the years: breaking norms. Corruption persists because we keep breaking norms.

"Corruption" is one of the most elastic words in the English language. To every individual, it is something of which he or she disapproves. Some years ago, at a seminar of the International Bar Association held in Berlin, Jeremy Pope (of Transparency International) gave what then struck me as the most comprehensive and yet the most concise definition: "Corruption is the misuse of public power for private profit."

How right he was, or so it seemed then. But subsequent events have shown that his definition was not as all-embracing as I had once thought it was, because there are simply no limits to where, when, or how corruption rears its ugly head. For example, with the revelations of match-fixing and drug-related scandals in the world of sports. Cricketers, footballers, cyclists, etc., do not hold any public office, and yet they exercise *moral* power—the power to instil idealism among millions of sport-loving fans. Such fans feel cheated when a player, due to corrupt motives, plays badly or does not play well.

The word "corruption" now embraces the *misuse of power of any kind for private gain*. Pope's definition needs restructuring. In fact, the definition of corruption keeps requiring restructuring as time passes, as more ways to be corrupt are invented. But meanwhile, I have a suggestion.

Jean Monnet, father of the European Union (which is a bit shaken these days), used to say there are two types of people in this world: those who want to be somebody and those who want to do something.

My suggestion is to let us praise those who have done something or want to do something, even if they don't completely succeed. When good people, people in positions of power, sometimes do the right thing, believe me, it does have a trickle-down effect for us all—for the common man, the proverbial man in the street, and the uncommon man and woman as well. As the great book says: "Whatsoever a great man doeth, that other men also do; the standard he setteth up, by that the people go."

The need of the hour is great men (and women). And quite frankly, they are, as yet, in extremely short supply.

Section II
JUDICIARY

1

Technology to Enable Accessible and Speedy Justice[1]

The importance of lawyers learning from other disciplines was emphasised many years ago by the then secretary-general of the Commonwealth, Sir Shridath S. Ramphal, Q. C., when he sent a message to the Ninth LAWASIA Conference held in New Delhi way back in 1985. He urged lawyers to wander into pastures beyond a lawyer's domain. "By what superior law are its gates locked against you?" he asked rhetorically, and then added, "Remember we are all heirs to a noble tradition of intellectual inventiveness in our response to changing needs."

The inventiveness of which Sir Shridath Ramphal spoke was of modern technology, which has outstripped the law, and the law must now run faster to keep pace with the inventions of modern science. Although I do claim to have kept pace with improvements in the law, I have not bothered too much with the modern instruments that science has provided. Many of my colleagues poke fun at me because I do not carry even the most harmless and the most effective instrument of modern technology: the cell phone! So, I am afraid I cannot speak authoritatively on technology. We have today many distinguished persons who can do so. However, I will say something about the need for accessibility of justice in this country.

The opening words of India's Constitution, "We the People," tell us at the start who this Constitution is for. Those who read the newspapers every morning can be pardoned for exclaiming, "But oh, what a people!" But the people we read about in the newspapers are not the people mentioned in the opening words of the Constitution. They are those who presume to lord over us, to govern us. They are continually, almost daily, weighed in the balance and found wanting.

In a pluralistic society like ours, in a vast subcontinent like this, in a land of a million mutinies, as the Nobel Prize winner, V. S. Naipaul, described it: "Who really are the people? For me, they are typified by the renowned cartoonist R.K. Laxman's endearing representative of Indian humanity, 'the common man'!" Unfortunately for the past few years, we haven't seen or read about the mystical "common man" in the *Times of India* as we used to do. But we still have something to remind us.

Some years ago, a former President of India, K. R. Narayanan, unveiled in Pune, an eight-foot high bronze statue extolled as the "world's tallest metal statue of a cartoon character." It typifies, as no other single manifestation does, the quizzical doubts of the "common man" about whom this Constitution of ours is for. Each generation throws up its common man and a generation, as you know, is usually computed at thirty years. Hence, by this computation, there have been two generations since 1950 and if we are to show the present generation (typified by the common man) our document of governance or tell him about it, he is bound to ask: "Tell me what has it done for us? How are *we* better off?"

These are some difficult questions that arise because the answer to them might help us in the very difficult, seemingly impossible quest, viz. accessibility of justice for the common man. One of our former chief guests, Justice Lokur, has contributed significantly to enhancing accessible and speedy justice for the common man, and we in the Supreme Court are very proud of him.

Aleksandr Solzhenitsyn, the great Russian critic of the communist system of government (when it was unpopular and dangerous to be a critic), said something very significant: "A man used to riding in a car cannot understand a pedestrian." I like to think that we would have been able to comprehend the needs of the poor (and really done something about them) if we had followed the path laid for us by the founding fathers.

Every constitution must have an ideal and purpose, and the more I get acquainted with this longest constitution in the world, the more I believe that its heart is in Part IV. If we look for the reason why we have floundered over the last few decades, why we have not been able to successfully work the Constitution, despite the efforts of politicians, lawyers, commissions, and committees, it is only because we have not had the will to implement the directive principles of state policy—principles declared fundamental in the governance of the country. The Constitution had imposed a duty on the state to apply these principles in making laws but had precluded courts from enforcing them.

It is for me a matter of great regret that our Constitution which borrowed from a host of written documents around the world did not choose to adopt those fine evocative words in that renowned democratic declaration of modern times—the Declaration of Independence by the American colonies. The material part reads:

> "We hold these truths to be self-evident, that all men are created equal, that they are endowed by their Creator with certain unalienable Rights, that among these are Life, Liberty, and the pursuit of their Happiness."

Note the emphasis on the pursuit of their happiness which is and should be the prime aim and object of every government and every document of governance. A start was made on "easy access to justice" by the provision for legal aid establishment of consumer forums where there are no court fees and where lawyers are not encouraged. But the general condition of the litigant even in these forums is not very uplifting.

A few years ago, a young friend, Dr S. Muralidhar, later a robust judge in the Delhi High Court and then chief justice of Orissa High Court[2], wrote a book titled, *Law, Poverty, and Legal Aid,* which contains a foreword by the great protagonist of legal aid, Justice V. R. Krishna Iyer, wherein he says: "The law is what law does and so justice is what justice does." It is on this not-very-secure foundation that the life and liberty of what he calls "the little Indian" depends. Unfortunately, the law as it stands does little for the little Indian, and justice does even less.

We need not merely technology but more. We need civil society initiatives, such as encouraging law students to represent litigants in small cases, particularly in the criminal courts. Law students, I am happy to say, have still not lost their idealism. They have experimented with this, with some success, in the Philippines. Students have the ability to critique the system. They and the paralegals are as yet unspoilt by the system—a contrast to we the members of the traditional, black-coated fraternity. They want justice for the people, and they want it fast.

There is a chapter in the book by Justice Muralidhar which is quite terrifying and needs to be read and digested by one and all. It is under the title, "Legal System as Oppressor." In it, the author criticises the system where at the end of a long criminal litigation, a person who emerges as innocent—which happens in more than 80 per cent of criminal cases that enter the criminal justice system—is neither compensated for the incarceration nor awarded the costs of the lengthy and tortuous litigation. A very important passage in this chapter reads:

> "The mere provision of legal services may not alter the way in which the poor are treated within the criminal justice system without fundamental changes in the behaviour of the personnel manning the institutions that comprise the criminal justice system."

Certainly, a very pertinent comment. Just as we need more and more inspired judges to push civil and criminal cases along to a final conclusion, we also need judges and lawyers with compassion to appreciate the plight of people who are caught up in the tentacles of the system and innovate at they go along in the quest for justice.

In the Rajiv Gandhi assassination case (*State* vs. *Nalini,* 1999 (5) SCC 253), a bench of three judges heard death reference cases where, after a marathon trial lasting several years, all twenty-six accused were convicted by the designated court (special judge), who sentenced them all to death. The assassination occurred in May 1991, and a year later, the charge sheet was filed. The special judge pronounced his verdict seven years later, in January 1998, and the final judgement of the Supreme Court was delivered in May 1999.

The Supreme Court ultimately held, eight years after the twenty-six accused were first charged, that, in view of the paucity of material to prove that the conspirators intended to overawe the Government of India or to strike terror in the people, they were unable to sustain the conviction of offences under Section 3 of TADA (the anti-terrorist law then in force). Each of the judges wrote separate judgements, which make for tedious reading. But at the end of these long judgements, the Supreme Court held that the conviction of *seven* of the accused for conspiracy to murder should be upheld but that the remaining accused, nineteen of them, (they said) must be set at liberty forthwith. Most of them had also been convicted of relatively minor offences, invoking a sentence of two years imprisonment, but they had all remained in prison long after—two years due to the murder charge—of which they were ultimately acquitted. However, there is not a word in the 237 closely printed pages of judgements as to why the persons who were (as it turned out) innocent of the capital offence should not receive from the state, which put them up for trial, at least their costs of the entire litigation, let alone compensation for their unduly prolonged incarceration.

We only speak about "human rights" but do little to make it meaningful. I believe we sorely need more judges like Justice Krishna Iyer in vantage positions of judicial power; judges with feeling who are able to respond to the expectations and aspirations of litigants in the lower strata of society.

In the quest for speedy justice, a quick recapitulation of the breakdown scenario of the criminal justice system must never be lost sight of. It is given by S. Muralidhar in his book, although a bit dated. The figures are for the year 2004, but there have been little improvements since then.

1. On average, 50 lakh crimes (or 5 million cases) are registered every year, which are sought to be investigated by a totally inadequate police force.
2. The pendency of criminal cases in the subordinate courts is in the region of 1.32 crore (i.e., 13.2 million) but the effective strength of judges is 12,177.
3. The number of undertrials whose criminal cases are pending is 1.44 crore (or 14.4 million) and of these, over 200,000 (or 2 lakhs) are in prisons.
4. Around 63 lakhs (or 6.3 million) get arrested every year, and more than 2,500 are victims of custodial violence including deaths and torture in police custody.
5. On average, the courts are able to dispose of only 19 per cent of the pending cases every year.
6. The budget for legal services is in the region of only Rs. 3 crores (Rs. 30 million) a year for all the states and union territories and other legal services committees in the country. And yet, much of this amount remains unutilised. Of that which is utilised, no accounts of expenditure are available.

Muralidhar's book annexes in an appendix a scheme proposed by the former advocate general of Madhya Pradesh, N. C. Jain. He was a member of the eleventh Finance Commission on clearance of the backlog of pending cases. At the heart of this scheme is the suggestion that instead of employing new judges, retired sessions judges or additional sessions judges be appointed as ad hoc judges specifically for disposing of pending sessions cases.

Jain had worked out the details and concluded that the exercise required to work out the modalities to be settled by the law ministry for amendment of the laws making rules of appointment of ad hoc judges, their selection, appointment, and for the construction of courtrooms etc., could be completed by the year 2005, and if a beginning had been made immediately, concrete results would have been attainable (even without modern technology) and most of the backlog would have been cleared by now. But alas, as in everything else, we just don't have the will. We are already in the beginning of the year 2013 but not even a start has been made on this proposal. The detailed recommendation, though emanating from a report of the eleventh Finance Commission on clearance of the backlog of pending cases, is gathering dust. I am despondent that there is no idealism left in any of the judges or lawyers—the idealism that inspired our founding fathers in the framing of our Constitution.

I have been to innumerable colleges around the country and have spoken to literally thousands of law students, and I am always stimulated by their sense of purpose and drive. More accessible and speedier justice can be achieved by recruiting law students and new law graduates. The poor don't need legal aid in the form of charity; they need legal aid as a professional duty of the state and the young law students and fresh law graduates take their professional duty far more seriously than those who are older in the profession.

There is no use saying that the poor will help the poor of the country. I have noticed in my practice of now more than sixty years that people in the lowest strata of society, once they rise a step higher, show little concern for the poorer and the more impoverished. There is no sense of concern for those on the lower rung. Otherwise, how does one explain the "creamy layer" amongst the backward classes who climb over the backs of their poorer brethren, reaching the top and then going on claiming privileges for themselves at the expense of their erstwhile fellow members?

We all speak glibly and constantly about the rule of law. But in his exhilarating Hamlyn Lectures, Justice Stephen Sedley, who retired as a judge of the Court of Appeal in England, reminds his readers that the rule of law, of which we all glowingly speak about, is a necessary but not a sufficient condition for a just society. There is more to a just society than the rule of law for instance. Judicial enforcement of rights by courts of law does not necessarily guarantee public understanding and support for those rights; such understanding or awareness needs to be inculcated and is only achieved when a larger percentage of our people who are without means can truly exercise their legal rights and are enabled to do so by lawyers with enthusiasm and by judges with vision.

Through his judgements, Justice Krishna Iyer revealed that this Anglo-Saxon system of jurisprudence that we have adopted and adapted in this country *does* work if only you know how to make it work. Decide as you must according to law, but never forget that law without justice is like an egg without its yolk, and much of its salt.

I hate to disappoint, but in India, if you want easier accessibility to justice, you will not get it with the adoption of modern technology but only with a basic change of attitudes of those who operate the system, particularly the criminal justice system.

I mentioned above Justice Sedley. An English Lord Chancellor, Lord Hailsham, would not appoint him as a high court judge because of his leftist leanings, but his successor, the Scottish Lord Mackay, took the chance of appointing him immediately on assuming office as Lord Chancellor, and he never regretted it. During his entire tenure of twenty years, Judge Sedley performed admirably, and he was reckoned as one of England's brightest judicial minds. Sedley was listed in *Who's Who* as having one of his hobbies: "Changing the world."

For the practicing lawyer, for the in-house lawyer, for the draftsmen of documents and of laws, and for law teachers of the twenty-first century, there can be no better motto: "Changing the World"—the world of attitudes in the law first needs changing.

2

Conduct of Junior Members of Bar before Court[3]

We are a free country, so free that we can discuss freely and publicly anything that is topical, without restraint. I would like to remind you of the width of this freedom in India. In Singapore and Malaysia (both democracies), even for a talk as innocent as about the conduct of junior lawyers in court, you require a police permit. It is not required in India because of the freedom we enjoy under our 1950 Constitution, which, thank God, has never been abrogated. Always remember that when people tell you that there is no rule of law in this country and everything has gone to rack and ruin, you must say that there is *hope* as long as you and I have "Freedom Under the Law," which was the title of the very first Hamlyn Lecture delivered by Lord Denning more than half a century ago.

As for the subject of this chapter about the conduct of young practising lawyers in court, considering that old lawyers like me never retire (they only drop dead), the first question is: how young is a young lawyer? I can assure you that calling a lawyer young has little to do with his age. He or she can be a five-year-old graduate, or he or she can be as old as the hills and yet he (or she) may remain young in the art of how best to argue cases in court. And this is the young lawyer that I write for today.

When David Pannick, the leading English barrister in the UK, wrote a book called *Advocates,* he dedicated it to two sets of people he was closest with:

1. His father-in-law, who was a non-lawyer, and yet (as Pannick wrote) "he could argue either side of any proposition with equal force"—in other words, a true advocate, though not a qualified one.
2. The other people Pannick was closest with were his wife and members of his immediate family, each of whom could tell him—and never missed an opportunity to tell him—whenever he made a bad point in the conversation!

Let this be a lesson for you, viz. to encourage members of your family to be critical of you, not worshipful of you. It will teach you humility and stimulate in you a sense of humour, which is so essential in life to all human beings, especially in modern India, where, at present, we appear to have completely lost our sense of humour and our ability to tolerate people with views different from our own. Hence, in this profession particularly, you must be able to laugh at yourself and your foibles. And since this is not possible because each of us has such an enlarged ego, you—which means you and I—must consciously cultivate the ability to laugh at ourselves. The first lesson that a practicing lawyer has to learn is to *subordinate his ego* in court, since the judge who sits above you also has an ego. His ego is more important than yours. Remember this, always remember this, if you wish to succeed in practice.

In your role as an advocate, I commend you to be *argumentative, inquisitive, indignant,* or *apologetic,* yet always be ready to accept criticism of yourself, because this will ultimately help you develop the art of persuasion. Remember that the best advocate is the one who is the best prepared and who is able to persuade—persuade the judge with logic and argumentative skills, to their client's point of view.

And this is when I bring in the presiding judge. If you want to know how an ideal judge must function in India, where each judge is often overburdened, you can watch one who goes and sits in his court on any day. You will find him or her firm but always receptive to a plausible argument. This exemplifies the well-known expression: "Straight as a judge."

Coming back to the lawyers, in a criticism of advocacy as a vocation, Socrates once emphasised that, "The orator does not teach juries and other bodies about right and wrong—he merely persuades them." If you are intelligent and have prepared your case extremely well, you will realise, only then, the superlative pleasure of a magician.

Alan Dershowitz is a prominent US defence lawyer whose claim to fame has been that he once described the flawed decision of the US Supreme Court in *Bush* vs. *Gore* (the infamous election case) as *fraudulent* and *dishonest.* Despite this, he escaped any citation for contempt of court, not because he was such a famous lawyer, but because the US Supreme Court (older than our court by more than 200 years) is a court suffused with wisdom and lives up to the ideals of freedom enshrined in the US Constitution. The court will embark on a contempt of court action only where it is certain it will not have to withdraw or drop it!

Well, Alan Dershowitz's son is a professional magician, and this is what he candidly tells his father: "You and I do the same thing father—sleight of hand. We make things appear to be what they are not." Dershowitz records this in his autobiography, *Reversal of Fortune*[4]. Read it if you can get hold of this book. I am afraid that becoming a magician, or almost, in the practice of law will take you a long, long time. But you must try. It must be your ideal to strive for. And if you fall short, it must not be for want of trying!

The best advice to young lawyers is that you must imbibe on your own by intelligently watching and listening because that is the advice generated on your own which you can never forget! But next to that, let me list a few bits of advice which I have learnt in the school of hard knocks—which is the school of life's experience.

- **Advice Number 1**

If you have chosen law practice in court as your career, then be regular in court. And when you attend court, keep your mind alert and receptive, your wits sharpened, but not your tongue. Don't talk too much simply because empty vessels make the most sound. When wearing a black coat and gown, the less you speak at the initial stages of your career the better. Like that wise old owl who lived in an oak. The more he saw, the less he spoke, and the less he spoke, the more he heard. Why can't you be like that bird?

Young lawyers tend to talk a lot and a lot of rubbish as well. Don't worry, I am not being pompous. We all (myself included) did the same but realised it only much later. Speak to your brief, not outside it, and make your point in the first few sentences of your argument. I know it is difficult when you start, but try to jot down on paper what you are going to say and then say it with clarity. This will help.

Justice R. S. Bachawat, who sat many years in the court, used to say: "State your argument in *capsule form*." He constantly telling us this helped us to cut out irrelevant embellishments from our speeches in court. Cultivate the art of brevity. Come and sit in the lounge where everyone is assembled. Remember that, in his time, the great jurist Motilal Setalvad, whose excellent portrait hangs in Lounge II, was the soul of brevity and for twelve long years, when he was India's first and its best attorney general, the Supreme Court judges—all very eminent men—were not able to resist the beguiling charm of his brevity.

Even if you are only briefed to take an adjournment in a case, get familiar with it because the judge may well ask you (yours being a new face) as to what the matter is about and that's when you must score and claim your right to fame. In a couple of sentences that you have previously rehearsed, you must say what the case is about, what the lower courts have said, and the point that is sought to be canvassed in the court where you appear. This is a frequent question many judges ask very young lawyers who appear before a bench of the Supreme Court and request for an adjournment because the senior who is briefed is on his legs elsewhere. I have seen this myself and I am most disappointed when I often find these lawyers either say that they have not read the brief or do not know what the case is about. That's a shame—not knowing what the case is about, even if you are only asked to have it adjourned. My own experience when I was one year old at the Bar was as follows (I have recorded it in my autobiography, *Before Memory Fades*, but I reproduce it here verbatim):

> "Chief Justice M. C. Chagla was the brightest and the best of the judges in my time. He had a fine mix of all the qualities of an ideal judge. He was highly intellectual and very judicial. And his treatment of juniors was exemplary. When I was only a year old at the Bar, Nani Palkhivala, then the wonder boy of the Bar, had entrusted me with an appeal from a judgement in a writ petition under the Bombay Land Requisition Act, which had been dismissed by a single judge. I was to look up the matter and prepare for him the law on the points involved in the appeal. Palkhivala had another engagement before the Income Tax Appellate Tribunal. As my luck would have it, the appeal reached a hearing (in his absence) before a bench consisting of Chief Justice Chagla and Justice P. B. Gajendragadkar (later to become the Chief Justice of India)—at that time about the strongest division bench in the country. I shuffled into court and weakly mentioned that Palkhivala was appearing in the matter and would hopefully arrive in a short while, and could the case stand over. Chief Justice Chagla courteously said that they did not know what the matter was about and that this was a great opportunity for me to begin. Of course, I knew it was not, since from what little I had read, it appeared to be a pretty hopeless appeal. I bravely went on, stated the facts, read the legal provisions, and did not have much more to say. I could see the solicitor and clients behind me, wringing their hands in despair! Fortunately, one of them had the good sense to go fetch Palkhivala post-haste, but by then, I had already made a perfect mess of the appeal. Palkhivala arrived whilst judgement was being delivered (my argument having concluded in about half an hour and the other side not being called upon). Palkhivala interrupted the judgement to mention (more felicitously than I

could) the interpretation of the relevant section, that our clients had been canvassing for. Justice Chagla did not like interruptions when he was dictating judgements but permitted this one. He listened to Palkhivala, gave an answer to the interpretation, and then said, 'Mr Nariman very ably put forward the same point and we have rejected it.' I knew I had done nothing of the sort. Justice Chagla then went on to add, 'I don't think, Mr Palkhivala, you can add anything more to what Mr Nariman has so well presented.' I knew how 'well' I had presented the point! But not a smile escaped Justice Chagla's lips and he made it appear that he was dead serious in the compliment he paid to a junior whose face he had never seen before, and whose name he had never heard before! The graciousness of the man was abounding. I have not seen such a combination of knowledge and graciousness, not until I met and came to know and respect (in later years) Justice M. N. Venkatachaliah— Chief Justice of India—another great judge and a great human being."

We are not all born orators and oratorical flourishes are never appreciated in the courtroom. State anything you have to say simply and clearly. The practice of law is not an elocution competition, but you do get marks for not shouting but only for speaking up. And don't use the mike that is in front of you. I have found that most judges don't like it.

- **Advice Number 2**

Attend court even when you have no work. And I mean attend in the courtroom and not sit and gossip in the Bar library. Carefully watch what senior practicing lawyers *say* and *do*, not necessarily out of adoration or with hopes of emulating them but particularly with a view to *remember* what not to say or not to do! Even the great and successful often falter in the cut and thrust of battles in court and you must cultivate the discernment to detect this.

When you see some of us arguing in the court, you must be perceptive, you must be able to discern what made the judge turn against us in the case at hand—a wrong phrase, an erroneous argument. This experience of seeing before your very eyes senior practicing lawyers losing cases or making a hash of their cases will stand you in good stead in later years. You will then be able to develop the art of *what not to say* and *when not to speak.*

- **Advice Number 3**

The waiting period in the practice of law is long and weary, almost like the waiting period of cases pending in the court. So always be well-equipped. For the practicing lawyer, the motto of the Boy Scouts applies: "Be prepared. Always be prepared."

Jot down and get familiar with the growing volume of case law (on various subjects) which will mean that you have to constantly read, digest, and remember reported cases decided by the high courts and by the Supreme Court. Know the references at your fingertips. And this is how you can be useful to the *big guys* who are handsomely paid—and often, more than handsomely paid—to argue cases in court. When they find you useful, they help you, not out of charity but out of need. And then you can safely look back to the bad old days when you were starving. "Stay hungry, stay foolish" was the message conveyed by Steve Jobs (when dying of cancer to young students at his college). In the law, stay hungry if you have to but stay smart—never foolish!

The law is a profession with cut-throat competition. Don't feel sorry for yourself. Legal aid is for clients not for young lawyers who must fend for themselves. The rich rewards are never at the beginning of your career and are only found near the top rung of the ladder, never at the bottom rung. But you have to begin as we all began at the bottom.

We, in the 1950s and 1960s, were fortunate that we had judges in the high court who always encouraged us. But senior lawyers can and must help, not by giving out dole, but by paying for effort well spent. You must earn your way to the top of the Bar by being both proficient and useful.

- **Advice Number 4**

Know your judge—not by calling on them or by becoming what we call a *chamcha* for that will only demean you. When you meet a judge at a tea party or outside the court, when some colleague of his or hers has retired, and you speak with them, make sure that you don't talk of matters of the court. This way, you will earn the respect of the judge.

Know your judge is used in an ethical sense because every judge sitting in court is different. Each judge has his own background of experience and the judge before whom you are privileged to appear must be addressed and handled with care. Addressing a judge correctly is extremely important. In a big constitutional case, perhaps it does not matter, but in the run-of-the-mill cases, it does.

In my time, there used to be Justice J. M. Shelat, who was first a judge in the Bombay City Civil Court, then in the high court, and finally in the Supreme Court of India from February 1966 to April 1973. Now, in the city civil court, a judge is always addressed as "Your Honour." In the high court, he (or she) is always addressed as "My Lord." Shelat was sensitive about the change in forms of address when he became a high court judge and he was so allergic to being continued to be addressed as "Your Honour" that lawyers who inadvertently addressed him as such would suffer by losing their cases.

It happened to me in my young days when I opposed another young lawyer. The opposing advocate (he is today a well-known commentator on public affairs) kept referring to Justice Shelat as "Your Honour" and so brittle did the judge become that he delivered judgement in my favour! It was of course a wrong judgement and when the appeal came up for hearing before a bench presided over by Justice Mudholkar in the Bombay High Court, the appellant was not called upon, and as I was appearing for the respondent, I was asked to defend the judgement (Of course, the judgement was reversed). But to his credit, Justice Shelat worked himself out of this blemish and became a fine seasoned judge in the Supreme Court. He had a literary bent and wrote a book on the life of the third Mughal emperor, Jalal-ud-din Muhammad Akbar, and it was published by Bharatiya Vidya Bhawan in 1959. The example of Justice Shelat is only to indicate to you that some judges are more sensitive and more apt to take umbrage than others.

- **Advice Number 5**

To be a successful young lawyer, you must have a pair of good watchful eyes and above all, good ears. Generally, when there is a bench of two or more judges, you can train yourself to *see* and *listen* and thus hear and divine what the judges are saying to one another, which is helpful. You must be able to pick-up even a whisper of one judge to another! There is no such thing as eavesdropping in court. You can hear and note whatever is said in the court with impunity. To overhear what one judge whispers to another or to his colleagues on the bench is not bad form and rather, it can be helpful. This way, you can tell which way the court is going in your case, and if need be, change tack and adopt a different line of action!

- **Advice Number 6**

Try to be a good judge of faces and moods, a skill which you can only develop if you sit in court and listen (even when keeping your own big mouth shut). When you do open it, i.e., your mouth, and speak in court, the judge must carry a good impression about you. Believe me, the memories of judges are like the proverbial memory of elephants; they never forget a slight. They may forgive it, but be sure that they will never forget it. Judges are also most receptive to a good argument. They will never forget a good logical argument, even though you may have lost the case, in which you made it because the next time you appear, the judge will expect you to speak equally sensibly and will appreciate what you say. Don't let him down.

- **Advice Number 7**

Don't show off. "Humbly does it" as the saying goes. And never give the judge an opportunity to mentally "blackball" you by making a wrong statement of fact or suggesting an erroneous proposition of law. You have to think before you argue a case of what are the points of law and the authorities that you can possibly take in support of it. Justice S. R. Tendolkar of the Bench High Court (1947 to 1958), who was a judge as sharp as nails, once said in a speech that he mentally blackballed a lawyer who misled him on facts of law. So, beware not to mislead, even inadvertently.

- **Advice Number 8**

This advice is most important for young lawyers to remember. Don't be funny in court. It doesn't pay to be funny. If you feel compelled to say something funny, let it be something disparaging about yourself, never about your colleague or any other member of the Bar. However, the sitting judge can and does sometimes indulge in levity. So, it is good policy to laugh at all the judges' jokes, however corny. Just as the judge's point (or the point suggested by a judge during an argument) is always the best point in the case, so also the (poor) jokes that judges sometimes crack in court are by definition (and by order of the court) the funniest! Never comment adversely on them except in the precincts of the Bar-room where the laws of libel and slander are by common consent inapplicable.

- **Advice Number 9**

You must be bold when arguing cases—bold but never rude. You must cultivate the art of being respectful. Never be familiar with a judge before whom you regularly practice, either in court or outside of it.

- **Advice Number 10**

Never lose your temper and if you have to lose it, because of some proposition stated by a judge with which you disagree, never show it. Take it out on the assistant who sits next to you. Get angry with him but never, never lose your temper at the presiding officer of a court. Losing your temper will only help you lose your client's case.

- **Advice Number 11**

Don't be boring. Don't go on and on as some advocates do. Once you realise the judge has understood your point, then shut up. Whether he or she accepts your argument or not is up to the judge. You have to make your point; it is for the judge to accept or reject it. If you go on and on and the judge is polite and looks out of the window, it only means you have bored him. I have in my study some pictures of an American courtroom where the judge, apparently bored by the counsel's argument, has gone to sleep. So, counsel leans forward and tells the court clerk, "Charlie, wake him up" and Charlie cheekily responds, "You wake him up, since you put him to sleep in the first place!"

The Bar is a great place—enjoy every moment of it. And may God be with all of you in your endeavours.

3

150 Years of the Bombay High Court: Reflections and Insights

A famous jurist, Professor Otto Kahn-Freund, had coined a striking metaphor about the role of judges: "They build up the law and the institution brick by brick." The prestige of the High Court of Bombay was because we had in the past and are fortunate to continue to have in the present, judges and advocates who by dint of hard work and integrity have helped to erect and maintain the temple of the law brick-by-brick. Architecturally, the structure is unique and beautiful from without, but it has made its mark only because some of our judges and lawyers over the years—over a century and a half—have helped to strengthen it from within.

Exactly fifty years ago (in 1962), the Bombay High Court was a hundred years old[5] (and I was twelve years in practice at the Bombay Bar). Chief Justice H. K. Chainani and his companion judges resolved to celebrate the event by commissioning a history of the court. Advocate and scholar P. B. Vachha was requested to undertake the work. He stipulated, at the very start, that he should have a free hand to write in his own way and to freely express his views and comments on men and matters. This being agreed, the work, later titled *Famous Judges, Lawyers, and Cases of Bombay*[6], was duly completed.

In the chapter on historical cases (Chapter XV), Vachha described the facts and events relating to the trial for sedition of Bal Gangadhar Tilak (in the central court of the high court building) in respect of articles published in the popular daily, *Kesari,* in May-June 1908. Tilak defended himself at the trial, and in his address to the jury (in those days there was always a jury in a notable criminal trial), Tilak made some very good points. In his charge to the jury, the presiding judge, Justice Dinshaw Davar, summed against Tilak: "A journalist could criticise the government as strongly as he liked, but he had no right to attribute dishonest or immoral motives to it." The jury, by a majority of 7:2, returned a verdict of guilty. On being asked by the judge whether he had anything to say, Tilak uttered the following—now memorable—words:

> "All that I wish to say is that, in spite of the verdict of the jury, I still maintain that I am innocent. There are higher powers that rule the destinies of men and nations; and I think, it may be the will of providence that the cause I represent may be benefited more by my suffering than by my pen and tongue."

The judge then sentenced Tilak to six years' "transportation" (i.e., confinement in the Andaman Islands) and a fine of Rs. 1,000. While passing the sentence, the judge indulged in some scathing strictures about Tilak's conduct. He condemned the articles as seething with sedition: "preaching violence and speaking of murders with approval."

According to Vachha, Tilak's trial, even if legally justified, was a grave political blunder aggravated by the judge's intemperate strictures on the popular patriot, whom Justice Davar had described as a man with a "diseased and perverted mind." All this was said by Vachha in felicitous prose, and it was acceptable to the committee of judges under whose auspices, the history of the high court was being written. But then Vachha added a postscript to Tilak's trial. In it, he also criticised an event that took place at the unveiling of a marble tablet fixed outside the central court where Tilak was tried. On the tablet is inscribed Tilak's protestation of innocence: 'In spite of the verdict of the jury . . . I still maintain that I am innocent." Chief Justice M. C. Chagla unveiled the tablet in Tilak's memory.

In the postscript, Vachha not only criticised Chagla's speech at the unveiling of the tablet but also the very idea of a memorial tablet in the high court that atoned "for the misdeeds of previous generations." He characterised Chief Justice Chagla's speech as "admirably patriotic, or patriotically admirable, but legally and judicially inexplicable and indefensible," and as being delivered from a wrong platform. Vachha said that the tablet, taken in conjunction with the speech, was also unfortunate as it established a very undesirable precedent. And he went on:

> "If successive generations of judges, with fluctuating loyalties and ideologies, are to be at liberty to put up memorial tablets, 'atoning' for the misdeeds of previous generations, there would be no end of such memorial tablets; and judges henceforth will have to decide cases with an eye not to the law and evidence, or even to the Supreme Court, but to the 'inevitable verdict of history,' which, of course, is to be taken as always infallible and final. Pace Herodotus, Tacitus, Gibbon, and Macaulay! In point of fact, the verdicts of history are no more inevitable or infallible than those of judges and juries, and, in any case, are utterly irrelevant in the context of judicial pronouncements. It is also an irony of human life that the 'inevitable verdict of history' occasionally overtakes us sooner than we anticipated."[7]

Chief Justice Chainani and his colleagues (which then included Justice Tarkunde and Justice Y. V. Chandrachud) bridled at this criticism of Chagla, as well as at Chagla's tribute to Tilak, when unveiling the memorial tablet outside the court where he was tried. Vachha claimed the historian's privilege of writing whatever appeared to him to be correct, and he refused to omit the postscript or alter any part of it. He told the judges that he had followed the advice which was given to India's great historian Ferishta by Ibrahim Adilshah, when Ferishta migrated from the Nizam Shahi court at Ahmadnagar to the Adil Shahi court at Bijapur. "Write," that liberal monarch had said, "write without fear or flattery." Vachha said that fear and flattery for the powers that be are the worst enemies of historical truth and vitiated history at its very source: "If a writer is influenced by these unworthy and unmanly emotions and motives, his work becomes not only dishonest, but insipid, humdrum, and featureless."

All this, of course, led to an impasse. The judges remained adamant, and so did Vachha. As a result, the history of the Bombay High Court for the first hundred years had to go without the imprimatur of being an official version but no matter. Headed by K. M. Munshi, H. M. Seervai, and one or two more seniors, along with some juniors like R. J. Joshi, Atul Setalvad, and myself, a committee was formed which was entrusted with the task of having the book published privately. Funds were collected and ultimately this book was published by law publishers N. M. Tripathi Pvt. Ltd. The book has remained a classic, and fortunately, it is in print again.[8]

The Chartered High Courts of Calcutta and Madras are as old as the Bombay High Court but the histories of those great institutions have not found their Boswell. The Bombay High Court alone has the distinction of having an admirable record comprehended and penned by a single author of its *Famous Judges, Lawyers, and Cases of Bombay*. I am proud to have been associated with the publication of this book.

The central court on the second floor, where sessions trials took place (before my time) till the establishment of the civil and sessions court in the building adjacent to the high court, was a hallowed place. It was here that the entire Bar assembled in October 1958 to bid a tearful farewell to its favourite chief justice who had laid down office at his prime minister's request to go as India's ambassador to the United States—an event that evoked much praise and some controversy. One of the stalwarts at the Bar, S. V. Gupte, was critical of Chagla accepting an ambassadorial assignment from the executive whilst holding high judicial office, and he publicly made his views known!

It was in the same central court that the constitutional validity of the order of the governor of Bombay suspending the sentence, imposed by a division bench of the high court on Commander K. M. Nanavati, was heard in 1960 by a bench of five judges. Nanavati was a brave, bright but extremely impetuous officer in the Indian Navy who shot dead his wife's lover, Prem Ahuja. In view of an impassioned plea by his counsel, Karl Khandalavala, one of the leading criminal lawyers of the time, the jury, despite the summing up by the sessions judge, brought in a verdict of not guilty of murder 8:1.[9] Since the judge did not agree with the verdict of the jury, the case was referred to a division bench of the high court for reappraisal. The evidence led in the case was reconsidered by a bench of two judges of the Bombay High Court—Justices J. M. Shelat and Naik. They reached the unanimous conclusion (though for different reasons) that Commander Nanavati was guilty of cold-blooded murder and sentenced him to imprisonment for life (Y. V. Chandrachud, then government pleader, successfully argued the reference for the state—a success that was the stepping stone to much greater things).

At the instance of higher-ups at the centre, the governor of Bombay promptly intervened and passed an order (in March 1960) suspending the sentence imposed on Nanavati till he filed his appeal in the Supreme Court. Arguments about the constitutional validity of this order of the governor were heard for several days in the central court by a specially constituted bench of five judges presided over by Chief Justice Chainani. Since the order of the governor was not shown to be unconstitutional or contrary to law, the bench of five judges upheld the same and directed that the warrant of arrest of Commander Nanavati (which had been returned unfulfilled) should not be reissued, until Nanavati's appeal in the Supreme Court had been disposed of. But in September 1960, the Supreme Court of India held that the governor's order of suspension of the sentence was invalid and required Commander Nanavati to surrender to proper jail custody like all other convicted felons.

Of Oliver Cromwell (April 1599—September 1658), England's first and only dictator, it has been said that he told his portrait painter: "Mr Lely, I desire you would use all your skill to paint my picture truly like me, and not flatter me at all, but remark all these roughnesses, pimples, warts, and everything as you see me, otherwise I will never pay a farthing for it." Well, if you walk from the central court to the chief justice's court at the southern end of the corridor on the second floor, you will see there a portrait—an exact likeness of a great chief justice, "pimples, warts and everything", though he had fewer warts than many other guardians of the law!

The trouble with great chief justices is that they cast a shadow over their successors, howsoever erudite and competent they may be. Many years ago, the chief justice of the New York Court of Appeals, in his inaugural address to a conference of the International Bar Association held in that city, told his audience how he had proudly shown his wife the room of his illustrious predecessor-in-office, of nearly half a century past, and with what result: "See my dear," he said reverentially to his wife, "this is Cardozo's room, and this is where I will sit."

And his wife responded (not very reverentially): "Yes—and after fifty years and five more chief justices, it will still be Cardozo's room!"

To me, the chief justice's court in Bombay will always remain the court where M. C. Chagla sat. The fact that the Bombay High Court is still reckoned as one of the premier courts in the country is in no small measure due to the man who was its chief justice from the year 1947—even before I joined the Bar—until October 1958.

I recall that when, as additional solicitor general of India at Delhi, I appeared in the High Court of Calcutta back in the 1970s, Chief Justice Shankar Prasad Mitra told me (when I cited before him a judgement of Chagla's) that he and all his colleagues always welcomed citation of a judgement by that great judge. He also said in open court that the Bombay High Court was known and respected because of the judgements of its great chief justice. A handsome tribute by the chief justice of one chartered high court to the chief justice of another.

Chagla was not only a master of law and the English language but also had an abiding sense of justice, which is vitally important for all who sit in judgement. Moreover, he possessed a rare gift that few have: the art of gentle persuasion. Men in flourishing practice, men like Y. V. Chandrachud, Dahyabhai Patel, V. M. Tarkunde (who practiced on what was known in my time as the appellate side), N. A. (Nalin) Mody, and the three Desai's— Sunderlal (ST) Desai, Kantilal (KT) Desai, and Kapil (KK) Desai (who practiced on the original side)—were all in top practice, but they just could not, dare not, say "No" to Chagla. When he called on them to become judges, they yielded. And they had no regrets (Y. V. Chandrachud, when the chief justice of India, himself told me so!). They accepted because they genuinely felt that, upon their appointment as companions of Chief Justice Chagla, they would be really *elevated* to sit in a court presided over by India's most distinguished chief justice. Chagla's extraordinary kindness to members of the Bar who practiced before him rubbed off on all persons whom Chagla recommended and got appointed as judges.

If the Bombay High Court is to survive and survive with glory in the future decades of the twenty-first century, I suggest that it must grapple with, and tackle, grave domestic problems of the three C's: the besetting problems of corruption, caste, and costs.

Bribery and corruption are so rare in English tradition that when, in the last century, in a debate in the House of Lords, the Lord Chancellor referred to a judge taking a bribe, the reporter of *Hansard* was so shocked that he wrote "bride." Taking a *bride* he could believe, but taking a *bribe* was thinkable! But that was decades ago.

In his autobiography, Chief Justice P. B. Gajendragadkar[10] recalls an incident on the appellate side of the high court when one of the senior members of the appellate side Bar, Hormazdiar Coyajee (father of Justice N. H. Coyajee), was arguing before a bench consisting of Justice Rangnekar and Justice Maclean. To an appeal from the judgement of a district court, Coyajee told the court: "My Lords, this is one of those cases in which court fees having been paid, the decree had to be passed."

Justice Maclean asked what this meant: "Surely, Mr Coyajee, in every case, court fee has to be paid."

Rangnekar, the more experienced, the more worldly-wise, whispered into Maclean's ear that the judgement under appeal was delivered by a judge whom Coyajee believed to be corrupt. Coyajee's mode of presentation was by innuendo, suggesting that the decree was illegally procured. Justice Gajendragadkar recalls this incident as an anecdote. But today, this story in the Bombay High Court is no longer just an amusing anecdote; it is a seriously disturbing one. Corruption has permeated all facets of life, including the judicial. And it is no use pretending that it has not reared its ugly head even in the echelons of the higher judiciary.

Justice Benjamin N. Cardozo, former associate justice of the Supreme Court of the United States, once confessed that the hydraulic pressure of great events does not fail to influence judges, "they do not idly pass them by." So, it is with the canker of corruption. Hence, it must be rooted out not by the dilatory and virtually impossible process of "impeachment" (i.e., in constitutional terms "removal for proved misbehaviour"[11]) which has been attempted in recent times. For example, in the case of a sitting judge of the Supreme Court, a sitting judge of the Calcutta High Court, and a sitting chief justice of the Karnataka High Court. Each of the attempts has been ineffectual because, in the case of Justice V. Ramaswami, the motion to remove him was defeated since members of the ruling Congress Party, as a bloc (and as a matter of policy), deliberately abstained from voting, thus ensuring that the requisite two-thirds majority could not be secured. In the case of Justice Soumitra Sen of the Calcutta High Court, the motion for his removal was passed by an overwhelming majority of members in the Rajya Sabha, but before it could be brought up in the Lok Sabha, the judge tendered his unqualified resignation. In the case of Justice Dinakaran, formerly chief justice of the Karnataka High Court, after the decision of the statutory committee appointed under the Judges Inquiry Act, 1958, holding him guilty of proved misbehaviour, he too pre-empted his removal from office by resigning. A new methodology has to be devised *by* judges *for* errant judges. I have in the past recommended the institutionalisation of an ombudsman system for the higher judiciary.

"Impeachment" (or compulsory removal from high office) is a powerful but blunt instrument. It is the heaviest piece of artillery in the constitutional arsenal, and because it is so heavy, it is virtually unfit for use. In the United States, they have the same problem with superior judges in state and federal courts. So, they have devised an alternative method. Under the US Judicial Council Reforms and Judicial Conduct and Disability Act, 1980, the primary responsibility for disciplining judges rests with the "council of judges" in each circuit and ultimately in a select body of superior judges known as the "Judicial Conference." Neither body may remove the judge from office, but they may request that he voluntarily retire or direct that no cases be assigned to him for a limited period. When more severe action is warranted, the Judicial Conference sends the case to the House of Representatives to consider, initiating the constitutional process of removal.

Then there is the problem of caste. Take appointments to the subordinate judiciary. They are of great significance because a large number of high court judges are drawn from the cadre of district judges. Under the Constitution of India, though appointments to the posts of district judges are made by the governor (i.e., the state executive), they are always done in consultation with the high court. The subordinate judiciary in the state is entirely under the control of its high court, as one of the judgements puts it, "under its care and custody." The power to confirm, the power to promote, the power to determine seniority of service, in respect of these judges, rests entirely with the high court. When the executive has interfered, it has often come to grief.

But there have been complaints, more frequent of late, that some high courts, when dealing with the subordinate judiciary, nay, that some judges even when deciding cases, act on the basis of caste to subserve parochial interests. The late Justice D. P. Madan once told me that after he was appointed chief justice of the Bombay High Court, he found, upon a perusal of the confidential files, that there were a large number of district judges who were kept back by some of his predecessors (a few of them illustrious) merely because of their caste, although they deserved to be elevated to the high court on merit! And he said that he was trying to set this right.

Many years ago, a Lord of Appeal, Lord Davey, said of English judges that though they were all impartial, "not all have the power of divesting themselves of prejudice." Very deftly put! So, it is with some of our judges. We must *be aware of,* and then *beware of,* these traits if we mean to plan for the survival of this high court as a great and prestigious institution of democracy.

Corruption and caste are primarily matters for the judges to resolve, while the problem of costs (and delays) is for the legislature and the legal profession. We lawyers must make a concerted effort to find a solution to the overpowering problem of delays and costs. Prominent lawyers, practicing in the high courts, must be accessible to all those who can afford them and even those who cannot. The legal profession is service-oriented. It cannot survive unless it is seen to be of service to those who need them. In addition to being accessible to all, the lawyer must also be proficient and competent as he is the fuel in the engine of justice. It is the quality of the fuel that determines how effectively the engine will work.

But the lawyer is something more than just the fuel in the engine. The lawyer who practices in court functions as a catalyst between those who judge and the vast majority of those whose cases are to be judged. A catalyst, as you know, is an agent that causes activity between two or more forces without itself being affected. Though the lawyer's functions have vastly varied, this is still his main function.

A lawyer can fulfil this function only if he (or she) is *efficient* and *honest*. Each attribute is as important as the other. An inefficient but honest lawyer is not much use to either the client or society. An efficient but dishonest one is positively dangerous.

Way back in 1859, before the Bombay High Court was even established, an act was passed by the state of Jersey. Its provisions are extracted in one of the volumes of *Moore's Privy Council cases* (Vol. 13, page 263). The Preamble to the 1859 Act is worth quoting because the sentiments it expresses are as applicable today as they were more than 150 years ago.

> "PREAMBLE:
> Considering that the interests of justice require admission at the Bar of all those who offer substantial guarantees of capacity/ that the monopoly of the profession of advocates limited by considerations other than those of capacity is a Bar to intellectual emulation, indispensable to the useful exercise of that profession; that the profession of advocates being a *public* function depending above all on the *confidence of suitors,* it behoves that the public be not exposed to place the protection of its interests in the hands of those who cannot show proofs of undoubted special capacity."

We legal practitioners must exhibit "undoubted special capacity," as we must be a bit like proficient surgeons. Both the legal and medical professions are subjects of mystique: making "life and death" decisions, using skills that others do not have or understand. The patient being wheeled into the operating theatre and the litigant being directed into the courtroom, are similar. They submit themselves to experts who can help them or destroy them, bring them into the light or leave them in perpetual darkness! The "victim" whom we (at the Bar) call "the client," doctors call him "the patient," but in the hands of each, he is the "victim." The victim must feel confident that he is in safe hands and that the professional will perform his role adequately and competently, uninfluenced by external forces or by greed or avarice. The survival of the high court as an institution where justice is administered depends a great deal not merely on advocates practicing in it, but on advocates who believe that they also serve society whilst they make their living, and who practice their profession with a conscience.

No celebration of the high court can be complete if it ignores the subordinate judiciary. It was the Privy Council who first realised the importance of district judges in our scheme of administration of justice. How often have we read how those exalted personages preferred the judgements of the sub-judge or district judge to those of the high court who reversed them (!), complimenting (along the way) the subordinate judge on the lucidity and learning of his judgement. Alas, in our preoccupation with the writ jurisdiction and the plethora of cases on administrative and constitutional law (that now abound), the district judge is ignored until, of course, he has the good fortune to be promoted to the high court.

At the district level, where the district judge should know much more about how the administration works, our Constitution has deprived him of all jurisdiction to enquire into the acts of district officials. That, I think, is a pity. It was a mistake not to associate the district judges with that branch of the law which, in the post-constitutional period, has been called administrative law. Incidentally, this was the pronounced view of Justice E. S. Venkataramiah, one of India's very learned chief justices. Contrast this with the position in the United States. The district judge there is still a very important functionary and has jurisdiction to supervise the acts of officials within his jurisdiction. At a seminar held in Srinagar to celebrate the bicentennial of the United States Constitution (in 1987) a US district judge, Judge Kane, informed the gathering of the width and ambit of his powers in his own circuit. As a district judge, he had the power to fix his board and carry on with matters taken up from day to day. He told us that only two weeks before coming to Kashmir, he had fined a lawyer $15,000 for "delaying proceedings without cause." So long as we don't give the subordinate judiciary the place it deserves, it will continue to function as it currently does—almost as a stepchild in the important business of administering justice according to law.

In times of stress, a brave judge, though sometimes in a minority of one, has changed the course of his country's judicial history! So too the dissentient judge—the one who speaks for the brooding conscience of future generations. Let me remind you of *Liversidge* vs. *Anderson*[12] (that infamous decision given in times of war which the majority of our Supreme Court in *ADM Jabalpur*[13] wrongly relied on in times of peace!). It is now more than eighty years since the decision in *Liversidge* was rendered, and the majority view, which was embarrassing to English lawyers and judges, was officially buried in 1980 by the House of Lords. Lord Atkin's dissent has been finally vindicated. When it was delivered, however, the popular view was the majority view. And it is necessary to recall the context in which the House of Lords heard the case. The argument took place in September 1941, and the speeches (i.e., judgements) were delivered on 3 November. It was at the lowest point of the Second World War. The Balkans and Crete had been overrun. The invasion of Russia had carried the Germans close to Leningrad and Moscow. The British summer offensive in the Western Desert had failed. The Japanese menace on the Malayan Peninsula and Singapore was already being felt. Pearl Harbour was to follow (in a month), and the United States were not yet at war with Germany or Japan! Viscount Maugham's speech (the majority view) reflected the atmosphere:

> "All the circumstances of national safety to which this House adverted in *R.* vs. *Halliday* (1917) are present in this war, only with vastly increased urgency and gravity, because German methods for effecting the prisoners infiltration among British or allied subjects of their purpose and schemes have been immensely more subtle and ingenious than in the last war. Even

> a judge may be allowed to take notice of the import of words like fifth-columnists and quislings and the like."

But Lord Atkin would not take notice. Instead, he reminded his colleagues of that oft-quoted purple passage that in England "amid the clash of arms, the laws are not silent. They may be changed, but they speak the same language in war as in peace." Brave words, heroic words, but not at that time. Lord Atkin suffered as his colleagues refused to speak to him because, in his dissent, Atkin had hit out at them:

> "I view with apprehension the attitude of judges who, on a mere question of construction, when face-to-face with claims involving the liberty of the subject, show themselves more executive-minded than the executive.
>
> . . . I know of one authority which might justify the (their) suggested method of construction (of Reg.18B). 'When I use a word,' Humpty Dumpty said in rather a scornful tone, 'it means just what I choose it to mean, neither more nor less.' 'The question is,' said Alice, 'whether you can make words mean different things.' 'The question is,' said Humpty Dumpty, 'which is to be the master—that's all' (*Alice Through the Looking Glass,* c.vi)."

Atkin was also contemptuous of his colleagues:

> ". . . In this case, I have listened to arguments which might have been addressed acceptably to the Court of King's Bench in the time of Charles I!"

And he knew that the consequences of what he had written would offend and would cause hurt. On 2 November 1941, he told his daughter, Gaven: "I am giving off my dissenting judgement in the Home Security Cases tomorrow and haven't spared the others. I hope I shall be on speaking terms with them afterwards." He was not. He was criticised by his senior colleague, Lord Maugham, in an unprecedented open letter to *The Times*. He was requested by the lord chancellor (Lord Simon) to delete his scornful reference to the Humpty Dumpty attitude of his colleagues on matters of statutory construction. He was upbraided, almost branded a traitor. But Atkin remained tight-lipped. He refused to be drawn into controversy over his dissent. He refused to go to the press. He was amply rewarded, first in private and much later by posterity.

Dr C. K. Allen, the famous author of *Law and Orders*, which contained a forceful account of the administration of Emergency Regulation 18B, and who was always a vehement champion of the individual against the encroachments of executive power, wrote to Lord Atkin three days after the judgement:

> "Dear Lord Atkin,
>
> I expect that this is a very improper letter to be written even by a non-practicing member of the Bar, but I cannot refrain from saying that it will be remembered as not the least distinction in your great judicial work that you alone among other judges have raised your voice against a gross abuse of power. Such cries in the wilderness have strong and long echoes. There is no real answer to the simple point of language on which you took your stand."

In 1980, Lord Diplock spoke for posterity. "For my part," he said in his speech in the House of Lords (in the *Rossminister case*[14]), "I think the time has come to acknowledge openly that the majority of this House in *Liversidge* vs. *Anderson* were expediently and, at that time, perhaps excusably wrong and the dissenting speech of Lord Atkin was right."

I would respectfully remind the judges of our high court that cries in the wilderness do have "strong and long echoes."

One other important point about which the Bar and the bench need to be reminded is that we must never forget how attempts were made to dim the great "searchlight" provision of our Constitution (Article 226) during the dark days of the internal emergency from June 1975 to March 1977, and how this was averted. A committee, which included three prominent lawyers, was set up by the centre to clip the wings of the high courts by proposing drastic changes in Article 226. The chairman of the committee, Swaran Singh, who was India's foreign minister in Indira Gandhi's government, told his colleagues that when he was himself a minister in Punjab, he found that, as a minister, it was just not possible to render justice in individual cases because of the pressures and pulls of party politics and that it was far better that courts were left to do the job, and that was why it was best that Article 226 remained in the Constitution with a few changes. Swaran Singh[15] was the one person, a non-practicing lawyer, who set his face against the abolition of Article 226, not when times were good, but when times were bad. Real bad! And we must all be grateful to him for having saved the writ jurisdiction of the high courts.

It is a sad commentary of our times that it was the practicing lawyer-politicians on the Constitution Committee who so fervently wanted not just to amend but to scrap Article 226 "in obedience to the wishes of the high command." The moral of the story is that we should avoid relying on high-profile lawyers (who have political interests or ambitions) to guide our destinies, because it is they (with their argumentative skills) who are able to rationalise anything, including all forms of tyranny!

Judicial independence is a byword in every democracy. In British India, with the establishment of the high courts in the middle of the nineteenth century, the concept of an independent judiciary took root. But till 1947, one-third of the area of this subcontinent was being administered by what came to be known as the princely states. The judges in those states, often described as the "jee-huzoor judge," were required to function in the time-honoured tradition of judicial subservience, so characteristic of Mughal and pre-Mughal times—an aspect poignantly emphasised two decades ago at a seminar titled, "Administration of Justice in the Year 2000 AD," held in Bombay under the joint auspices of the International Bar Association and LAWASIA. The then president of India, Zail Singh (who inaugurated the seminar), eloquently and graphically described in Hindi the conditions under which judges functioned in the erstwhile Indian states. The president gave his own example of the ardent young Zail Singh, a keen nationalist, who was put in jail on not one, not two, but on innumerable occasions by the ruler of one of the princely Patiala states. On one occasion, in his youthful exuberance, Zail Singh protested to the judge against his fresh detention on the evidence of a tutored witness who had deposed to his allegedly illegal activities on each of several previous occasions when he had been imprisoned. He demanded that he should be permitted to cross-examine this tutored witness and, for that purpose, to engage a lawyer from British India. The judge (who was a kindly person) adjourned the hearing in court and asked the young Zail Singh to see him in his chambers. In chambers, the judge asked him why he was so impetuous, and when informed that it had become intolerable to be detained multiple times on the false testimony of the same person, the judge said (and this is the president speaking):

> "Zail Singh *tōō boodhoo hai* (You are foolish Zail Singh). What's all this talk about cross-examination of the witness produced by the police? They have only acted because the Maharaja has asked them to. Don't you know? If he asks me to acquit you, I will acquit you. If he asks me to convict you, I will convict you. So, let's have less talk about lawyers from British India and get on with the case."

When we framed our Constitution, we chose the British model and not the one India's president had complained about. It is this British model that we most cherish and preserve. It is preserved more by example than by words. There will always be assaults on the independence of the judiciary. But do remember that the citadel never falls except from within. It is up to us— lawyers, judges, and citizens—to help maintain the independence and integrity of the court.

As for the tasks before the union judiciary, I recall the words of Lord Harry Woolf, lord chief justice of England and Wales from June 2000 to October 2005: "Like old clocks, our judicial institutions need to be oiled, wound up, and set to true time."

The reach of India's highest court is all-pervasive. The Supreme Court sits in final judgement over the decisions not only of the high courts in the states but also of hundreds of tribunals (central and State) functioning throughout the country. And the law declared by the Supreme Court, including its pronouncements on the constitutional validity of enacted law (including constitutional amendments), is binding on all other courts and authorities in the country (Article 141). There is virtually no area of legislative or executive activity that is beyond the highest court's scrutiny. Its writ extends to all two million square miles of Indian territory and over its (now) more than its 1.40 billion inhabitants. Empowering itself with the trappings of modern technology, India's Supreme Court has been striving to perform its arduous task. But what of the future?

First and foremost, the judiciary as an institution needs to preserve its independence, and to do this, it must strive to maintain the confidence of the public in the established courts. The independence of judges is best safeguarded by the judges themselves through institutions and organisations that the law empowers them to set up to preserve the image of an incorruptible higher judiciary that would command the respect of all right-thinking people. In the United States, under the Judicial Councils Act, 1980, this task has been gladly undertaken by the judges. But regrettably, so far, there is no law in India to guide our judges, only "guidelines." There is a felt need for a *law*. The 1980 US Act confers powers on bodies comprised of judges to take such action against a federal judge "as is appropriate, short of removal." Under this law, some time ago, a committee of fellow judges had investigated complaints against a federal district judge, John McBryde. The judicial council reprimanded him and suspended him from hearing new cases for a year. McBryde challenged the decision. He argued that the 1980 law violated the judicial independence that the US Constitution guaranteed to life-tenured federal judges. He argued that it also interfered with the mechanism of congressional impeachment that the US Constitution had established for removing judges. A one-year suspension from hearing new cases, he argued, was nothing but a "temporary impeachment." But a US Court of Appeals rejected all these pleas, and a petition for certiorari against its decision was denied by the US Supreme Court. It accepted the argument of the US solicitor general that judicial independence, protected by Article III of the US Constitution, was meant "to insulate judges from interference from other branches of the government, not from oversight by other judges."

An American judge once famously said about the judiciary that "some things will sometimes go wrong." In India, in the past and in recent times, some things *have* gone wrong, and citizens need the reassurance of a system of judicial accountability, a remedial mechanism which will protect the higher judiciary from some of its own members who have gone astray. Such reassurance can only be provided by enacting a law along the lines of the American model.

Other aspects of judicial reform are not lacking for want of ideas. We have been overwhelmed with innumerable reports of law commissions (more than 200 of them!) on all aspects of judicial governance. And a bench of three justices of the Supreme Court (in a judgement delivered by its then seniormost puisne judge in August 2005) had drawn up a fine blueprint on case management on how to make recent amendments in our procedural laws work on the ground and how to get more cases moving along. For instance, in three different tracks: fast track, normal track, and slow track. In the *Salem Advocates Association case,* the justices had *requested* the high courts to implement the detailed blueprint. Most of them have not. They could not *direct* the high courts to do so because, under our constitutional scheme, the latter are autonomous constitutional bodies not subject to administrative directions of the Supreme Court. It is in the high courts that there are now left the largest number of roadblocks and delays. In their administrative functioning, the high courts are answerable to no one but themselves. This often enables the Supreme Court to plead helplessness. Hardly a good augury for integrated court management.

It is time that the Supreme Court be entrusted with direct responsibility for the functioning of the high courts. Only then can the highest court be an effective apex court. Only then can the Supreme Court be made answerable (as it should be) for judicial governance for the entire country. And judicial governance means that all judges who are constitutionally entrusted with the responsibility of protecting the rights of citizens must also be seen as persons of rectitude. They must make annual financial disclosure statements, not privately to their respective chief justices, but publicly. This is done by justices of the Supreme Court in the world's oldest democracy (the USA), and it is appropriate that all such disclosure statements of its judges be made and then published in the world's most populous democracy (India). Judges must set an example for ministers (central and state), for members of Parliament and of state legislatures, and for all high officials of the government to follow. As stated in the Annie Besant translation of the third discourse in the Bhagavad Gita: "Whatsoever a great man doeth, that other men also do; the standard he setteth up, by that the people go."

4

Questions of Consequence

Over many years that I have been speaking at various forums, I have been asked numerous questions—a few of much consequence, some of little consequence, and most of no consequence. In this chapter, I am listing some of the pertinent ones which I feel are rather important. These will encourage young advocates, who are hardworking, to display their skill in writing about different aspects of the law, because writing about law is vastly different from speaking it. It requires close attention to minute detail, which will be excellent training for a "would-be" successful lawyer.

A question that I have repeatedly been asked is that in India's legal system, despite the simmering fault lines in the administration of justice, is there a typical or unique flavour of "Indian justice"?

The answer is "Yes." But you, readers, must know why. It is because:

i. The legal system that originated a few centuries ago in British India and has been continuing under the Constitution of India, 1950, was one in which system and language were inextricably linked. It was originally introduced in British India as a transplant. It had Anglo-Saxon roots. But over time, it got nourished in typically Indian soil. What was initially intended (by the British) to grow into an *English* oak tree had, by the early years of the twentieth century, turned into a large, sprawling *Indian* banyan tree, whose aerial roots had descended to the soil to become new trunks!

ii. India's legal system and English concepts of law were most closely interlinked. India's Constitution was also drafted in English in October 1947 (by Constitutional Adviser B. N. Rau) and then debated, clause by clause, in the Constituent Assembly by its members. Ultimately, the Constitution of India, 1950, was enacted for independent India in English, with a simultaneous translation in Hindi in the Devanagari script, described as the Constitution of Bharat, 1950.

iii. The guiding principle of early Anglo-Indian administrators (and of judges) was not to interfere with the local laws and practices of the country unless they were iniquitous or unjust. It was this principle that inspired the first royal charter of the Supreme Court of Calcutta (1774), Clause XVIII of which had ordained:

> The Supreme Court should be a court of equity and shall and may have full power and authority to administer justice, in a summary manner, as nearly as may be, according to the rules and proceedings of our High Court of Chancery in Great Britain.

The clause conferred on the judges of the Supreme Court of Calcutta the power to administer justice and equity. The High Court of Calcutta (established later in 1862) inherited this right from the Supreme Court of Calcutta. High courts established in Bombay and Madras were also conferred the same powers separately by a royal charter.

Accordingly, in British India, in a case governed solely by Hindu law, since the shastras (scriptures) did not provide a clear answer, judges assumed authority to decide it on principles of "justice, equity, and good conscience." In a celebrated case from Madras that went up all the way to the Privy Council, the question at issue was whether a murderer could succeed to the estate of his victim. The High Court of Madras held that the murderer did not have title and that the succession to the estate of the victim could not be traced through him, and there being no Hindu law that governed the matter, the judges of the high court took recourse to the "principles of equity, justice, and good conscience," i.e., rules of English law modified to suit Indian conditions. Before the Privy Council (the final Court of Appeal from high court decisions in India), it was argued that since the parties were Hindus and the matter was governed by Hindu law, and since no provision was made under that law for disqualifying a murderer from succeeding to the estate of his victim, it must be taken that according to this law, he must succeed! But the judicial committee of the Privy Council (all Englishmen) held, in agreement with the high court, that since Hindu law made no provision on this subject, "the principles of equity, justice, and good conscience" had been rightly invoked, and on these principles, the murderer would be excluded. They also held that no title could be claimed through the murderer, who had to be treated as non-existent and not as one who formed the stock for a fresh line of descent!

iv. Incidentally, this appears to be the origin of JUSTICE in the Preamble to India's Constitution and also explains why "the simmering fault lines of Indian justice" must also be contrasted with the euphoria with which Indian judges were welcomed in British India![16] For instance, Whitley Stokes (1830-1909)[17], Irish lawyer and Celtic scholar—more importantly, a law member in the Governor General's Council and one of the draftsmen (with Macaulay) of the Penal Code 1860—had written his famous treatise on *The Anglo-Indian Codes* 1887 (as well as the introduction and notes to clauses of the Penal Code, which had been the source of the original intent of its framers).

v. The concluding portion of the general introduction to the IPC by the Irish lawyer Whitley Stokes needs to be quoted so that it is known and remembered by all current students of law (including young lawyers): "Decisions of Indian judges not only throw light on the ideas and customs of the people of India but are, as a rule, admirable for their logicality and learning. Of these judgements, none can be read with more pleasure and few with more profit than those of the Hindu Muthuswamy Iyer (judge in the High Court of Madras)[18] and the Mohammeden Sayyid Mahmud" (judge in the High Court of Allahabad)[19].

   Stokes ended his praise of Indian judges with these eloquent words:

   > "For the subtle races that produce such lawyers, no legal doctrine can be too refined, no legal machinery can be too elaborate."

vi. The typical or unique flavour of "Indian Justice" post-1950 is apparent from the language deliberately introduced in Article 142 of India's Constitution:

   > "142. Enforcement of decrees and orders of Supreme Court and orders as to discovery, etc.—(1) The Supreme Court in the exercise of its jurisdiction may pass such decree or make such order as is necessary for doing complete justice in any cause or matter pending before it, and any decree so passed or order so made shall be enforceable throughout the territory of India in such manner as may be prescribed by or under any law made by Parliament and, until provision in that behalf is so made, in such manner as the President may by order prescribe."

   The language used in Article 142 (though adapted from Section 210, Enforcement of Orders of the Federal Court of

British Parliament's Government of India Act, 1935) was with the addition of the following italicised words, viz. "*Make such order as is necessary for doing complete justice in any cause or matter pending before it*" (words that were missing in Section 210 of the 1935 Act).

vii. The italicised words in Article 142 have been construed by different justices of India's Supreme Court differently at different times—individual judges expressing differing views. For instance, in a bench decision of five justices in *Union Carbide Corporation* vs. *Union of India* (1991 (4) SCC 584 at page 634-635), Justice Venkatachaliah, speaking for the court, held that: "The constitutional power of the apex court cannot be limited or restricted by provisions contained in statutory law . . ."

However, in a later decision, also of a bench of five judges reported in 1998 (4) SCC 409, it was held that: "Statute law must always prevail over the court's decision to do complete justice in a given case . . ." The bench expressed some doubt as to whether substantive provisions in enacted law could be ignored.

However, judges of the Supreme Court, sitting in benches of two and/or three to administer justice in individual cases, have often *cocked a Nelson's eye to* statute law in a desire to do substantive justice (a class of judges described by the great Lord Denning as "bold spirits") and other judges (described by him as "timid souls") are reluctant to depart from or ignore statutory law.

Perhaps, the only guide in such cases is the judge's conscience. Renowned scholar Ronald Dworkin (writing in the *Harvard Law Review* about "hard cases") had once opined: "Some cases raise issues so novel that they cannot be decided even by stretching or reinterpreting existing rules. So, judges must sometimes make new law, either covertly or explicitly. But when they do, they must act as deputy to the appropriate legislature, enacting the law that they suppose the legislature would enact if seized of the problem."[20]

An important question that I am often asked is that since India's courts are faced with a docket explosion and an unworkable caseload, it is often suggested that private disputes between individuals should be resolved through alternate dispute resolution (ADR) mechanisms, and as to what do I feel about the ADR framework in India, particularly about mediation?[21]

The working group in India that was entrusted with the task of drafting independent India's new arbitration law (to replace the old Arbitration Act of 1940) had before it three separate adaptations of the UNCITRAL Model Law, 1985 (adopted unanimously by the UN General Assembly in December 1985):

a) Adoption of the UNCITRAL Model Law and its incorporation: Countries like Canada (Federal), Australia, and Hong Kong adopted the Model Law, attaching it to their respective national laws;
b) Adaptation of the UNCITRAL Model Law: Countries like the Netherlands and the United Kingdom, which did not adopt it, took special care to make their own national law compatible with it; and
c) *Adopting* many of the provisions of the Model Law and *adapting* some other provisions with amendments. In territories like the province of British Columbia (1986) in Canada and the state of California in the USA, a legislation was framed based principally on the UNCITRAL Model Law but using the local drafting format for giving effect to many of the provisions of the Model Law.

Item (c) above was chosen in the new draft of India's Arbitration and Conciliation Bill, which was prepared and later became the

Arbitration and Conciliation Act of 1996. But after several later amendments added to the act, it has lost its punch and effect. There has been much rethinking on the part of the Government of India as to a fresh legislation being adopted as suggested by a high-level committee in June 2023, but no final decision has been reached.

Regarding ADR: What General Charles de Gaulle, former president of France, once said (in French) is just as eloquent in English: "One must not confuse the light breezes of fashion with the winds of history." In the sphere of ADR, the winds of history are with traditional arbitration. But the art and (the) practice of mediation does show that the winds are a-changing! As mentioned earlier, there is a growing body of opinion around the world that arbitration, both domestic and international, even arbitration that is well conducted by competent arbitrators, is not necessarily the most successful way of resolving disputes, especially commercial disputes. Other ways have to be explored.

Skilled mediators are now able to achieve results satisfactory to both parties, far beyond the power of lawyers and even of courts! A few years ago, I was invited to speak at a conference of the Global Indian Diaspora in Singapore and the topic was "Arbitration and Business Dispute Resolution: The Way Forward." In the materials provided by the organisers, mention was made about an action filed in a court (in Singapore) by British Airways (BA) against Singapore Airlines. BA had alleged a patent infringement of their first-class sleeper beds, and the action was reported in local newspapers with the heading "Let Sleeping Beds Lie." But there was more to it than just the title. The interesting bit of information offered was that the suits were *mediated* for just over two days, and an amicable compromise was reached. Both airlines issued identical press statements to the effect that they would look forward to continuing competition through their products and services, rather than through law courts and arbitration. This is the way *sensible* people (and *responsible* corporations) resolve business disputes. And this is why an enabling new chapter (Part III: Conciliation) was added to India's Arbitration and Conciliation Act, 1996.

I believe that there has to be a conscious (and constant) attempt by arbitrators themselves (at the moment there is not) to invoke Section 30 of the 1996 Act, simply because it encourages parties to get into a mediation-friendly frame of mind at the earliest. This section provides that with the agreement of the parties, the arbitral tribunal may "use mediation, conciliation, or other procedures at any time during the arbitral proceedings to encourage settlement." And the best way to "encourage settlement" is to initiate it. As every practicing lawyer knows that suits get compromised, more often than not, simply because the presiding judge, after familiarising himself (or herself) with what the case is all about, *suggests* and later *guides* parties to an amicable adjustment of the entire case.

Unfortunately, experienced arbitrators appear to be inclined to be dismissive of ADR, taking the rather lofty view that whilst it would no doubt work well enough in family disputes, it is quite unsuited to disputes of a commercial character. That view is now proved to be misplaced. ADR in the form of mediation is growing. It is a great deal quicker and cheaper than litigation, (or even arbitration). And attempts at ADR are generally successful, ending in some form of agreement. Besides, ADR (including mediation) is not constrained by strict legal rights. It facilitates even non-legal forms of relief, such as the offer to the aggrieved party of a substitute contract (unthinkable in a traditional arbitration proceeding) or the resuscitation of an agreement that has been already terminated (impossible to justify on strict legal principles).

Lord Mustill (in my experience one of the finest legal minds England had produced in the last century) once complained at the Millennium Conference of the Chartered Institute of Arbitrators in London (on 19 November 1999) that: "We have now lost the culture of compromise." He was right. Arbitration has lost its best ally. Until the resolution of a dispute by settlement is considered once again to be a constituent function of arbitration, it is ADR that will completely take over and will displace arbitration as a pragmatic and workable alternative.

In my view, arbitration must never be considered as excluding from its purview at any stage during the *settlement* of the dispute. Recent years have seen English courts take proactive steps to promote the use of ADR alongside the formal court system. In December 1993, Justice Cresswell made the following statement at a sitting of the Commercial Court:

> "While emphasising the primary role of the Commercial Court as a forum for deciding commercial cases, the judges of the court wish to encourage parties to consider the use of alternative dispute resolution (ADR), such as mediation and conciliation, as a possible additional means of resolving particular issues or disputes. The judges will not act as mediators or be involved in any ADR process but will in appropriate cases invite parties to consider whether their case, or certain issues in their case, could be resolved by means of ADR. By way of example only, ADR might be tried where the costs of litigation are likely to be wholly disproportionate to the amount at stake."

This statement was later reproduced as a practice note in the Law Reports (See 1994 (1) All E. R. 33).

In January 1995, another practice direction was introduced by the Court of Appeal in the UK. The practice direction required a solicitor in a high court action in England to sign and lodge with the court a checklist (with answers) to the questions:

1. Have you or counsel discussed with your client(s) the possibility of attempting to resolve this dispute (or particular issues) by ADR?
2. Might some form of ADR procedure assist to resolve or narrow the issues in this case?
3. Have you or your client(s) explored with the other parties the possibility of resolving this dispute (or particular issues) by ADR?

Whilst the practice directions in the UK are careful to highlight the voluntary nature of the submission to an ADR process, the requirement of a checklist has recognised the professional duty of every lawyer to give thought to the suitability of ADR as a means of resolving the dispute. The willingness of the English courts to put their weight behind the active consideration of ADR processes at all stages of a dispute, up to and including the appellate stage, has been regarded (in the UK) as one of the more "welcome developments in legal reform." But unfortunately, it has not been reciprocated in India. This needs to be emulated by judges in India.

Although mediation and conciliation have been encouraged by law over the past twenty-five years by the introduction of Part III in the Arbitration and Conciliation Act, 1996, and later by an amendment to the Code of Civil Procedure, 1908 (S.89), practicing lawyers and many judges remain unenthusiastic and not supportive of ADR.

Mediation is not only about law (although legal knowledge is essential in almost every mediation) but also about skills in negotiation and how to develop expertise in the fine art of bringing two (or more) parties together to resolve amicably the problem at hand, thus helping to reduce the crippling burden of litigation in courts. Section 89 (Settlement of Disputes Outside the Court) was inserted by parliament in the Code of Civil Procedure, 1908 (by the Code of Civil Procedure (Amendment) Act, 1999) with the purpose of preventing suits from proceeding further, except when parties could not get their disputes settled through any of the methods of alternate dispute resolution mentioned therein. The objects and reasons for Clause 7 (Section 89) of the Code of Civil Procedure Amendment Bill, 1999, made this clear.[22]

The opening words of Section 89 ("where it appears to the court that there exist elements of a settlement which may be acceptable to the parties") left the initial satisfaction about "elements of a settlement" to the court and not to the agreement or consent of the parties.

In the *First Salem Advocates Bar Association case*[23] (2003), the Supreme Court of India, whilst clearing the constitutional challenge to the 1999 Amendment (to the Code of Civil Procedure, 1908) and holding that it was not ultra *vires*, explained the true rationale of Section 89 as follows:

> "9. It is quite obvious that the reason why Section 89 has been inserted is to try and see that all the cases which are filed in court need not necessarily be decided by the court itself. Keeping in mind the law's delays and the limited number of judges which are available, it has now become imperative that resort should be had to alternative dispute resolution mechanism with a view to bring to an end litigation between the parties at an early date."

It then accepted the suggestion at the Bar that a committee should be constituted to consider devising model case management formula as well as rules and regulations that should be followed while taking recourse to the ADR referred to in Section 89. After these rules were formulated[24], the case came back to the court in the (second) *Salem Advocate's Bar Association case* (2005).[25] The court there said that the intention of the legislature behind enacting Section 89 was where it appeared to the court that there existed an element of settlement "which may be acceptable to the parties," they, at the instance of the court, should be made to apply their minds so as to opt for one or other of the four ADR methods mentioned in the section, and "if the parties do not agree, the court shall refer them to one or other of the said modes." Thus far, the court was supportive of ADR.

However, in a still later, and now binding decision of the Supreme Court of India (in *AFCONS Infrastructure Ltd.*, 2010 (8) SCC 24) handed down in July 2010, there has been a complete setback. A strained construction was placed on one of the most important and salutary provisions in the code.

In *AFCONS* (2010), the trial court had heard an application under Section 89 by one of the parties and recorded that the plaintiff was agreeable for "arbitration" (one of the modes of ADR prescribed in the section). It also recorded that the defendants were not agreeable for arbitration. The trial court then allowed the application by a reasoned order, holding that since the claim of the plaintiff related to a works contract, it was appropriate (*in its view*) that the dispute *should* be settled by arbitration, thus indicating its satisfaction in terms of the opening words of Section 89. The defendants filed a revision petition against this order of the trial court but the same was dismissed (in my view correctly) by the High Court of Kerala (in a decision reported in 2007 (1) Arbitration Law Report 405). The high court held that the apparent tenor of Section 89 permitted the court, in appropriate cases, to refer even unwilling parties to arbitration, and that the concept of a pre-existing arbitration agreement, necessary for a reference to arbitration under the Arbitration and Conciliation Act, 1996 (Section 7), was inapplicable to references by a court under Section 89 of the code. But unfortunately, on a further appeal by special leave under Article 136 of the Constitution of India, the Supreme Court of India set aside both the order of the trial court as well as the judgement of the high court holding: "That unwilling parties could not be compelled to go to arbitration absent in an arbitration agreement," even though Section 89 did not so prescribe. The Supreme Court even went further to say that as far as conciliation was concerned (a synonym for "mediation"), "the court cannot refer the parties to conciliation under Section 89 in the absence of consent of all parties," overlooking the express provisions of Section 61 in Part III (Conciliation) of the Arbitration and Conciliation Act, 1996. That section provides that the provisions in Part III (Conciliation) *shall* apply to the conciliation of disputes arising out of legal relationships, whether contractual or not, and to all proceedings relating thereto "unless the parties have otherwise agreed!"

After the decision of the highest court in *AFCONS* (which remains good law), there is not much help to be expected in the future from courts promoting ADR! Mediation and conciliation must now stand on their own; their success being judged on their own record, unassisted by judges.

When my book *God Save the Hon'ble Supreme Court* published, by Hay House Publishers in 2018, was released, interweaving global and Indian experiences into a tapestry of jurisprudence to comprehend the challenges before the nation's highest court, I was asked as to what from 1950 to 2023 are the vantage points showcasing the best of India's Supreme Court in terms of its judgements as also the advocacy by eminent lawyers.

Since human memory is short, and my memory at my advanced age is getting even shorter, let me try to answer regarding "the tapestry of jurisprudence."

Article 124(1) in the Constitution of India as enacted (and as currently applicable) had provided that there shall be a Supreme Court of India "consisting of a chief justice of India" and "not more than seven other judges," until parliament by law prescribes a larger number.

In a series of Supreme Court (Number of Judges) Amendment Acts, the number of judges in India's Supreme Court has increased periodically and at present, stands at thirty-four. This is unlike the Supreme Court of the USA, which originally consisted of six justices—the total number of justices changing six times after the year 1790—before arriving at the current total of nine judges from the year 1869. There have been seventeen chief justices during the entire history of the US Supreme Court, since the first chief justice, John Jay, in 1789. The current chief justice, John Roberts, has been in office since the year 2005. In the USA, there is no prescribed retirement age for federal judges or Supreme Court judges.

In India (where judges of the Supreme Court hold office up to the age of sixty-five years), there have been fifty chief justices so far, with India's first chief justice being Sir Harilal Kania. The current chief justice of India, D. Y. Chandrachud, assumed office in November 2022 and will retire at the age of sixty-five in November 2024.

It was in the 1880s that Chief Justice Melville Fuller of the US Supreme Court set up the tradition of the judicial handshake, a tradition that exists even today when the nine justices of the Supreme Court of the US gather to go on the bench or to meet in conference.

Each justice making it a point to shake the hand of the other eight justices is a tradition that is followed "to remind the justices that despite their differences, all members of the court share a unity of purpose" (see *Oxford Companion of the Supreme Court of the US*, Oxford University Press, Second Edition, page 1153). There is no such tradition in India, although I do recall that Chief Justice Y. V. Chandrachud (CJI from 1978-1985), after concluding each day's hearing in his court and on his colleagues leaving the courtroom, would courteously express his thanks to each one of his colleagues who sat with him that day. An admirable tradition, though not followed since.

The Supreme Court of India supervises the decisions not only of the high courts in the states (there are twenty-two high courts for the twenty-eight states and nine union territories) but also of all tribunals (central and state) functioning in different parts of India. And it does this through its extraordinary jurisdiction, conferred by Article 136, of granting special leave to appeal from any decision or order of any court or tribunal in the country. The Supreme Court of India is empowered by the Constitution to issue all manner of writs, orders, and directions for the enforcement of a wide range of fundamental rights guaranteed under Part III of the Constitution (Article 32). High courts in each state (including union territories) are likewise empowered, and they have also the power to issue writs order and directions for enforcing fundamental rights and in addition, "for any other purpose" (Article 226).

The Supreme Court of India is also invested with a special advisory jurisdiction (Article 143) to answer questions of law or of fact of public importance, but only those referred to it by the president of India (in effect, by the central government)—a jurisdiction invoked especially when the centre wants to pass on to the judicial branch of the state a "hot political potato." But the court is also aware of this. It is not bound to answer a presidential reference, and it may respectfully decline to do so, as it did in the now-famous reference of the Ayodhya dispute. The question posed to the court by the executive in the presidential reference was: Whether a Hindu temple or any Hindu religious structure existed prior to the construction of the Ram Janmabhoomi-Babri Masjid (including the premises of the inner and outer courtyards of such structure) in the area on which the structure stood?

The Constitution bench of five judges, though divided (3:2) on the constitutional validity of the act of parliament known as The Acquisition of Certain Area at Ayodhya Act, 1993, were unanimous in (respectfully) declining to answer the reference.

At the inaugural sitting of India's Supreme Court in New Delhi on 28 January 1950, India's first chief justice, Sir Harilal Kania, had said that the foremost task of the judges would be to interpret the Constitution but, "in no narrow spirit" and "with an enlightened liberality" and not in "a spirit of formal or barren legalism." The reported judgements of the court interpreting the Constitution over the last seventy-odd years have been, generally speaking, in tune with the course charted out for it by India's first chief justice. "Generally speaking" because, as in the life of any institution, the Supreme Court too has had its dark moments, like during the nineteen-month period of the Internal Emergency of June 1975, which came to be known (because of its unpopularity) as the "Phoney Emergency." "Phoney" also because the Emergency was contrived—the executive power to declare it (under Article 352) was invoked only to rescue a prime minister who had lost an election petition filed against her in the Allahabad High Court. During that so-called "Internal Emergency" (from 26 June 1975 to March 1977), fundamental rights were suspended, draconian laws were enacted, and judges in the highest court (with a few notable exceptions) buckled under the fiats of a seemingly omnipotent executive.

However, in the period after March 1977 (when the Emergency was lifted with a change of government at the centre), there emerged a remarkable resurgence of enlightened liberalism. In retrospect, the years after March 1977 have been the best years of the court. One of the unintended benefits of the Emergency regime (after it ended) was the spurt in judicial activism and intervention, with an enlargement of the scope of judicial review. In one decision after another, since

March 1977, the court has built around itself (step by step, case by case) a virtually impregnable fortress of judicial inviolability.

In the early years of the working of India's Constitution, the Supreme Court had consistently held that whatever was intended by the framers of the Constitution was expressed in the language used in its provisions and that there was no scope for intendment, and the court eschewed a positivist approach when interpreting constitutional provisions. No attempt was made to ferret into the crevices of the Constitution, to plumb the depths of its silences so as to ascertain a judge-oriented meaning. That was to come only in later years, when the confidence of the court in the wisdom of the legislatures had been consistently weakened, and when the legal presumption of executive acts being regularly performed had worn thin.[26]

The late 1970s and early 1980s, and ever since, have marked a turning point in the way in which the court looked at and read the Constitution. Consistent legislative and executive encroachments on judicial power ultimately alerted the court to its true role—that *of the conscience keeper of the nation*. It was only after this realisation that the judges in the highest court embarked on a "broadly expansive" interpretation of the constitutional provisions. I hope and trust it will continue.

Tribunals across various specialised jurisdictions have come to stay. Hence, how does one perceive the proliferation of tribunals, and the growing number of youngsters engaged in tribunal appearances as their mainstay?

(Tribunals—Articles 323A [Administrative Tribunals] and 323B [Tribunals for other matters] Part XI-A were added by the Constitution 42nd Amendment Act, 1976 [w.e.f. 3 January 1977] during the Internal Emergency of June 1975.)[27]

I am all for "youngsters" advancing in the profession. But I have a grim perception of the increasing proliferation of tribunals, which of course, have come to stay. They only add to the enormous delays in final disposals. Tribunalisation of the Indian legal system is totally counterproductive and adds to the law's proverbial delays. Besides, as explained below, giving finality to the decision of a tribunal (without the intervention of the high court and the Supreme Court) renders the decision of each and every tribunal unconstitutional, except for inter-state water disputes tribunals that had been (and continue to be) set up under the Constitution of India, 1950, as enacted.

The Law Commission of India, in its Report No. 272, dated October 2017, gave its *Assessment of Statutory Framework of Tribunals in India*. But in my view, tribunalisation of the legal system has not been a success since the confidence of litigants and of the public remains—as it was before—with the established courts. Tribunlisation and compartmentalisation of the legal system in India have been a failure. Besides, litigation has proliferated. Almost everyone who fails before tribunals approaches the high courts under Article 226 of the Constitution to rectify the so-called "wrong." And therefore, almost every matter decided by a tribunal has to be vetted again for its validity by the high court, which is an enormous waste of public time and money.

Besides all this, the Supreme Court of India in *L. Chandra Kumar* vs. *UOI* (AIR 1997 SC 1425) (a special bench of seven judges) held that clause 2(d) of Article 323A and clause 3(d) of Article 323B, to the extent that they excluded the jurisdiction of the Supreme Court under Article 32 and of the high courts under Articles 226 and 227, were unconstitutional since they adversely affected the *basic structure* of the Constitution and correspondingly, some provisions of the Administrative Tribunal Act, 1985 (w.e.f. 2 October 1985), enacted pursuant to the insertion of Articles 323A and 323B, were also declared to be unconstitutional. But then, the bench of seven judges (at the same time instead of leaving it at that) unfortunately went on to hold that the tribunals created under Article 323A and Article 323B of the Constitution do remain possessed of the competence to test the constitutional validity of statutory provisions and rules, but that all decisions of these tribunals would be subject to scrutiny before a division bench of the high court within whose jurisdiction the concerned tribunal was situated and that the tribunals would nevertheless continue to act like courts of first instance in respect of the areas of law for which they had been constituted and that this not open for litigants to directly approach the high courts, even in cases where they question the vires of statutory legislation (except where the legislation that created the particular tribunal had been challenged).

In *Madras Bar Association* vs. *Union of India*, a judgement of a bench of five judges, reported in 2014 (10) SCC 1, it was held:

1. That the jurisdiction to adjudicate upon substantial questions of law by the high court could (under ordinary law) be transferred to an appropriately constituted tribunal, and therefore the validity of the Constitution 42nd Amendment Act, 1976, inserting Article 323B in the Constitution of India, was upheld.
2. At the same time, the National Tax Tribunal Act, 2005, was declared unconstitutional because salient characteristics of a court had been sought to be replaced and not incorporated in the tribunals created by the new law.
3. That the ultimate power to adjudicate upon questions of law/substantial questions of law was the sole province of the superior court of record, viz. the high courts and the Supreme Court and that jurisdiction could not be transferred to any tribunal/court. On this ground also the National Tax Tribunal Act was held to be ultra vires and unconstitutional. In *Madras Bar Association* vs. *Union of India* (2014 (10) SCC page 1), a Constitution bench of five judges of the Supreme Court declared the National Tax Tribunal Act of 2005 (an enactment in pursuance of Articles 323A and 323B) as unconstitutional. It was held that the "basic structure" of the Constitution would stand violated, if while enacting legislation pertaining to the transfer of judicial power, parliament does not ensure that the newly created court/tribunal conforms with the salient

characteristics of the court sought to be substituted. And in the same case, in a (concurring) judgement on page 243, it was held (and this is the true ratio of the case): "In view of the constitutional scheme and the jurisdiction conferred on this court under Article 32 and on the high courts under Article 226 of the Constitution, the power of judicial review being an integral part of the basic structure of the Constitution, no Act of Parliament can exclude or curtail the powers of the constitutional courts with regard to the enforcement of fundamental rights."

Then, citing Lord Atkin's observations in 1931 Appeal Cases 310 (PC), the concurring judgement went on to say that "time alone will not validate an act which, when challenged, is found to be ultra vires, nor will a history of a gradual series of advances till this boundary is finally crossed avail to protect the ultimate encroachment." The concurring judgement finally concluded as follows:

> "179. *L. Chandra Kumar* and *Madras Bar Association* have allowed tribunalisation at the original stage subject to certain safeguards. The boundary has finally been crossed in this case. I would, therefore, hold that the National Tax Tribunals Act is unconstitutional, being the ultimate encroachment on the exclusive domain of the superior Courts of Record in India."

In my view, there is a need for more expertise amongst existing benches of judges in the established courts, for example, an arbitration bench, a labour bench, a commercial bench, a Constitution bench, etc., with experienced judges who handle such matters. They could be assisted by experts recruited from other disciplines, who would sit along with the judges.

Another common question I am often asked is, "Having written several books over the years that uniquely blend law and literature, which five books by other writers would you suggest every lawyer should read?"

It is not so easy to answer such a question. There are "no top five books." There are many, many more. Justice Felix Frankfurter was a judge of the Supreme Court of the United States (from 1939-1962)[28]. He was a name that is, or should be, familiar to all lawyers in India. He was the judge whom India's Constitutional Adviser B. N. Rau had consulted when first drafting the Constitution of India. But he is famous for another reason.

In May 1954, a twelve-year-old American student living in Alexandria, Virginia (USA), wrote a letter directly to the judge and said that he was "interested in going into law as a career" and he requested for an advice of the judge. Judge Frankfurter's now-famous advice to a young man interested in going into law is in the public domain for all to read. It is, in my view, compulsory reading.

> "The best way to prepare for the law is to come to the study of the law as a well-read person. Thus, alone can one acquire the capacity to use the English language on paper and in speech, and with the habits of clear thinking which only a truly liberal education can give. Stock your mind with the deposit of much good reading and widen and deepen your feelings by experiencing as much as possible the wonderful mysteries of the universe, and forget all about your future career."

This was Frankfurter's frank advice to a young American. It remains important for every young Indian lawyer too. You will find Frankfurter's advice to a law student mentioned in the two volumes of *The World of Law*, Volume I: *The Law in Literature* and Volume II: *The Law as Literature*. The two volumes comprise extracts of essays, opinions, stories, records of famous trials, etc., all compiled by a distinguished English constitutional lawyer, Ephraim London. While in the first volume, there is a section on cases and trials in fiction, coupled with writings by lawyers, judges, jurors, etc., in the second volume are accounts of notable and notorious cases, as well as extracts from judgements, observations, and reflections on the law.

These two volumes contain a mine of very useful and excellent writing in English[29], which lawyers must read and digest so that they come up to scratch in the profession. They will then be Frankfurter-trained in the law because the very first rule on becoming an advocate in India is: be proficient in English by stocking your mind with good reading, i.e., reading about the law *as* literature and reading about the law *in* literature.

Next, keep yourself informed and be up to date with Indian case law, i.e., decisions of the Supreme Court and of the high courts, particularly your own high court. This is essential for the profession you have chosen. In this way, you will be useful to your senior in the profession and later to yourself as well when you appear in court. However, even when you or your senior are not briefed in a case, you can be useful to someone, unknown to you, who is arguing a case in the court. You can be of help to him because when you are of help to him by giving him some very recent judgement relevant to his case, he will remember your good deed and will surely be of help to you!

Sir Jamsedji Kanga, a doyen of the Bombay Bar, in whose chamber I had the privilege to read, had little work in the first few years of his practice (in those days, long before the Constitution of India, 1950, there was far less work for juniors than there is today). He told us that he spent his time reading all the then-current decisions of the Privy Council and of the Indian high courts. He would sit in various courts, seeing and listening, and so learning how to argue and how not to argue, merely by watching other lawyers presenting their cases in the court. This is the best way to become a successful advocate.

Parkinson's law applies in the profession of law more than in any other. The less work there is, the less inclination there is to put your mind to it, and so the less will be your experience. Then, the less clients will seek you out as an advocate, and so you will have less work. All in all, a downward spiral! But the more you are engaged in work, the better will be your application of mind, the sharper will be your intellect. Then, everything will be in an upward spiral with only the sky being the limit. And "work" here means being occupied, not necessarily paid work.

The worst enemy of hard work is a fixed monetary reward. There is no "incentive" when your senior pays you a stipend. Of course, if it is necessary for you to survive, then take the stipend, but don't depend on it forever because you are then in the position of an employee or an office clerk. You will soon begin to work less and less, and only in office hours, and then, in the company of other young lawyers, you will begin to complain how poorly you are being paid.

There are no office hours for a practicing advocate as you have to be mentally engaged day and night. Remember that when you assist another person to argue, you must be of real use to him. This you can do only if you have looked up or studied the facts, made short notes, and looked up the entire law pertaining to the case in hand—not only relevant law, but also law having even some remote connection with the facts. In the USA, this is known as the Brandeis brief.[30] This is because, although in a court of law, only relevant facts are to be stated, there is one very important but least known section of the Indian Evidence Act—Section 165 which states:

> "The judge, in order to discover or to obtain proper proof of relevant facts, may ask any question he pleases, in any form, at any time, about any fact relevant or irrelevant, and neither the parties nor their advocates shall be entitled to make any objection to such question."

This is because a judge, at a trial or in any proceeding, is expected to explore all avenues open to him or her in order to discover the truth. Hence, in an Indian court of law, as an advocate, you must be prepared not only with the facts of your case but all possible permutations and combinations that can be imagined. So, when you have a brief, you must always go beyond it and be ready with answers to the judge's questions—relevant or irrelevant. And you can be sure that a judge will ask many irrelevant questions, and you have to patiently and politely answer them. You will not be able to answer them unless you have mentally prepared yourself.

Of late, I have been repeatedly asked as to what is my overall opinion of the Kashmir judgements delivered by the Supreme Court, and if I have been impressed by the judicial arguments presented or if I am concerned about some of the reasoning and its implications.

My overall opinion on the decision in the Article 370 case is that it is politically welcome but constitutionally flawed. It is welcome only in so far as it has facilitated the complete integration of the state of Jammu and Kashmir into the Union of India, which, for India, is a good thing. It is constitutionally flawed because, in my personal view, what has been done by the court is not at all according to the provisions of the Constitution. But (more importantly) it is also not in accordance with settled principles of federalism. The public must know that, since the year 1994, it is settled law—settled by a decision of a bench of nine judges of the Supreme Court—that India is a federal state, or more correctly, a union of quasi-federal states, and that federalism is a basic feature of India's Constitution.

On the same subject, I was asked a few more pertinent questions that have been highlighted below:

- **Question 1:**

"Let's come to the details, and because they are complicated and difficult to follow, I will speak slowly and carefully. Also, with your permission, I will read the questions because it's important that I get the language right and not just approximate the right words. First, it's been brought to my attention that Constitutional Order No. 48 of 1954 amended Article 368 to say that no amendment to the Constitution via that article can take effect unless it's applied through Clause (1) of Article 370. This clause specifically requires the concurrence of the state government. Clearly, no state government would give its concurrence to any amendment deleting Article 370. And for parliament, under President's Rule, to have claimed that the state government has given concurrence is surely a fraud and a deception?"

I feel that the terms "fraud" and "deception" on the part of the centre are too strong. I will put it a little differently. Presidential Order No. 48 of 1954 (which means the Central Government Order of 1954) had clearly said that an amendment under Article 368 of any provision of the Constitution would only have effect in relation to the state of Jammu and Kashmir if it was applied by a Presidential Order under Article 370. And the same Presidential Order of 1954 also provided that Article 3 of the Constitution (which permits parliament by law inter alia to diminish the area of any state) would apply to the state of Jammu and Kashmir with a super-added condition that in the case of Jammu and Kashmir, the area of the state could not be diminished by the executive or even by parliament without the consent of the State Assembly of Jammu and Kashmir. This is very important. Unfortunately, the judgements of the court do not even mention that, in the year 1950, when Jammu and Kashmir state was set up as a Part B state, the area of the state was 39,145 square miles, and with the diminution of that area in August 2019 (when the orders and laws challenged were passed) to 22,856 square miles, out of which the new union territory of Ladakh was created.

The exact depleted area of Jammu and Kashmir state is simply not referred to in any of the three judgements of the Supreme Court. What is also not mentioned in any of the three judgements is that not only was the area of the state substantially diminished (from 39,145 square miles in January 1950 to just 16,304 square miles in August 2019), but more significantly, it is assumed that reducing a state to a union territory was permitted by Article 3. It is not. A change of status from state to union territory is just not contemplated nor even mentioned in Article 3 or in any other provision of the Constitution.

- **Question 2:**

"Let's now come to the court's decision to uphold what's popularly called the abrogation of Article 370. On the one hand, the majority judgement, written by Chief Justice D. Y. Chandrachud, says that a critical part of Constitutional Order 272, reading down Article 370, is ultra vires because it wrongly uses Article 367 to interpret the Constituent Assembly as the Legislative Assembly. Since that is the process, the government argued that Article 370 could also be read down by the use of Clause 3 and, therefore, upheld what the government did. This means the court ruled that what the government did was wrongly done, but if it had done it differently, it would be right and, therefore, upheld what the government did. What do you make of that?"

Regarding the abrogation of Article 370, a very important safeguard in the Constitution was provided. It is contained in the proviso to Clause (3) of Article 370, which said that the president (and in the Constitution, the word "president" meant the central government) may, by public notification, declare that this article shall cease to be operative or shall be operative from such date as he may specify (only if the necessary recommendation has been made by the Constituent Assembly of the Jammu and Kashmir state). This proviso to Article 370(3) was in existence continuously from January 1950 right up to 6 August 2019, and if the government wanted to avoid the operation of this condition precedent, it could and should have first removed the proviso by moving an amendment in parliament to delete the proviso under and in accordance with the strict conditions mentioned in Article 368, viz. that two-thirds of the members present had to vote in favour of the amendment for it to become operative. Instead, the centre proposed an addition to Article 367 (the interpretation article in the Constitution), claiming to alter the proviso to Article 370(3) to read: instead of the words "the Constituent Assembly of J&K" (which had ceased to exist since

26 January 1957) to add the words "legislative assembly of the state." However, this was really a totally ineffective amendment since, to the knowledge of the centre, the legislative assembly of the state had already been dissolved by the centre itself in December 2018. There was, in fact, no legislative assembly of J&K state in existence since then, nor was it in existence at any time thereafter. Yet surprisingly, the court proceeded to strike down this pretty worthless amendment as unconstitutional.

I would describe this so-called amendment to Article 367 as purely a diversionary tactic on the part of the centre and the court should have seen through this and should have said so! Unfortunately, it did not. Instead, it proceeded to strike it down.

- **Question 3:**

"Even the Supreme Court's argument that Article 370 can be legitimately read down by use of Clause 3 hinges on the court's claim that the dissolution of the Kashmir Constituent Assembly only means that the power of the assembly to recommend ceased to exist, but that it didn't affect the power of the president of India to act, whether he had such a recommendation or not. Do you agree with that claim, or is it disputable?"

This claim that it didn't affect the power of the president to act is not correct. Let me make this clear. There had been no Constituent Assembly of Jammu and Kashmir since as far back as January 1957 when the Jammu and Kashmir Constitution was brought into force, but yet this proviso to Article 370(3) had remained on the statute book, and it was a condition precedent to the president exercising the power to abrogate Article 370. In law, a court cannot say that a provision in a statute or in a constitution is *otiose* (i.e., of no practical purpose). If the government wished to avoid this, the only way was to delete the proviso to Article 370(3) first by resorting to Article 368 (amendment to the Constitution) so that the president (i.e., the centre) could unilaterally and uninhibitedly declare Article 370 as inoperative. There is authority for this. It has been held by a bench of three judges of the Supreme Court of

India, a decision that remains good law. It is reported in AIR 1962 SC 1543 on page 1552: "The function of the legislature is to enact laws which courts are not permitted to ignore. The courts are only empowered to interpret laws." Courts, therefore, cannot ignore any part of enacted law. It is for parliament to delete the provision if it has become otiose.

- **Question 4:**

"Let's now come to the Supreme Court's refusal to determine whether the reorganisation of the state was permissible under Article 3, i.e., whether the government had the power to demote Jammu and Kashmir from a state to a union territory. The court has relied on two arguments. First, it says: "We do not believe that the court ought to sit in appeal over every decision taken by the president during the imposition of Article 356 . . . (because) if every action taken by the president and parliament on behalf of the state was open to challenge, this would effectively bring to the court every person who disagreed with an action taken during President's Rule." Do you accept that as a legitimate reason for not determining whether the reorganisation was constitutional?"

I have already answered this. The central government, i.e., the president, had no power or authority to reduce what was state to a union territory, neither under Article 3 nor is this permitted under any other article in the Constitution. And the court should have so held. Therefore, in any event, and particularly because there was a very substantial diminution in the area of the state of Jammu and Kashmir, there was no power at all conferred on the centre or on parliament to also reduce an existing state (recognised as a state since 1950) to a union territory, particularly because whilst every state under the Constitution must have an elected legislative assembly, a union territory need not have one.

The second reason for not determining whether the reorganisation of Jammu and Kashmir was done constitutionally under Article 3 is that the recommendation of the state legislature is not binding on parliament. No doubt. But it's still a stipulated procedure required by the Constitution. Can it be circumvented and overlooked just because it's not binding?

I have a different approach to what you call "second reason." Article 3 states that a bill to diminish the area of a state must be introduced only on the recommendation of the president (i.e., the central government) and *only after* the president has referred the bill to the legislature of the state for expressing its views on the bill, and there is a judgement of five judges of the Supreme Court from the year 1960 that the state assembly's views are not binding on parliament. But the important point is that the bill cannot be introduced in parliament unless the president has first referred the bill to the state assembly. In the present case, the bill to reorganise the state admittedly was not referred to the Legislative Assembly of J&K because there was no such assembly in existence. Therefore, the conclusion must be that such a reorganisation bill could never have been introduced in parliament and no Reorganisation Act passed. Article 3 is very clear: there must be a functioning legislative assembly of the state prior to a bill for reorganising the state's territorial area because the views of the state legislative assembly must be communicated to parliament to justify the invocation of Article 3. The fact that its views are not binding on parliament is of no consequence. The existence of the state assembly is a condition precedent to the bill for reorganisation of the state to be even introduced in parliament.

- **Question 5:**

"One consequence of the Supreme Court refusing to determine whether the reorganisation of Jammu and Kashmir was constitutional is that this process of reorganising a state can now be used to reorganise other states. The government can declare President's Rule in opposition states like Bengal, Kerala, and Tamil Nadu, transfer the powers of the assembly to parliament and thereafter parliament can decide to abolish the state or demote it to a union territory as it wishes. That precedent has now been set."

The judgements are dealing only with a unique case of the repeal of a temporary provision in the Constitution. None of the observations of the court apply to any other state. It is erroneous to even suggest that the judgement sets a precedent for the centre to adopt for other states. I do not agree with what is stated in this question nor with anyone who takes the same view. The judgements are a precedent only for the state of J&K, which was, till 6 August 2019, governed by a temporary provision that is now revoked. It is this revocation that is unconstitutional.

Section III
CONSTITUTION

1

The Silences in Our Constitutional Law[1]

Milton's *Paradise Lost* is one of the great epic poems in English literature. It is also one of the longest. Milton's critic, Dr Samuel Johnson, once said that "he could not wish it longer." The same can be said about our Constitution. As enacted, it contained 395 Articles (with a Bill of Rights) and an appendix of eight schedules, occupying in the official edition 251 printed pages. And yes, one could not wish it longer!

Produced after two-and-a-half years of debate and discussion, the Constitution of India did not find much favour with the leading Commonwealth historian of the time, Sir Ivor Jennings. In 1951, the University of Madras requested Jennings to deliver a lecture on the Indian Constitution. Jennings commenced his address by summing up our Constitution in one cynical sentence: "Too long, too rigid, too prolix." And to add insult to injury, he also said that the dominance of lawyer-politicians in the Constituent Assembly had contributed to the complexity of its provisions! But harsh words, like chickens, sometimes come home to roost!

In the 1960s, the same Ivor Jennings had been commissioned to write a new Constitution for Sri Lanka, then known as "Ceylon." Despite all precautions taken in its drafting, that Constitution lasted only seven years. Hence, the first lesson about written constitutions, then, is that they do not function on their own. A special effort must be made by their custodians—those entrusted with their functioning—to work them.

It is under this "lawyer's Constitution" (as Jennings sneeringly characterised it) that we have regularly held elections every five years on the basis of adult franchise, in which millions go to the polls. And despite the misgivings of constitutional historians, whenever governments have been voted out of office, whether i n the centre or in the states, the transfer of power has been according to its provisions, even if occasionally not in consonance with its true spirit.

I recall with pride Prime Minister James Callaghan's tribute when Prime Minister Indira Gandhi was defeated at the polls in March 1977. Callaghan said that the ultimate mark of a true democracy is the willingness of a government defeated at the ballot box to surrender power peacefully to its opponents. This is what happened when the Janata Party swept the polls. And this is what happened again when those who held power since March 1977 were, in turn, defeated in the elections of 1980, and Mrs Gandhi was swept back to power. Truly then, this Constitution of ours, embodying a parliamentary form of government, was not only a compulsion of geography, shaken and divided by the "earthquake" of the partition in 1947. It was also a compelling accident of history. In 1947, the British hurriedly left us, somewhat in pique. Amidst the trauma of the partition that followed, the members of India's Constituent Assembly, motivated by the urgent need to preserve the political and cultural unity of what was left of British India, valiantly rose to the occasion and forged the document that became the Constitution of India, 1950.

The life of a written Constitution, like the life of the law, is not logic (or draftsmanship) but experience. And years of experience since independence on this subcontinent have shown us that it is easier to draft a constitution than to work it. Pakistan and Bangladesh have drafted and crafted different written constitutions at different times, but they have been interspersed with long periods of martial law and civil and military dictatorships. We will never be able to piece together a new constitution in the present day and age even if we tried, because innovative ideas, however brilliant, howsoever beautifully expressed in consultation papers and reports of commissions, cannot give us a better constitution. In constitution-making, there are other forces that cannot and must never be ignored—the spirit of persuasion, of accommodation, and of tolerance. All three are at a very low ebb today.

This is one reason why I believe that the great commentary of Dr Durga Das Basu on our written Constitution will never become obsolete nor dated. Long as our Constitution is, the commentaries of Dr Basu from Kolkata and of H. M. Seervai from Mumbai are longer, but they are both erudite and informative. The two commentators had vastly different approaches to the subject. Seervai was more historical and critical of many of the interpretations of the Constitution by India's Supreme Court. Basu had the distinction of writing a comparative study, which made it the more interesting since he gave ready references to comparable texts of constitutions from different parts of the world. In fact, by his work, he introduced a new school of jurisprudence in India, which goes by the name of "constitutional comparativism."

When Justice Chittatosh Mookerjee once asked me to deliver what he told me was to be the first Durga Das Basu Endowment Lecture, I felt honoured because I had known the judge for several years and had come to respect and admire him. His judicial wisdom is now legendary, ever since his novel but successful handling, as chief justice of Bombay, of a complaint made by about 200 lawyers regarding the questionable conduct of four of its sitting judges. No one could have handled it better, but that's another story. When I was asked to deliver this lecture, I could not help thinking to myself that the request was perhaps fifty years too late. On further reflection, however, I think it is not, because in this, as in other fields, distance does lend enchantment to the view. After half a century, a written constitution takes on a life of its own, especially in a country that is wedded to the concept of judicial review. That has been the case with our Constitution. Today, I believe we are a little wiser about its provisions.

The treatment by the two great commentators of our Constitution are different and divergent, and someone, someday, will doubtless assess the respective contributions of these great jurists to our constitutional law. It will be a fascinating exercise, but for a memorial lecture, one can only choose a particular aspect of the Constitution that is of special interest to the speaker. Hence, at that time, I chose to speak not on the length or structure or even on the main aspects of our written Constitution, but on its silences. A practicing lawyer always looks for precedents, and in choosing my subject, my precedent is a decision of the Privy Council in a case originating from Ceylon (now Sri Lanka). It is known as *Liyanage's case* (1965). It concerned a group of appellants who took part, in the year 1962, in an abortive coup against the established government. The appellants were put up for trial, not under the ordinary criminal law, but under a special law, not before the ordinary courts, but before a special court of three high court judges nominated by the chief justice of Ceylon. They were to be tried under the special law, which altered the fundamental law of evidence so as to facilitate their conviction—a law that deprived the judges of their normal discretion as to appropriate sentences. The judges appointed under the special law were compelled to sentence each offender, upon conviction, to not less than ten years' imprisonment and were compelled to order the confiscation of each one's possessions, even though his part in any conspiracy might have been trivial.

After a very extensive trial, the appellants were duly convicted and sentenced under this special law, which was confirmed by the Supreme Court of Ceylon. But on appeal, the Privy Council held that the convictions could not stand because the special law violated a basic unwritten premise in the Constitution of Ceylon, viz. that judicial power was exercisable only by the established judicature, not by an ad hoc court as constituted and as constrained by the limitations imposed by the special law, even though the court comprised sitting high court judges. The plea of counsel for the Government of Ceylon was that under the then Constitution based as it was on the Westminster model (like the Constitution of India), there was no express vesting of judicial power in the established courts, such as was to be found, for example, in the Constitution of the United States or in the Constitution of Australia. But the Privy Council said that this circumstance was not decisive. After tracing the establishment of the judicial system in Ceylon from the days when it was a British colony, it said that although there was no express mention made of vesting judicial power in the established courts of the land, there was, under the Westminster-type constitution, provision for the appointment of high court judges and a provision that they would not be removable except by the governor-general on an address of both houses of parliament. "These provisions," said Lord Pearce[2], "manifest an intention to secure in the judiciary a freedom from political, legislative, and executive control. They are wholly appropriate in a Constitution which intends that judicial power shall be vested only in the judicature. They would be inappropriate in a constitution by which it was intended that judicial power should be shared by the executive or the legislature. The constitution's silence as to the vesting of judicial power is consistent with its remaining, where it had lain for more than a century, in the hands of the judicature. It is not consistent with any intention that henceforth it should pass to or be shared by the executive or the legislature."

Inspired by this passage in *Liyanage's case*, the subject I have chosen for this chapter is "The Silences in Our Constitutional Law." It is a subject prompted also by years of our own constitutional history and experience. The silences in the Constitution of India are as profound as are its written provisions. Let me explain. Take the opening words of our Constitution: WE, THE PEOPLE OF INDIA (hereby adopt, enact, and give to ourselves this Constitution). If it means the people of India who were born long before 1950 (as were the Constitution's founding fathers), then it must surely be out of tune with most of the people of India, born after 1950. But no, there is hidden magic in these words "WE THE PEOPLE." The same three words are also the opening words of the world's oldest constitution that of the United States. And the answer to the conundrum as to what relevance a written constitution has for the overwhelming majority of its people, who were not born before its promulgation and therefore not included in the phrase "WE THE PEOPLE," was provided by a shrewd political observer of the Constitution of the US. The Congresswoman said:

> "'We the People' is a very eloquent beginning. But, when that document was completed on 17 September 1787, I was not included in that 'We the People.' I felt somehow, for many years, that George Washington and Alexander Hamilton just left me out by mistake. But I realise that it is through the process of interpretation and court decision that I have been finally included in 'We the People.'"

Original thought. Nicely put. Well, that, in a nutshell, describes what has been the role of *our* Supreme Court. By interpretation and court decision, it has broadened the reach of our Constitution's provisions. It has included within the range of its beneficent provisions those who were not born when India gained independence. That is why I am proud of our judges, past and present, who have interpreted and sustained this Constitution, framed for only 350 million people, most of whom are not alive today. That is why I am proud of people like Durga Das Basu, who made it his life's ambition to interpret and explain its provisions to the people of India—to lawyers and non-lawyers alike. This is one of the ways in which a written Constitution grows into a dynamic, living document.

Next to the opening words of the Preamble, perhaps the single most effective example of "hidden meanings" was provided by our own Supreme Court when it fashioned what is now known as the basic structure doctrine. Let me briefly expound on it. Although supreme, the Constitution of India (1950) is not immutable. Article 368 expressly provides that, notwithstanding anything in this Constitution, parliament, in exercise of its constituent power, may amend any provision of the Constitution (mark the word "any") in accordance with the procedure laid down in that article, i.e., by the same body which enacted laws at the centre: the two houses of parliament—the House of the People (Lok Sabha) and the Council of States (Rajya Sabha).

Within a year of the Constitution being brought into force, parliament passed the Constitution (First Amendment) Act, 1951. It consisted of the same members who, sitting as a Constituent Assembly, had adopted the Constitution on 26 January 1950. The First Amendment dispensed with the payment of compensation for taking over large estates, mainly zamindaries, which were large estates permanently granted over a century ago to families loyal to the Mughal emperors or to the British Raj. The First Amendment introduced two new articles in the Fundamental Rights Chapter (Part III): Article 31A and Article 31B which provided that legislations for effectuating agrarian reforms were outside the pale of protection of Article 19(1)(f) (the fundamental right to property), and the acquisition of such property as part of a measure for agrarian reforms did not need to comply with the requirement of payment of compensation guaranteed under Article 31. Article 31B was an innovation. It provided that whatever enactments (whether of parliament or of state legislatures), which by constitutional amendments, were included in the Ninth Schedule to the Constitution should be deemed never to be void or to have never become void because of any infringement of fundamental rights, notwithstanding any judgements of the courts to the contrary.

It was the challenge to the First Amendment that raised, for the first time, the question whether parliament could, by a special majority and after following the requisite procedure prescribed in Article 368, amend the Constitution so as to abridge or take away any of the fundamental rights set out in Part III of the Constitution. In a unanimous opinion handed down in October 1951, a bench of five justices of the Supreme Court (in *Sankari Prasad* vs. *Union of India*[3]) unhesitatingly answered the question in the affirmative. With further constitutional amendments making more inroads into fundamental rights (like the Fourth Amendment of 1955 and the Seventeenth Amendment of 1964), the question of judicial review of constitutional amendments was attempted to be reopened. In October 1964, in the case of *Sajjan Singh* vs. *State of Rajasthan*[4], a bench of five judges of the Supreme Court was not so emphatic in its view as it was in October 1951. It reiterated that parliament could, by constitutional amendment, abridge or take away fundamental rights, but it did so only by a majority of 3:2. The strong reservations of the minority of two justices prompted Chief Justice Subba Rao to constitute a larger bench (in fact, a full court of eleven judges) to reconsider the constitutional validity of the First, Fourth, and Seventeenth Amendments to the Constitution.

Chief Justice Subba Rao never needed much prompting to constitute a larger bench to overrule a judgement that did not give full play to the chapter on Fundamental Rights. S. R. Das, chief justice of India, upon his retirement in September 1959, made an amusing farewell speech, which is published in the Law Reports. After referring to some of his other colleagues in a lighter vein, he was particularly jocular about "Brother Subba Rao":

> ". . . and then we have Brother Subba Rao, who is extremely unhappy because all our fundamental rights are going to the dogs on account of some misconceived judgements of his colleagues, which require reconsideration."

Well, the full court of eleven judges, constituted and presided over by Justice Subba Rao, sat in *Golaknath* vs. *State of Punjab* (1967)[5], and the judgement rendered in that case gave rise to an acute controversy between the legislative and judicial branches of the state. It was held, by a narrow majority (6:5), that constitutional amendments were "laws" under Article 13 of the Constitution and as such subject to the mandate of that article. The state could not abridge or take away fundamental rights by enacting laws, whether in the exercise of legislative power or in exercise of constituent power. The First, Fourth, and Seventeenth Amendments were declared invalid, but only prospectively. Part III of the Constitution (the Bill of Rights Chapter) was placed on a pedestal beyond the reach of the amending power.

John Marshall was chief justice of the Supreme Court of the United States from 1801 to 1835 and is known in America as "the

Great Chief Justice." He once said: "Never seek to enlarge judicial power beyond its proper boundary, nor fear to carry it to the fullest extent that duty requires." Inspired by the second part of the dictum and by his own conception of the pre-eminence of fundamental rights, Chief Justice Subba Rao (in *Golaknath*) carried judicial review to the fullest extent—in fact, almost to the breaking point! Many reasonable people regretted that the great judge did not pay heed to the first part of Marshall's dictum. At first, the reaction to *Golaknath*, especially in the halls of the legislatures, was one of stunned surprise. The pace of constitutional amendments slowed down. But as the implications of the judgement became more widely known and more openly criticised, the attitude of the elected representatives of the people changed from a state of initial shock to one of defiance.

In 1971, parliament passed, in quick succession, the 24th, 25th, and 29th Constitutional Amendment Acts. It was declared that the power of amendment was a constituent power and that the provisions in Article 13, empowering courts to declare laws passed in contravention of fundamental rights void, would not apply to laws enacted under the constituent power of amendment. Next, the fundamental right requiring payment of compensation for the acquisition of property (Article 31(2)) was substituted. The new provision declared that property of any description, whether large or small, could be acquired for public purposes if the law provided for payment of an amount, and no such law could be called in question in any court on the ground that the amount fixed or determined by the law was not adequate or that the whole or any part of such amount was given otherwise than in cash.

An angry response to what was believed to be a misuse of the power of judicial review also produced another piece of heavy artillery: Article 31C. Introduced by the 25th Amendment, it provided that, notwithstanding anything contained in Article 13, no law could be challenged which gave effect to the policy of the state towards securing two of the main objectives of State Policy mentioned in Part IV of the Constitution, viz. towards securing that the ownership and control of the material resources of the community were distributed for the common good (Article 39(b)) or towards securing that the operation of the economic system did not result in the concentration of wealth and means of production to the common detriment (Article 39(c)). Any law giving effect to such policy was deemed not to be void on the ground that the law took away or abridged the fundamental rights conferred either by Article 14 (equality clause) or by Articles 19(1)(f) or 31 (the property clauses). The Constitution (29th Amendment) Act, 1972, further added enactments in the Ninth Schedule—mainly acts of state legislatures so as to save them from attack under Article 14, 19, or 31 on the ground of contravention of fundamental rights.

The stage was now set for the grand challenge. If *Golaknath* was rightly decided, the 24th, 25th, and 29th Amendments were void; if not, the powers of parliament (and the powers of future parliaments) were severely curtailed. The full court (then consisting of thirteen justices), presided over by Chief Justice S. M. Sikri, sat from 30 November 1972, hearing arguments on the correctness of the decision in *Golaknath* and as to whether there were any limitations on the power to amend the Constitution. The hearing lasted almost continuously till the third week of March 1973—a period of four months. As one of the justices put it: "The largest bench sat for the longest time to decide issues of grave moment not only to the future of this country but to the future of democracy itself."

The case was titled *His Holiness Kesavananda Bharati* vs. *State of Kerala* (1973)[6] but is better known as *Kesavananda* (or the Fundamental Rights case). Almost at the start, the reasoning in *Golaknath* was given up. What was pressed, however, was that there had to be some limitations on the amending power. The debate centred around the extent of such limitations. The judges plumbed the depths of the "Silences in our Constitution" to search for limitations, but there was no unanimity, as the court was once again sharply divided, except in the opinion that *Golaknath* should be overruled. Six judges (S. S. Ray, Palekar, K. K. Mathew, M. H. Beg, Dwivedi, and Y. V. Chandrachud JJ) held that the power of amendment conferred by Article 368 was wide and unfettered. It reached every part and provision of the Constitution, including the Chapter on Fundamental Rights, and there were no inherent limitations on the amending power. Six other justices (Chief Justice S. M. Sikri, J. M. Shelat, K. S. Hegde, A. N. Grover, Ray, and Jagmohan Reddy JJ) held that the power of amendment was limited, but they did not all agree on the extent of such limitation. The court was thus evenly divided.

It was Justice H. R. Khanna's judgement that tilted the balance. The great Justice Khanna held that the power of amendment under Article 368 was plenary, that it included the power to amend various articles of the Constitution and was not fettered by any provision in Part III (the Fundamental Rights Chapter), that no fundamental right (only because it was a fundamental right) could claim immunity from the amending process, and that the power to amend included within itself the power to add, alter, or repeal the various articles of the Constitution. BUT (with a capital B-U-T) he also held (and this is now the ratio in the Fundamental Rights case) that the power to amend under Article 368, wide as it was, did not include the power to abrogate the Constitution or to alter its basic structure or framework: hence, the doctrine of basic structure.

The opinions first in *Golaknath* and then in *Kesavananda* were products of divided courts. They aroused controversy and contention. But the basic structure theory has come to stay. It evolved from the great silence in our constitution. After all, the Constitution did provide that it could be amended, but surely it did not say that it could be abrogated, or that its basic features could be thrown to the winds! Though an innovative doctrine in disputes relating to property rights, the basic structure doctrine has long survived the deletion of the right to property from the Fundamental Rights Chapter.[7]

Durga Das Basu himself was critical of the judgement in *Kesavananda.* In his commentary, he wrote: "The court took upon itself the task of differentiating between the essential and non-essential features of the Constitution. No such power was vested in the court by Article 368, either expressly or by implication." Basu's view was that of a strict legal constructionist. But the Supreme Court was not bound by a literal view of the Constitution. Great cases are often shaped by events. As Justice Cardozo famously said: "the hydraulic pressure of great events do not pass judges idly by." Though of doubtful legal validity, the basic structure theory was the reaction of a court that was apprehensive of an over-enthusiastic and an over-powering one-party majority in parliament. But the doctrine, even though illogical, has come to stay and was firmly cemented in 1975 because of an over-enthusiastic response from the government of the day to a verdict of the Allahabad High Court.

As has been explained earlier too, Prime Minister Indira Gandhi lost the election petition filed against her in June 1975 in the Allahabad High Court. Her advisers (too ready to please) recommended not only an appeal to the Supreme Court but also a drastic constitutional amendment. Whilst Mrs Gandhi's appeal was pending in the Supreme Court, a bill amending the Constitution was rushed through parliament. The Constitution 39th Amendment Act, 1975, provided, among other things, that disputes regarding the election of a person who becomes prime minister were not to be decided in courts but by a special body named by parliament. It also provided that election laws would not be applicable to the prime minister and would not be deemed over to have been applicable to the prime minister and that notwithstanding any order of any court, the election of the prime minister would never be deemed to have become invalid or void. It would continue to be valid in all respects.

Strange as it may sound, it was this *monstrous* amendment that helped save the basic structure theory from death and destruction. The 39th Amendment of the Constitution was a crude attempt to pre-empt the Supreme Court from deciding the election appeal of Mrs Gandhi. But fortunately for the country, the court successfully resisted the attempt, relying for the first time after the Fundamental Rights case on the basic structure theory. In *Indira Gandhi* vs. *Raj Narain* (1975)[8], the court established that judicial review and free and fair elections were a fundamental part of the Constitution beyond the reach of the amending power. The Constitution does not say so, but this was inferred by the Supreme Court from the Constitution's silence. Later, in 1980, the court applied the doctrine of basic structure in a challenge to a provision in the Constitution 42nd Amendment Act, 1976. This provision shut out all judicial review of constitutional amendments: No amendment to the Constitution (it said), made in accordance with the procedure in Article 368, could be called in question in any court on any ground whatever. But in *Minerva Mills* (1980)[9], a Constitution bench of the court, following the ratio in the *Fundamental Rights case,* declared that the exclusion of judicial review violated the basic structure of the Constitution and struck down this part of the 42nd Amendment.

"The power to declare the law," said a great American judge, "carries with it the power and, within limits, the duty to make law where none exists." In reading implied limitations in the amending power, the Supreme Court of India had made new law. As Dr Basu put it in his classic commentary (on the Constitution of India[10]): "The doctrine of basic features had been invented by the Supreme Court in order to shield the Constitution from frequent and multiple amendments by a majoritarian government." The assumption of power by which one organ of government is enabled to control another has been characterised as political power. In asserting the basic structure theory, the Supreme Court of India has, in this sense, asserted political power in the guise of judicial interpretation. That is why there are so many critics of the basic structure theory. By propounding it, the guardians *of* the Constitution had at one bound become guardians *over* the Constitution. Constitutional adjudicators had assumed the role of constitutional governors. It must be admitted that the criticism is valid. But equally valid is the stark fact that parliament, in its wisdom, has not sought any confrontation. If it had, the casualty would have been the Supreme Court. When the Janata government endeavoured to recast Article 368 (the amending clause) and introduced provisions for a referendum for effecting changes in the basic features of the Constitution, the attempt failed.

The 45th Amendment Bill could not secure the requisite two-thirds majority in the Rajya Sabha only because the opposition party in parliament—the Congress (I)—which had been the most vociferous advocate of an unlimited power of constitutional amendment, simply would not vote for it! Strange are the ways of politics and of politicians. Parliament has also not chosen to re-enact a fresh constitutional amendment containing an ouster of jurisdiction clause in Article 368 after an earlier attempt at such an enactment (part of the 42nd Amendment) was struck down by the court in 1980. As a matter of fact, five years after the basic structure theory was first propounded in the Fundamental Rights case, parliament gave implicit recognition to it in the Constitution (44th Amendment) Act, 1978. This amendment provided that the fundamental right to life and liberty guaranteed by Article 21 of the Constitution could never be suspended (by law or constitutional amendment), even during an emergency, simply because the right to life and liberty was *basic* to the constitutional framework. The basic structure theory had been woven into our constitutional fabric.

In July 1986, just before his retirement, Chief Justice Warren Burger of the US Supreme Court was interviewed on television by Bill Moyers. In the course on his interview, Warren Burger said: "Congress (he was speaking of the US Congress) can review us and change us when we decide a statutory question, and frequently do. But when we decide a constitutional issue, right or wrong, that's it until we change it. Or the people change it. Don't forget that. The people made it, and the people can change it. The people could abolish the Supreme Court entirely by a constitutional amendment."

He was right. If the people really willed it, they could. But no one in the United States is going to abolish the US Supreme Court, and one can safely predict with equal confidence that no one is going to abolish the Supreme Court of India or the concept of judicial review. Judicial review will remain an integral part of Indian constitutional law and practice simply because the Supreme Court, relying on popular opinion, has definitively said so. Undoubtedly, primary control of governmental activity in this, as in any other democracy, is with the people. The power that the Supreme Court of India exercises ultimately rests upon their tacit approval. But experience has taught us to take (what Madison once described as) "auxiliary precautions."

The basic structure theory was the response of an anxious and activist court to the experience of the working of the Indian Constitution during its first twenty-three years. It remains as an auxiliary precaution against a possible tidal wave of majoritarian rule. Do remember (and if you are too young to remember, do make note of a stark fact in our constitutional history) that majoritarian rule was the political order of the day for nearly forty long years, from 1950 right up to the late 1980s.

However, it is not only judges who have plumbed the depths of silence in our Constitution; so have our presidents. The constitutional position of India's president is similar to that of England's sovereign, described in elegant prose more than 150 years ago by a great political journalist of his time:

> "To state the matter shortly, (says Walter Bagehot) the sovereign has, under a constitutional monarchy, three rights: the right to be consulted, the right to encourage, and the right to warn. And a king of great sense and sagacity would want no others. He would find that having no others would enable him to use these with singular effect. He would say to his (First) minister: 'The responsibility of these measures is upon you. Whatever you think best must be done. Whatever you think best shall have my full and effectual support. But you will observe that, for this reason and that reason, what you propose to do is bad; for this reason and that reason what you do not propose is better. I do not oppose; it is my duty not to oppose. But observe that I warn.' Supposing the king to be right, and to have what kings often have, the gift of effectual expression, he could not help moving his minister. He might not always turn his course, but he would always trouble his mind."[11]

India's first president, Dr Rajendra Prasad, tried very hard to influence India's first prime minister, Pandit Jawaharlal Nehru, but did not succeed either to "turn his course" or "trouble his mind." He had complained to Minoo Masani that Panditji did not allow him to exercise the powers which he thought he had under the Constitution. Years later, Masani shrewdly observed that Rajendra Babu did not have the force of Nehru's personality, gave in too readily, and yet went on shaking his head and grumbling (as he gave in), saying: "this is not the way we framed the Constitution." Masani also said: "When people say what is wrong with this Constitution, I say nothing is wrong. What is wrong is us. We have destroyed the Constitution because people in Delhi love power too much to tolerate either a strong president or a strong state." Minoo Masani was a member of India's Constituent Assembly, of which Dr Rajendra Prasad was president, but his views about a "strong president" do not find support in the Constitution they together helped to frame. And yet, the Constitution of 1950 did not and does not envisage a mere cipher or figurehead as president. And this is because of the silences in our Constitution about the powers and functions of the president.

The president, as you know, is a constitutional functionary with no political power. Though the president is bound by the advice of his council of ministers regarding bills passed by both houses of parliament and regarding the promulgation of ordinances when parliament is in recess. In order to emphasise that the president as a constitutional head could not override his council of ministers, a proviso was added to Article 74(1) in our Constitution by a constitutional amendment (the 44th Amendment in 1978), which said that despite the fact that the president was mandated to act in accordance with the advice of his council of ministers, he could require his council of ministers to reconsider such advice, either generally or otherwise. However, when such advice had been reconsidered and again tendered to the president, he had to act in accordance with that advice. At the time, when the tenth Lok Sabha had, in all but name, been dissolved, the Narasimha Rao government placed two ordinances before the then President

Shankar Dayal Sharma for promulgation namely, one for shortening the period of poll campaigns from three weeks to two weeks, and the other was to extend reservations in public employment (or quotas) to Dalit Christians. President Sharma, relying on the proviso to Article 74(1) of the Constitution, sent back the draft ordinances to the government with a note dated 19 March 1996, which read: "I would like to inform you that, independent of the relative intrinsic merits of the ordinances proposed, promulgating these ordinances would appear to be inappropriate and contrary to the canons of constitutional propriety in the view of circumstances existing at this particular juncture."

Since nothing a prime minister or president says or does in our country remains a secret, the contents of the communication of President Sharma to the prime minister soon became known. And the wisdom and sagacity of a president (even though a constitutional head of state) often trump the political compulsions of an elected government. That is how a constitutional democracy functions and must function. The government of the day dropped these ordinances and did not press for their promulgation, fearful as always, of those opening words in the Constitution: "WE THE PEOPLE."

A second instance that I recall occurred during the tenure of President K. R. Narayanan when I. K. Gujral was the prime minister. The council of ministers, headed by Gujral, sent a proclamation to the president for promulgation under Article 356 of the Constitution for the introduction of President's Rule in Bihar. President Narayanan, acting under the proviso to Article 74(1), returned the proclamation for reconsideration, giving, as he always did, elaborate reasons for his view. Again, this became widely known, and the union government wisely refrained from reaffirming it and sending it back to the president. If he had, the public ("We the People") would have been against him. In politics, discretion is often the better part of valour!

I believe that the president provides a window (perhaps the only window or opening) in that wall of separation that divides those in governance from the rest of the populace. Even after the constitutional amendment obliging him to act in accordance with the reconsidered advice given by his council of ministers, there is no prescription as to the time when he should so act. Time runs in the president's favour and the astute President Giani Zail Singh used this to great advantage. When the Post Office Bill, 1987, was submitted to him for his assent, there was much criticism of its provisions, particularly the one that permitted interception of all communications through the mail by the government of the day. Although the bill was passed by both houses of parliament, Zail Singh paused and harkened to public opinion. He could sense the public outrage and responded to it by not giving his assent. Before demitting office, he wrote on the files that he hoped that his successor would not clear the bill.[12] As a consequence, the public outcry against the bill gathered greater momentum, and the bill remained unsigned even on President R. Venkataraman's desk, with the latter having expressed his own displeasure at the bill. He returned it to Prime Minister V. P. Singh in January 1990. The bill was then tabled again in the Rajya Sabha, where it remained, officially and only in name, a pending bill. In actuality, a parliamentary relic![13]

All of this illustrates how a head of state can successfully "choke off" unpopular legislation by simply doing nothing. Through a calculated process of deliberate inaction, an unpopular and regressive measure can be successfully prevented from becoming enacted law. And this achieved by exploiting one of the deliberate silences in the Constitution as to when a bill passed by both houses of parliament should be assented by the president. No one suggested that Zail Singh had defied parliament, no one moved for his impeachment. The obvious reason, of course, was that the president had the firm backing of public opinion.

The British Constitution is not written. But it recognises that the British monarch, on rare but important occasions, is entitled to intervene in public affairs in a way that may be decisive. As the constitutional historian of England, Walter Bagehot, once said: "the greatest wisdom of a constitutional king would show itself in well-considered inaction."[14] Gianiji may have been untutored in what went on at Westminster, but he had astute political horse sense; he could sense that the people were behind him when he delayed (and then withheld) assent to the Post Office Bill. And in politics, nothing succeeds like success!

On 25 February 2005, I was witness to a bit of constitutional statesmanship by our own President A. P. J. Abdul Kalam, who delivered the customary address to both Houses of Parliament to herald the new session. As you know, the Constitution provides for a presidential address at the beginning of each session. It does not say who is to prepare it, but this is decided by convention. Since the president acts only on the advice of his council of ministers, the address is prepared by the government of the day. But on the morning of 2 February 2005, President Kalam made a departure. He had with him the full text of the written speech prepared by the government, but he chose to begin with a poem in Tamil, composed by himself the previous night, titled "Where Are We?".

> "Where are we?
> Where are we now, dear friends,
> In the Maha Sabha that shapes as history,
> The call of heartbeats of Indian people,
> People ask us, people ask us
> 'Oh! Parliamentarians, the sculptors of Mother India,
> Lead us unto light, enrich our lives.
> Your righteous toil is our guiding light,
> If you work hard, we all can prosper.'
> Like King, so the people,
> Nurture great thoughts, rise up in actions,
> May righteous methods be your guide,
> May you all prosper ever with Almighty's grace."

It was a criticism of parliamentarians and their erstwhile manner of functioning, firmly but politely expressed in verse. It was meant as a gentle exhortation from the people's president to the country's representatives not to walk out of legislative chambers, but to work hard and do their job. Since the president could not alter the text of his address to both houses of parliament, he devised the expedient of saying (what he had to say) in verse, and it was well received! It was, once again, an instance of an enlightened head of state taking advantage of one of the great silences in the Constitution, to slightly amend a constitutional convention and exhort the people's representatives to perform their tasks as parliamentarians with honesty of purpose and dedication. No one could fault him for expressing the sentiments of the vast majority of India's thinking millions.

The president of India, as its first citizen, has the constitutional right, and correspondingly, the duty to interpose in public affairs of great moment, offering his wisdom privately, never publicly, quietly, never with fanfare. An elected president notionally represents the collective will of the people, which he can use (and must use) to temper the occasional excesses of its elected representatives. I believe that on those very rare occasions when parliament (or the government) chooses to do something which the president of India believes to be unconstitutional or even morally wrong or improper, it is his or her function, right, and duty to intervene and to make known his views. An illustrative instance in point would be an excessive prolongation (by a proposed constitutional amendment) of the life of an existing parliament, which would keep in office a government whose normal term has run out and which is anxious to avoid elections.

But then how must a president, as a constitutional head of state, express his disapproval? It was a former chief justice of Pakistan who provided the answer many years ago. He was asked by his country's president (during the country's initial experiment with democracy) whether he could constitutionally refuse to give his assent to a bill passed by the National Assembly (Pakistan's first Constitution after independence was like ours—fashioned on the Westminster model). Chief Justice Muhammad Munir's answer went something like this: "If you think it is a matter of the gravest importance, and you cannot in all conscience accept the measure presented to you, you can, and you must (if you are true to your oath) refuse assent.

But having refused assent, you must then resign. The system must go on. People will know why you resigned and will sort things out with their governments."

Pearly words of wisdom which show how important and how potentially effective is the great office of the president in a parliamentary democracy. However, they also show that the words of the Constitution, though important, are never decisive because the silences in our constitutional law speak louder than words.

2

How the Constitution Should Be Understood[15]

(Karan Thapar's interview with Fali S. Nariman ["arguably India's greatest living expert on the Constitution"] covers a broad sweep of issues, including the calls for a new Constitution, simultaneous polls, questions raised on the basic structure of the Constitution, the prevailing climate of intolerance in the country, the changing relationship between the judiciary and executive, opposition's role in a democracy, parliamentary functioning, among others. On the situation in India today, Nariman says it is like the Emergency of 1975, except "behind a veil." However, he adds that the one critical difference between the situation today and during the Emergency of Indira Gandhi's time is that today there's an anti-Muslim, anti-minority mood prevailing, if not increasing, in the country which "does not gel with India's prominence in world affairs." In his book *You Must Know Your Constitution,* Nariman provides a profound exegesis of every single article in the Constitution. So, if you want to know how the Constitution should be understood, this book that is a compulsory read for you.)

Karan Thapar: Mr Nariman, let's start with the Constitution. I will come to politics and politicians after that. Now, in chapter 3, you write the Preamble is the most important part of the Constitution. Given that most people tend to ignore it and Prime Minister Indira Gandhi, some people say, controversially amended it, why do you believe the Preamble is the most important part?

Fali S. Nariman: Well, for one thing, the Preamble is a statute. The Constitution is ultimately compared to a statute except that it is on a loftier footing. A Preamble gives you an idea of what is sought to be achieved by the document, whether it's a statute or it's a constitution. Generally, there are preambles to the Constitution, and this Preamble has been called by our Supreme Court the "conscience of the Constitution." Preamble's Part 3: Fundamental Rights, Part 4: Directive Principles of State Policy, which are not enforceable by the court but are nonetheless binding, they are all part of the conscience of the Constitution.

KT: So, you believe that the Preamble is conscious because it expresses the intent of the framers of the Constitution?

FSN: That's right.

KT: Now the interesting thing and a controversy at the moment is that the Preamble uses the word India, not Bharat. It says "We the People of India." Bharat appears in Article I, and does that suggest that in the minds of the framers of the Constitution, India was the prior name?

FSN: No, I don't think so. You remember that there was a grave controversy about whether there should be a national language for the new independent country, after the British left. The question always was what should it be? There were protagonists of Hindi in a Devanagari script or some other script. Then there was English, and then there were regional languages. It almost was that the Constitution never would have been framed. It was almost at the end of July 1949, when this question was again taken up about what should be the language. One of the chapters in the Constitution said: "We won't have a national language, but we will have two official languages"—Hindi in the Devanagari script and English. So actually, the mere fact that the Preamble says India doesn't mean anything except that when it's in English, but if you read it in Hindi, it will be Bharat. So, the fact that the word Bharat doesn't appear in the English version of the Preamble is not an important thing.

KT: Now, you also believe, and I am quoting you, that "it's the way judges have interpreted and helped sustain a Constitution that has been framed for only 350 million people, most of whom are not even alive today, that is one of the ways in which a written Constitution is made to grow into a dynamic living document." In other words, the breath of life comes from judicial interpretation.

FSN: Yes, absolutely correct! That is why it is "We the People." It is, of course, borrowed from the American Constitution: We the People. Now if you think of the people as those who were born before the Constitution, like I am today, you will find very few left. Most of them are subsequent to the Constitution. After seventy-five years, you hardly find many people. So, this "We the People" doesn't mean anything except that, as I have mentioned, one congresswoman in America said, "I was wondering why I was left out by the framers of the Constitution," and she then came to the conclusion that "Ah, I wasn't left out but because our Supreme Court has interpreted the Constitution as applying to every living person." That is, I have been included. Now that is exactly what has happened here. The interpretation of the phrase "We the People" incorporates people born long after the Constitution was promulgated. Otherwise, "We the People" would refer to those who were alive at the time and now dead. And all those who are not even alive today.

KT: This also means that you don't subscribe, I imagine, to the literalist interpretation of the Constitution, which is the present fashion in the United States. You believe that there is the duty to interpret the Constitution in the context of the time and in the context of the issues of the day.

FSN: Oh, absolutely! There has to be! Because it is a living instrument, a living thing. Although there are doubts about how long a constitution should last, etc., and it was expected that the American Constitution wouldn't last for more than nineteen or twenty years, it has now lasted for well over 200 years. We are in the 75th year, so hope we continue. The problem, of course, is that we will never be able to devise a constitution like this for or of any type at all.

KT: So, what you are saying is that judges have a duty to read richer, fresh meanings into the articles so that they remain relevant to the period of our time? This means judicial interpretation is critical to understanding the Constitution. It's not given in stone and frozen forever.

FSN: Yes, absolutely! Apart from it being critical, in fact, the only final interpreter of the Constitution is the judiciary. In India, the highest judiciary is the Supreme Court. It started off with only eight judges on the bench and now it's about thirty-four or thirty-five. The criticism that is made that judicial interpretation is going too far is actually mistaken. The object of a judge, the duty of a judge, is to interpret in the context. You can't say he's going too far. We have long passed 1950; we are now in 2023. An entirely different century, and therefore everything is different, and the judges are also different. Most of them were not even born in 1950. So, the interpretation that they give is what makes it a living Constitution, which it's meant to be. Courts, as you know, go by precedent, so what five judges say today, seven judges can say tomorrow or have nine judges say the contrary to that, two years later. This is what makes the Constitution a living, dynamic object.

KT: Now, this brings me to an issue that is of tremendous political salience at the moment. The retired chief justice has questioned, in public, whether there is a basic structure to our Constitution. In your book, not only do you cite the case of the *Kesavananda Bharati* judgement which first propounded the basic structure theory, but you also cite other instances such as *Bhim Singh, Kuldip Nayar, Indira Gandhi versus Raj Narain,* and, of course, the *National Judicial Admissions case,* in each of which the Supreme Court reiterated there is a basic structure. Then my question is a simple one: What do you say to the doubts Chief Justice Ranjan Gogoi has raised when clearly the Supreme Court judges and cases and precedents contradict him?

FSN: May I just first put it this way? You are absolutely right that in *Kesavananda,* which was in 1973 when this question, this phrase, first came in: the basic structure of the Constitution. It was by a very narrow majority: seven to six in a bench of thirteen judges, the largest bench that then sat. But there is one thing which is missed by most people that there was a postmortem on this judgement which took place at the instance of the then Chief Justice A. N. Ray, and he constituted once again a bench of thirteen judges who were entirely different because after 1973, eight out of the fourteen had retired. The question that he framed was whether we should now continue with this decision, which was a very troublesome decision. The answer given is very peculiar. There was no answer to this question. The bench of thirteen judges sat for the first time with these eight new judges on 10 November 1975. Arguments were carried on and on. On the 11 November, they once again assembled and sat the whole day. On the morning of 12 November 1975, when the courtroom was marked in, unknown to all the other colleagues of Mr Ray, he announced this bench was dissolved.

You won't find what happened because there was no tape recording in those days. Nobody knows who argued what because it was the great (Nani) Palkhivala who argued for the petitioners and Niren De for the other side. But the question only was what did this mean, what did he say, and hats off to our constitutional historian H. M. Seervai, who gives the answer in his book, and that's the only answer we have ever. The answer is that all twelve of the thirteen judges, except the chief justice perhaps, were of the considered view that the basic structure doctrine that had been propounded was not erroneous and ought to be followed. That's what he has said and that's always missed by everybody, including Chief Justice Gogoi.

The interesting point is that if twelve out of thirteen judges on that bench believe that the basic structure theory is not erroneous, it is correct. It must be followed. It would have meant that the chief justice would have been a minority of one. That's why he said that the bench was dissolved because he wanted to save his face. It would be embarrassing. Possibly! Because he was embarrassed and one other thing, please remember that H. M. Seervai at that time had argued this case on behalf of the government. This is most important. Most people don't know that H. M. Seervai had been especially asked to lead the attorney general (Niren De) and argue this case of *Kesavananda* in 1973.

KT: So, the findings were the opposite of what he was supposed to do. This actually underlines the point that he made that the vast majority of judges were not in favour of overturning the basic structure.

FSN: That's right! The chief justice acted to avoid embarrassment, but that was only the first instance. There have been several instances that the Supreme Court has stood by this. Right up to 2007, when, unanimously, a bench of nine judges again contested, and they unanimously affirmed the decision on the basic structure doctrine.

KT: Correct me if I'm wrong, but didn't the National Judicial Commission case happen when Justice Gogoi was at least on the bench?

FSN: No, he wasn't.

KT: He wasn't, but he was in the court. I mean he was a judge of the court at the time. So, when he now says or questions whether the basic structure theory holds, he's going against not just one precedent, but fifty other precedents set by the court.

FSN: Yes, absolutely. But quite frankly, people have their own views. They want to stick to them, and one can't say anything about it. It may well be that he genuinely believes this. You see, all that arises out of the fact that in India, people don't realise no one organ of the state is sovereign. Parliament in India is not sovereign, the judiciary also is not sovereign, and the executive is, of course, not sovereign at all. Apart from the Commonwealth countries, in England, the parliament is sovereign because it is called the High Court of Parliament. That's the other name for the English parliament. In fact, there was a very interesting case years ago in 1965, where in the Allahabad High Court, two judges were hauled up for contempt of the Legislative Assembly of Allahabad, and on a presidential reference specially made, ultimately the Supreme Court decided, with chief justice sitting on the bench unanimously, that India's parliament is not sovereign, unlike England's parliament.

KT: Is the Constitution sovereign?

FSN: Yes, absolutely. The Constitution is supreme. We don't say sovereign because it doesn't govern anything but supreme.

KT: So, in your opinion, has Justice Gogoi made a bad mistake claiming there's no basic structure?

FSN: I'm afraid so, but that's all right. Different people may have different views. I think so.

KT: People have a right to hold different things but his view in your opinion is wrong?

FSN: Yes, totally wrong!

KT: In this context, let me ask you. Would One Nation, One Election, which is again something that's being talked about at the moment, breach the basic structure of the Constitution? Because we assume state assemblies are autonomous and sovereign in their own right?

FSN: Autonomous, not sovereign.

KT: One Nation, One Election would require them to hold their elections synchronised with the Lok Sabha, which they may not want to do, which may mean that they have to curtail their terms or expand their terms. Would this affect the federal or quasi-federal structure of our country?

FSN: I haven't examined it, but perhaps it might or it might not. I mean that would depend upon how the Supreme Court looks at it. But I would like to only put this that one election business is going to be an extraordinarily difficult task for any government to hold. Namely, for this reason, there has to be security during every election, and we don't have all the personnel to have security for each and every constituency in the country, whether it is a state constituency or a Lok Sabha constituency.

KT: So, in a practical sense, this would be close to impossible?

FSN: Yes, and there is an article only in this morning's one of the newspapers which mentions all this.

KT: What about in terms of the Constitution? I know you haven't examined the matter, but what's your hunch? Would One Nation, One Election breach the basic structure because of the impact on state assemblies and their autonomy?

FSN: I can't say this offhand. Whether it would be a breach or not a breach. It is because of this federal structure that there's a problem with breaches.

KT: Because the federal structure is definitely part of the basic structure.

FSN: Yes, absolutely. That's been held.

KT: And central to the federal structure is presumably the autonomy of state assemblies?

FSN: Yes, absolutely, absolutely!

KT: And if that autonomy is impinged upon because you require them to curtail their time or expand their time, and . . .

FSN: You see apart from that, what happens when no-confidence motion is moved and passed in one state assembly? An election has to be held within a stated time and how does that coordinate with every other state? This is going to be a big problem.

KT: People say that the way around the fall of a government prior to five years is a German-style, what's it called, a constructive vote of confidence. The problem is in theory . . .

FSN: That is to say, who else will take its place?

KT: Absolutely! You can't vote out one government unless you can vote one in. In theory, it works. But what happens if the ruling party splits and the breakaway does not join the opposition?

FSN: And we have too many splits today!

KT: Absolutely! And remember, in that situation, you'll have a minority government which doesn't have a majority, but the opposition can't create one either because the breakaway refuses to join. You're left with an absurdity.

FSN: There's no governance, and that's the problem. Therefore, you see, this is some newfangled idea. I don't know whether or how it will work. Whether it's practical, whether it's legal, whether it undermines the basic structure.

KT: But do you have serious qualms about it?

FSN: I have serious doubts about whether it would work. Serious doubts, that's all I can say at this stage.

KT: You also make another important point. You hinted at it a moment ago. It has to do with the question of do we need a new constitution. I'm going to quote what you say in your book, "We will never be able to piece together a new constitution in the present day and age simply because innovative ideas, however brilliant and howsoever encouragingly expressed in consultation papers and reports of commissions, can never give us an ideal constitution. In constitution-making, there are hidden forces that must not be ignored." These are, you say, "the spirit of persuasion, of accommodation, and of tolerance in India as in the rest of the world is at a very low ebb today." Can you explain that further?

FSN: Yes, I will. See, I'll take the last first—the spirit of tolerance. Although we have the word "fraternity" in our constitution, the spirit of tolerance amongst us is getting worse and worse over the years. What is the reason? Why should it be? It is, at the moment, not relevant. The fact is that there is very little tolerance for any view which is contrary to an official view—call it a governmental view, call it a particular view, a group of individuals' view, etc. Therefore, the spirit of accommodation that your view may also be right, I may also be right, etc., is not there. That is why constitutionalists, people like Sir Ivor Jennings, who had written a brilliant book on cabinet government, have said that it is deliberate why in England, you have the leader of the opposition called the leader of his "Majesty's Opposition" or "Her Majesty's Office." Why? Her Majesty has nothing to do with the opposition. It's just the government, but it is essential in a democracy. According to the Westminster model that we have, you must have an opposition which opposes whatever the government does so the rest of the public may make their own decision.

KT: And for this to be possible, tolerance is essential. You're saying that *that* spirit of tolerance is missing today. We've become polarised. We see opponents as enemies. Therefore, in this atmosphere, it is close to impossible to devise and create a new constitution.

FSN: I regret to say this, but you see, over the years, ever since 1960-65 onwards, whether under the Congress party government or under the present BJP party government, makes no difference. This lack of tolerance has been showing and has been visible. I think even majoritarian governments, therefore, have not worked in India.

KT: You are saying that because this spirit of tolerance is missing, because the desire to accommodate other views is missing, we cannot write a new constitution. The environment to do that . . .

FSN: Yes, absolutely correct! Absolutely, because the environment to do that is just not there.

KT: The problem is that you've written this at a time when actually there are increasing calls for a new constitution.

FSN: Oh absolutely, for a presidential form of government.

KT: In fact, none other than the chairman of the prime minister's Economic Advisory Council, a gentleman called Bibek Debroy, has written an article suggesting the need for a new constitution. What do you say to Mr Debroy?

FSN: I say that this is a kite-flying exercise, that's all, with great respect to him. He's a very brilliant person, I really read all his articles, but the problem is that when you say, "I want a new constitution," I would ask, "How shall we frame it?" and "Who would be the person who would frame it?" In India today, among a large number of people, everybody amongst two people, there are four opinions. There are no two opinions. The whole thing breaks down at the very start. Please remember that it is this written Constitution that we have, that worked through, or half worked through, that keeps the country together. It's very important.

KT: Don't jettison it because you can get yourself in peril.

FSN: Yes! Because you won't be able to ensure that India won't be split up and that's such a disaster. Unity is the most essential element in our constitutional working. That is why we are not quite federal but quasi-federal.

KT: You're saying two very important things. First, you are saying we do not have people like the founding fathers who created the 1950 Constitution, who we respect and look up to, who can create a new constitution. Secondly, you're saying if you jettison this Constitution, the silken threads that bind us together as a nation will snap, and we'll split. Don't take that risk!

FSN: Yes, please don't. You see, because this idea of persuasion also has left us. Both parties, all parties, bully today. Everybody wants to make his word count. That can't be in any group that we're talking about. You look at the world today, and the world is in that situation.

KT: Let's at this point come, Mr Nariman, to how the Constitution and, perhaps more importantly, the rights that it confers on the citizens of India are defended by our judges. You quote in your book, Chief Justice Chandrachud—he wasn't chief justice at the time in 2017 in the *Puttaswamy* judgement—he said, and I'm quoting him: "A constitutional democracy can survive when citizens have an undiluted assurance that the rule of law will protect their rights and liberties against any invasion by the state, and that judicial remedies would be available to ask searching questions and expect answers when a citizen has been deprived of these most precious rights." But does the Supreme Court, leave lower courts, does even the Supreme Court live up to this? In 2019, when there was a state of habeas corpus cases from Kashmir, it virtually ignored them. In 2020, when tens of millions of people walking on the roads during the lockdown were trying to get home, their plight was ignored by the Supreme Court.

Critical issues like the Citizenship Amendment Act or electoral bonds are not being heard. It took about five years to hear the Kashmir case. Not just the Supreme Court, but all the courts down the hierarchy, have made it increasingly difficult to get bail. It should be "bail, not jail," but people stay in jail for years. Hence my question, Mr Nariman: Are these glorious resonant words from Justice Chandrachud just rhetoric?

FSN: You see, I know that from the Constitution that has worked for so many years, in America, it's the same thing. You look at one ten-year period, you look at another ten-year period, look at the third ten-year period—different judges state different things at different times, all over the world in the same situation. But we are today talking about a Constitution which has been framed, which is in existence, and which works in a way at least. So, whether we can now speak of some other constitution, ideally that will suit everybody, it can only be an autocratic constitution.

KT: I'm not using Justice Chandrachud's words to say we need a new constitution. I'm using them to ask do judges defend the rights of the Constitution? Are they dilatory? I mean, habeas corpus they ignore . . .

FSN: Sometimes yes, but hopefully no.

KT: I mean, there are people like Umar Khalid whose bail case is not going to be heard by the Supreme Court for weeks hence. The poor man's been in jail for two years. He's not convicted; he should have been out on bail, but there was no urgency.

FSN: You see, Justice Krishna's famous dictum was "bail, not jail!" Fortunately, I find one or two judges today do follow this, and they have, on that assumption, granted bail to various people. But if you look at the number of persons who are under detention or in jail before trial, they have not even been convicted which is most unfair.

KT: And languishing for fifteen-twenty years . . .

FSN: And languishing, yes! Then this is brought out by Mr Bibek Debroy himself.

KT: Absolutely, which is why I asked, do our judges do enough to defend the rights the Constitution confers on us? It seems to me, occasionally they do, but there are probably worrying instances when they don't.

FSN: Yeah, hopefully it will be better. Hopefully!

KT: Is this to do with the fact that we have an uneven quality of judges? Some good judges, but quite a few are not good judges.

FSN: You see, there is a question about the organ of appointments. How are judges appointed? That's another big controversy. Does the collegium system work? Did the original system work? Why did it break down? Although it is a different question on which I have written something here, as you will see, in the book itself. But these are questions to be solved, I say, and they can only be solved by a person who assumes the office of chief justice and decides that "I will continue to do something that will help the progress of the country."

KT: But the problem is, in the recent past, two or three years ago—I'm not talking about history—we've had judges even at the Supreme Court level, who whilst being judges, have been praising the prime minister.

FSN: That is extremely unfortunate. They should completely stay away from this. This is something which creates an absolutely wrong impression, that you are buddy-buddy with somebody high up in political office.

KT: Then you have the Justice Chalameswar case who organised a press conference because they were so concerned about the way rostering was happening. They organised a press conference which was unprecedented. Doesn't it suggest that there is a deep rot in the system that must be removed?

FSN: Must be removed, and who can remove it? Well, I don't know who can remove it. Not Parliament. I don't say this only because of one chief justice. There was a person whom we had many years ago, in my time, Chief Justice Venkatachaliah. Now, the judges themselves looked up to him as a person of great learning and of great integrity. The Bar looked up to him as a person of learning and of great integrity. That sort of thing helps a great deal because then he or she, whoever that person is, whoever heads the judiciary only, can deliver the goods. Not any collegium system or commission system.

KT: Mr Nariman, there is an impression that Justice Chandrachud is acquiring some sort of similar position. He's looked up to for his learning. The problem is that there are many instances, even when he's been head of the collegium, when recommendations made have been ignored by the government or delayed transfers have happened without permission and there was that dreadful case of Justice Muralidhar who was removed from Delhi, overnight sent to Haryana, and then retired pretty quickly there.

FSN: I wrote about it.

KT: Why doesn't our judge system, the collegium system, fight back? Why don't they hold the government guilty of contempt in court when the government deliberately refuses to give authority and approval for an error that's been reiterated, not once, twice, but three times even?

FSN: Worse still, why do they withdraw what they said before? Which is even worse! The gentleman was transferred as the chief justice of Madras, one of the premier posts in the country, and yet the government didn't approve. So, the collegium withdrew that recommendation. This is akin to self-destruction.

KT: Absolutely! This is what I mean. Judges don't stand up for their own rights. Leave aside the fact they don't stand up for my right or your right. We are secondary. They're not standing up for their own rights! Is there an element of pusillanimity or intimidation or fear? Why can't they stand up when nothing can be done to them?

FSN: Nothing can be done!

KT: So, do they lack a spine?

FSN: I don't know! But you see, we had the Emergency, and we had, if you remember, lived in through it, the bandwagon judges. We had what I used to call the bandwagon judges, who would jump on the bandwagon and say we must observe the twenty-point programme and things like that.

KT: And ADM Jabalpur was an embarrassment for the Supreme Court. Why are judges not standing up? I mean, afterwards they believe the collegium system is the right system? They overturn the National Judicial Commission. Now the very rules of the collegium system are being flouted by this government, and they're doing nothing. They're accepting it! Why does this not worry you?

FSN: Despite the fact that the major judgement of Chief Justice Verma in the *Judges* case was really that, if the government in a given case, refuses the assumption is that that refusal is mala fide. All the more reason to stand up.

KT: This is why I come back to this question a second time: Are our judges becoming pusillanimous? Do they lack a spine? Are they intimidated?

FSN: In England, they used to have a theory that judges are judges under the throne. You see now, unfortunately, there have been occasions when we've had these judges under the throne. Especially when I lived through the Emergency, this was definitely the position. Relatively, this situation continues from decade to decade.

KT: It's particularly sad, isn't it, when judges can't stand up for their own rights?

FSN: Yes, it is. I quite agree.

KT: So, this is a sad situation.

FSN: It is sad, but who can remedy it is a very difficult thing, except the judges themselves . . .

KT: Absolutely, and you need a couple of judges with spine. They need to be able to stand up because there's nothing the government can do to them. There's no way they can be punished.

FSN: Absolutely. There's no question about it.

KT: Let's come to how our governments respect and adhere to the constitution. In your book, with great approval, you quote Ambedkar. Ambedkar said, "However good a constitution may be, it is sure to turn out bad because those who are called to work it, happen to be a bad lot. However bad a constitution may be, it may turn out to be good, if those who are called to work it, happen to be a good lot." In your opinion, have our governments been a good lot or a bad lot?

FSN: You must put it on both grounds. If the judges have been a good lot or a bad lot, and has the government been a good lot or bad lot?

KT: Tell me the answers to both.

FSN: Yeah, quite right. Well, at times yes, at times no. One can honestly say that.

KT: This is like the wretched curate's egg.

FSN: That is quite right. It is good in parts.

KT: But at the end of the day, judges don't do as much damage, I imagine, as governments can do to the Constitution?

FSN: Tremendous.

KT: So, in the majority of cases, have we had good governments or bad governments?

FSN: The assessment, I think, varies from decade to decade. We have had at least one very important bad time which we have never ultimately remembered, and that was during the Emergency. You see, very few people today—probably many of them were not even born—remember the bad times during the Emergency. If you reflect on those bad times and think of how to improve things and which should never happen again, then perhaps there may be some way in which things could improve.

KT: Some people say that in the Emergency, you had outright censorship, outright intimidation of the courts, arrest of politicians, arrest of students. It was done outright. Because it was done outright, in a sense, it was done upfront. Today, you have virtually the same thing happening but by subterfuge.

FSN: In a veiled manner.

KT: Absolutely! Which is worse? Today, when it's happening in a veiled manner or then?

FSN: They are as bad, yeah!

KT: So, in other words, in your opinion, the situation today is like another Emergency?

FSN: Yes, you can say that. You can say that because, you see, internally we have a government which, unfortunately, despite everything, despite its great success outside the country, has no tolerance within the state, and this is reflected in the governments also in the states.

KT: Let me put one difference to you. Just as in the Emergency, we have intolerance, we don't like dissent, and we have a government battling against institutions and weakening them. Parliament itself is disregarded. All of that happened in the Emergency too, but there's one thing that's happening now that didn't happen in the Emergency: we have a mode of intolerance of minorities. There's an anti-Muslim atmosphere that did not exist in the Emergency. It is prevalent, and it's increasing today. Doesn't that make a significant difference?

FSN: Yes, it does. I don't know why this somehow doesn't gel with India's increasing prominence in world affairs. This doesn't somehow gel, but it has to gel. Someone has to bell the cat.

KT: We don't talk about it in our country because, by and large, our media and our channels are intimidated by the government. They don't want the rocks of Mr Modi to descend on them. However, the Western media is only too aware, and the Western media is frequently telling, whether it's Biden or Sunak or Macron, these are issues you should point out in India. The Western media chides their leaders for turning a Nelson's eye to the way Modi treats Muslims in India. The world is aware; we don't want to make ourselves knowledgeable of it!

FSN: Yeah, that's absolutely true. I quite agree with you.

KT: In your book, you make a very interesting distinction between two types of governments India has had: majoritarian, as you call them, when the ruling party had an outright majority, and coalition governments when they didn't have a majority unless they coalesced. Do I think that you believe coalition governments were better respecters of the Constitution than majoritarian ones?

FSN: Under present circumstances in India, yes, definitely! That's been our experience throughout. You just have to look at it.

KT: So, would you say, given the way we've developed and given the character perhaps of our politicians, particularly when they have outright power, that India's Constitution and the rights that Constitution confers are in better hands when we have a coalition than when we have a majoritarian government?

FSN: Yes, absolutely! There's no doubt about it, which is an unfortunate thing, but it is true. Autocracy, you see, is a trend in the world today, Karan. We all speak glibly of a democracy, but the autocratic trend is very distinct, and that wind is blowing, and it is very alarming, quite frankly. I mean, I've lived my whole life, but for the younger people, it's going to be quite alarming.

KT: Which is why a coalition government, which is necessarily a weaker government, is perhaps the best government.

FSN: Perhaps, in the state of affairs that we have, there is no doubt about it.

KT: I want to touch on one last issue because you've hinted at it a moment ago. You have, in your book, some very interesting things to say about the role of the opposition in a democracy. You're quoting Sir Ivor Jennings. He went on to be master of Trinity Hall, Cambridge, and you quote him with great approval. He says, "It is not untrue to say that the most important part of parliament is the opposition. The opposition is at once the alternative to the government and a focus for the discontent of the people. Its function is almost as important as that of a government. If there be no opposition, there is no democracy."

FSN: Absolutely correct!

KT: How would you persuade Mr Modi to accept this view?

FSN: I don't know. I'm too old to persuade anybody, quite frankly, and I'm certainly not in a position to persuade the prime minister. That's why I said that this move towards an autocratic state of affairs is not confined to this country. It is a trend all over the world.

KT: But in our country, with the exception of the Nehru years, mercifully there were seventeen of them, and perhaps with the exception of the Vajpayee years, the opposition has been looked upon as an enemy. Mrs Gandhi didn't tolerate them. She didn't like them, and she hardly consulted them and certainly, our present prime minister seems to look upon them with disdain. He mocks them, crudely at times, even customary politeness is missing. How do we teach our politicians that it is a critical sentence that "it is not untrue to say that the most important part of parliament is the opposition"? How do you convince the prime minister that you and the ruling party are not the most important—the most important part is your opponents.

FSN: I can't tell you. Perhaps you can answer that question. I wish I was the person who was asking the question.

KT: You go one step further, and once again you're quoting with great approval, Sir Ivor Jennings. He says, and I'm quoting him: "Attacks upon the government and individual ministers are the functions of the opposition." That's so important, I want to repeat it for the audience: "Attacks upon the government and individual ministers are the functions of the opposition," and then he adds, "The duty of the opposition is to oppose." So, when for example Rahul Gandhi . . .

FSN: May I just add here that exactly all this has been quoted in a book published by the Rajya Sabha itself. All these quotes of Ivor Jennings are not from England only; they have been adopted by our parliament. The Rajya Sabha itself has quoted this in a booklet which expressly says all this. The question is: Do we live up to it? That's the problem.

KT: Absolutely! When you say the Rajya Sabha has quoted this in a booklet, this is therefore part of our custom, practice, and belief.

FSN: That's how I've quoted it. I've quoted it from our book from the Rajya Sabha. It may be Ivor Jennings' words . . .

KT: But these are not British positions. These are Indian positions!

FSN: Yes! In the Westminster model of our Constitution, which is common to all the Commonwealth countries, is the only safeguard for the democratic setup.

KT: Something very interesting follows from this. When Rahul Gandhi vehemently and fiercely criticises the prime minister, and he does it with frequency and regularity, people turn around and say this is a personal attack, this is a vendetta. It's not. That is what an opposition leader is meant to do.

FSN: Therefore, we don't know. We all are not quite educated on what true democracy is. That's the problem. We have to be better educated.

KT: But you also have an important caution or warning for the opposition, and once again it may be from a British document, but I believe it's also part of our system. You say, and I'm quoting you: "The opposition has no right to obstruct in the sense of making parliament barren or unproductive," and that means, does it not, that the viewpoint originally propounded by Arun Jaitley and Sushma Swaraj that obstructing parliament is a legitimate parliamentary tactic is a completely mistaken view?

FSN: That's a mistaken view. That's absolutely correct.

KT: Opposition can oppose, and opposition can criticise. They can be vitriolic if they want to, but obstructing the functioning of parliament is not permitted.

FSN: Yes, and then carrying all those placards in the parliament is totally wrong. It never happened when I was there as a member, but this has all been subsequent to that, and it's getting worse and worse.

KT: The interesting message you're sending the opposition is: "I uphold, as Sir Ivor Jennings says, your right to oppose. You are perhaps the most important part of parliament. I uphold your right to criticise fiercely, rudely, however. But I do not believe you have a right to obstruct. You have to let parliament function. You can't shout it to silence."

FSN: You're absolutely correct because otherwise, the parliamentary system of government breaks down. These are things which ultimately lead to autocracy. Call it a dictatorship, call it what you like, but it has reached a type of autocracy, which is already unfortunate.

KT: This is very interesting, what you're saying. The opposition doesn't realise that if they carry on ceaselessly obstructing the parliament, they're paving the path to autocracy.

FSN: Yes, absolutely! This is being mentioned time out of number by those in charge of government—state governments or central government.

KT: If you make parliament futile and unproductive, the government will be given an excuse on a platter to take parliament non-seriously.

FSN: It's the sort of thing that happened in England when Cromwell came to power, if you recall.

KT: I do, indeed. "You have sat too long here for any good you have been doing. Depart, I say, and let us have done with you. In the name of God, go." Mr Nariman, thank you very much.

FSN: Thank you.

3

Evolution of Separation of Powers

"Separation of powers" was once thought to be the only sensible rule of constitutional behaviour. Fundamental differences between the three branches of government—the legislature, the executive, and the judiciary—prompted the conclusion that they should be separate and distinct. But this does not reflect how democratic governments around the world actually work. In 1920, British historian Albert Pollard, in his book, *The Evolution of Parliament,* wrote that the doctrine of separation of powers in politics "was an ingenious attempt to reduce the infinite complexity of government to the subtle simplicity of a constitutional rule of three."

In the first half of the twentieth century, academics, who were generally hostile to the traditional tripartite theory of separation of powers, argued for a system of government based on only two functions: *policy* and *administration.* This is because the problem at the centre of constitutional government today is how to achieve a balance between different branches of the government, a balance that will safeguard the freedom of the individual and at the same time ensure that governments provide their citizens with essential services, without which modern-day society cannot survive.

The initial doctrine of separation of powers had its roots in antiquity. Ancient Greek philosopher and polymath Aristotle (384-322 BCE) first mentioned the idea of "a mixed government" in his treatise, *Politics.* And Greek historian Polybius (200-118 BCE) later explained in some detail the system of checks and balances, crediting Lycurgus (king of Sparta) for having established the first government of this kind.

In more recent times:

1. An argument about the need for separation of powers within a monarchical state had been made by John Locke (1632-1704), who reasoned: "It may be too great a temptation to human frailty for the same persons who have the power of making laws to have also in their hands the power to execute them whereby they may exempt themselves from obedience to the laws they make, and suit the law both in its making and execution to their own private advantage."
2. One of the earliest and clearest statements of the separation of powers had been propounded by the French philosopher Montesquieu (1689-1755) in his now famous book, *The Spirit of the Laws* (1748). In it, he noted: "When the legislative and executive powers are united in the same person, or in the same body of magistrates, there can be no liberty . . . there is no liberty if the power of judging is not separated from the legislative and executive. There would be an end to everything, if the same man or the same body were to exercise those three powers." By way of illustration, he added that: "Among the Turks where the three powers are united in the person of the sultan, an atrocious despotism reigns."

   Since the British constitutional system functioned quite smoothly between the king, the parliament and the courts, Montesquieu boldly asserted that separation of powers was a necessary, if not a sufficient condition of liberty "since its absence promotes tyranny."
3. As to why the doctrine of separation of powers (more accurately, of "shared powers") was important and was considered worth fighting for, was also emphasised by the author of one of the Federalist Papers—a precursor to the formulation and later adoption, of the Constitution of the

United States of America (1789)—the modern world's shortest written constitution (less than 8,000 words). In his Federalist Paper No. 51, James Madison had written: "In framing a government which is to be administered by men over men the great difficulty lies in this: you must first enable the government to control the governed; and in the next place oblige it to control itself. A dependence on the people is no doubt the primary control on the government, but experience has taught mankind the necessity of taking auxiliary precautions."

4. In the Constitution of India, 1950, believed to be the world's longest document of governance after the Constitution of the state of Alabama in the USA, the doctrine of separation of powers is indeed recognised "but not in its absolute rigidity." This is what a Constitution bench of India's Supreme Court had said way back in 1955, adding: "But the functions of different parts or branches of government are sufficiently differentiated, and consequently it could be confidently said that our Constitution does not contemplate assumption, by one organ or part of the state, of functions that essentially belong to another."

   Since separation of powers *alone* does not operate as a canonical principle of constitutionalism, what is now proposed in the last two decades of the twenty-first century, by professor of law Jeremy Waldron (in an article published in the *Boston College Law Review* on 28 March 2013) is a close-knit set of rules that are designed to work both separately and together as set out below:

   a. The principle of the separation of the functions of government from one another (the separation of powers principle).
   b. The principle that warns against the concentration of too much political power in the hands of any

one person, group, or agency (the division of power principle).

c. The principle that requires the ordinary concurrence of one governmental entity in the actions of another, and thus permits one entity to check or veto the actions of another (the checks and balances principle).
d. The principle that requires laws to be enacted by votes in two coordinate legislative assemblies (the bicameralism principle).
e. The principle that distinguishes between powers assigned to the federal government and powers reserved to the states (the federalism principle).

Of course, none of these "principles" are made enforceable in written constitutions because every written constitution divides power in its own particular way. In 2023-2024, the separation of powers principle continues to survive, but under its more appropriate "umbrella term": division of powers principle.

Section IV
LAW

1

Is the Law of Contempt Being Stretched Too Far?[1]

In the branch of law relating to "insults to the court," the almost unlimited powers of judges need to be cautioned. I advisedly use the word "cautioned" and not "controlled." No one can keep this power under control except the judges themselves. The track record of the courts does show a marked tendency to use the power for committing persons for contempt (for scandalising the court) much too frequently. It is, in fact, being stretched too far, and it is time it was reined in by the judges themselves.

In an adversarial system of litigation like ours, there are always two parties—one must lose and the other must win. And when it goes through three tiers of litigation—again an unfortunate characteristic of our law—the party who ultimately loses sometimes harbours inbuilt (often unjustified) grievances against one or more judges down the line who may have decided against them.

People who propagate these grudges are often lawyers themselves. Top lawyers have big egos. And egotistical lawyers never like to lose, and when they do, some of them are not averse to blaming the judge or suggesting to their clients that there was some ulterior motive. Now, judging cases is a difficult business, and the occupational hazards of judging are many—the memory of a wrong decision (or what is ultimately found to be a wrong decision) sometimes festers. It also (though less often) gives rise to irresponsible, sometimes scurrilous comments, first about the case itself, and then inevitably about the judge or court that rendered judgement. The law reports are strewn with cases of disgruntled litigants (and occasionally lawyers as well) going to great lengths in making charges, often unfounded, against the judiciary.

The law of contempt—that part of which is so colourfully described as "scandalising the court"—is intended as a wall of protection against the vicissitudes of judging. Ours is a very litigious society, and there are (as you all well know) a number of "nuts" in the system—people who will make any type of allegation against anyone at the drop of a hat. This is why I believe that this part of the criminal contempt jurisdiction, though now obsolete in England, should remain in India. However, there are problems. In this branch of the law, the lines are thinly drawn and are not very clear, and they depend very much on the perception of the judge administering the contempt jurisdiction in the name of the court. The public, the men and women of the media, and lawyers are content to accept constraints imposed by the "rule of law" but are not prepared to accept ad hoc rules imposed according to the whims, vagaries, and idiosyncrasies of individual judges. This ad-hocism was typified in the V. C. Mishra case.[2]

No one liked what V. C. Mishra said and did in Allahabad, but the three-judge bench that decided his case, in their enthusiasm to teach him a lesson, deviated from the law. Ultimately, sobriety prevailed. The Constitution bench of the Supreme Court[3] also did not like what Mishra said or did and yet they overruled the punishment meted out to him and set out the true contours of the penalties that can be imposed in contempt cases. This case has set an example and prompted a word of advice to all, both lawyers and judges: *never* behave as Mishra did, and *never* lose your temper as the three-judge bench did in Mishra's case. Always keep your cool, as the five-judge bench did, and so earned the admiration of all.

Mishra's case has established (a fact overlooked by judges in the high courts) that the contempt jurisdiction must not and cannot be used to discipline a lawyer in the conduct of a case. This must be left to the Bar councils entrusted with disciplinary powers under the Advocates Act.

As for scandalising the court, there are no rules, there are no constraints. It is a mercurial jurisdiction. It was Jeremy Bentham (the theoretical jurist) who characterised the common law as "dog law."

> "When your dog does anything you want to break him off," (he wrote in 1823), "you wait till he does it, and then beat him for it. This is the way you make laws for your dog, and this is the way judges make laws for you and me."

The law of contempt of court in Anglo-Saxon jurisprudence, both in England in the past and in India in the past and present, has been no more, no less than "dog law." There are no rules, no constraints. No precise circumstances when the administration of justice is brought into contempt. The judgements are strewn with pious platitudes that give little guidance to the editor, to the commentator, to lawyers, and to members of the public. This part of the law of contempt, though necessary, is a standing threat to free expression. It leaves too much to the discretion of the particular judge (or judges). And at times, decisions do give rise to a strange feeling that the status of the person who scandalises the court perhaps did affect the ultimate result.

In 1988, a sitting cabinet minister made wide and improper remarks against judges of the Supreme Court:

> "Zamindars, like Golaknath (he was speaking of *Golaknath's case*), evoked a sympathetic chord nowhere in the whole country, except the Supreme Court of India. And the bank magnates, the representatives of the elitist culture of this country, ably supported by industrialists, the beneficiaries of independence, got higher compensation by the intervention of the Supreme Court in *Cooper's case* (1970). Anti-social elements, FERA (Foreign Exchange Regulatory Act) violators, bride burners, and a whole horde of reactionaries have found their heaven in the Supreme Court.[4]"

The minister then went on to say that because the judges of the highest court had their "unconcealed sympathy for the *haves*" (as opposed to the have-nots), they had interpreted the expression "compensation" in the manner they did, clearly attributing motives. And yet a bench of two judges (in *Duda's case*) exonerated him:

> "Bearing in mind the trend in the law of contempt (they were speaking of the liberal trend) established by the judgement of Justice Krishna Iyer in *Mulgaokar's case*[5], the speech of the minister has to be read in its proper perspective, and when so read, it did not bring the administration of justice into disrepute or impair the administration of justice. The minister is not guilty of contempt of the court."

Admirable. Laudable. Free speech upheld. But one cannot help wondering whether their lordships would have been quite as liberal if the criticism had been made by a less important personage than a cabinet minister! Again, when an important personage, Mohd. Yunus, chairman of the Trade Fair Authority of India, known at the time to be very close to Prime Minister Indira Gandhi, had criticised a judgement delivered by a Supreme Court judge in the *Jehovah's Witness case* holding that the singing of the national anthem for a particular sect of Christians was not compulsory, Mohd. Yunus said that this judge (Justice Chinnappa Reddy) "has no right to be called either an Indian or a judge."

An association of individuals called the Conscientious Group[6] filed a petition seeking a direction that Yunus should be hauled up for contempt. But close colleagues of Justice Chinnappa Reddy, daily sitting with him, suddenly found themselves powerless to even call for an explanation from Mohd. Yunus on the technical ground that when the attorney general was approached by the petitioners to give his sanction he had declined, and the solicitor general also demurred.

> "They knew that the power to issue notice *suo motu* for any contempt was plenary (not dependent on the fiat of the attorney general or solicitor general), yet they chose not to invoke it even though a sitting judge of the Supreme Court had been described as a person not fit to be an Indian, not fit to be a judge!"

Yet in a later case (also reported), a not-so-important litigant was held guilty of contempt for saying that a judge was anti-national. When a bench of the Supreme Court of India, hearing a miscellaneous application[7], said that it was inclined to think that a particular case should go before a bench which had earlier passed some orders, an inconsequential member of the public, Mohd. Zahir Khan (the litigant), addressed the court in a loud tone thus: "Either he is an anti-national, or the judges are anti-nationals."

A notice was issued, and the litigant was found guilty of contempt of court and made to suffer imprisonment for one month. These examples are given not to deride our judges or criticise previous decisions. It is only to illustrate very graphically that the true nature of this aspect of contempt jurisdiction is mercurial, unpredictable, and capable of being exercised (and therefore in fact exercised) differently in different cases and also differently by different judges in the same court.

The disturbing trend persists. In this branch of the law, the dice are loaded. At a conference held in Bangalore many years ago, a prominent American journalist recalled how he had been "cited" in the United States for contempt for reporting a pending case in colours too fanciful and garish for the judge. The journalist told the federal judge (somewhat brashly): "We want no accommodation from you. The First Amendment is on our side. We will fight it out." The judge responded, "Have it your way, but remember, who is the umpire in this battleground!"

Always, my friends, remember this: First, in this branch of the law, the judge is the prosecutor. Second, you are presumed guilty till you convince him of your innocence. And third, it is the judge against whom or against whose decision you spoke that will decide whether or not you should be sent to jail. The dice are loaded, and the great question is: should it be so loaded? Is this the right procedure or the right approach?

The origin of the branch of law known as "scandalising the court" is shrouded in antiquity. It has been described in textbooks as both "dubious and controversial."[8] It originates from a celebrated dictum of Justice Wilmot in his judgement in the *Wilkes case*[9] way back in 1765, a judgement which was never actually delivered, but meant to be delivered, and later published by Justice Wilmot's son when his father's papers were edited. It was a judgement reserved after argument, and when ready to be delivered, it was discovered that the writ against Wilkes was incorrectly titled, and since an amendment of the writ was not consented to, the case had to be abandoned. This is the real ancestry of that part of the law of contempt known today as "scandalising the court." It is based on a judgement never delivered in a case—a case which had already abated!

As for the constitutional angle, remember to never use this jurisdiction to suppress those who speak against the courts or judges nor merely to uphold the dignity of the court or its judges. The law of contempt is an exception to the fundamental right of free speech and expression guaranteed under Article 19(1)(a) of the Constitution. The law must then be justified on the ground that it is a "reasonable restriction" under Article 19(2). Otherwise, it would be unconstitutional.

There is a judgement of the Division Bench of the Calcutta High Court[10] delivered some years ago, which correctly appreciated this constitutional principle. It was not widely reported and deserves greater publicity than it has so far received. It is a judgement of a bench of two judges—Justice S. C. Sen and Justice U. C. Banerjee (each of whom became a judge of the Supreme Court of India). The fact that the law of contempt is an exception to the fundamental right of free speech has been nowhere more felicitously described than in this judgement (delivered for the bench by Justice Banerjee). In that case, the court was called upon to decide whether an article in a Calcutta daily, which had condemned a prior judgement of the Calcutta High Court, unread and by distorting facts, was contemptuous. The article had the disquieting heading: "Let the High Court Save Itself from Ignominy." A suo motu rule was issued by the high court. When it came up for hearing, no apology was called for or tendered. But the newspaper was exonerated and the contempt notice was discharged. The judges said: "None of the articles can be defended as fair comment made in temperate language about a court case. In fact, the distorted version of the judgement given and the language employed in the articles may have the effect of shaking the confidence of the people in the judiciary and thereby lowering the dignity and majesty of the law."

And yet, upholding the prime importance of freedom of speech, the Calcutta High Court held that the publication was not contempt, though the judges did say that the language used could have been better, polite, and more sober. Freedom to criticise (even wrongly and obtusely) a judgement of the court was upheld as part of the cherished freedom of speech.[11]

The judgement of the Calcutta High Court makes me recall what was said by Lord Denning in a now-famous contempt case. Quintin Hogg, son of a Lord Chancellor and a future Lord Chancellor of England himself, had written an article in a very critical and caustic tone about a decision of Denning in a gaming case. The litigant, Blackburn, moved for contempt, and this is what Lord Denning said[12] (it is a beautiful passage, the relevant part of which I must quote in full):

> "This is the first case, so far as I know, where this court has been called on to consider an allegation of contempt against itself. It is a jurisdiction which undoubtedly belongs to us, but which we will most sparingly exercise, more particularly as we ourselves have an interest in the matter. Let me say at once that we will never use this jurisdiction as a means to uphold our own dignity. That must rest on surer foundations. Nor will we use it to suppress those who speak against us. We do not fear criticism, nor do we resent it, for there is something far more important

> at stake. It is no less than freedom of speech itself. It is the right of every man, in parliament or out of it, in the press or over the broadcast, to make fair comment, even outspoken comment, on matters of public interest. Those who comment can deal faithfully with all that is done in a court of justice. They can say that we are mistaken, and our decisions erroneous, whether they are subject to appeal or not. All we would ask is that those who criticise us will remember that, from the nature of our office, we cannot reply to their criticisms. We cannot enter into public controversy, still less into political controversy. We must rely on our conduct itself to be its own vindication.
>
> Exposed as we are to the winds of criticism, nothing which is said by this person or that, nothing which is written by this pen or that, will deter us from doing what we believe is right, nor, I would add, from saying what the occasion requires, provided that it is pertinent to the matter in hand. Silence is not an option when things are ill-done. So, it comes to this. Mr Quintin Hogg has criticised the court, but in so doing, he is exercising his undoubted right. The article contains an error, no doubt, but errors do not make it a contempt of court. We must uphold his right to the uttermost.
>
> I hold this not to be a contempt of court and would dismiss the application."

Lord Denning in England, like Justices Sen and Banerjee in India, put free speech first in a conflict between this freedom and the contempt jurisdiction.

Now comes the question of personal insults which are uttered without malice or contempt. I recall the visit of Lord Templeman some years ago with a British team of judges and lawyers to participate in an annual feature called the Indo-British Legal Forum. Lord Templeman was then the senior-most sitting judge in the House of Lords in England, having since retired. One of the topics we discussed at the forum was "Freedom of the Press, including Contempt of Courts." It was shortly after the controversial decision in the *Spycatcher case*[13], which attracted worldwide attention. Lord Templeman believed that Peter Wright, who wrote *Spycatcher* and had it published in the UK, should be held fast to the undertaking given by him, which was not to publish confidential information obtained by him in his capacity as a member of the British Secret Service, notwithstanding that the information had, with the lapse of time, percolated into the public domain. Two of his colleagues (in the House of Lords) agreed with him, which put Lord Templeman in the majority. The press (the free press, if you will, but certainly not a responsible press) held them up to ridicule. The *Daily Mirror* published photographs of all three judges (Templeman included), and below the photographs was written in capital letters: "OLD FOOLS."

I pointedly asked him why no contempt proceedings were initiated against the *Daily Mirror*. And what has endeared him to me was his answer. He smiled and, without a trace of bitterness, said that judges in England did not take notice of personal insults uttered without malice. After all, he said, he was old, and though he believed he wasn't a fool, someone else who sincerely thought he was, was entitled to his opinion. Then his eyes lighted up, "But if they (he meant the editor and publisher) had said we were dishonest or not true to our conscience, I would have promptly hauled them up."

I said to myself: here is a Daniel come to judgement, a judge who was so conscious of his enormous power that he knew when not to use it; a self-restraining quality which (I believe) greatly enhances the prestige of all judicial power. I respectfully commend this attitude to all judges, present and future, both in the high courts and in the highest court.

Then there is another disturbing aspect of this branch of the law. Unlike defamation truth, it is not considered to be a defence. Does the law of contempt then impose reasonable restrictions on freedom of speech if you are not permitted to speak and establish the truth? India's noted constitutional historian, H. M. Seervai, had no doubt on the point. In the fourth edition of his famous book on the Constitution of India, he notes:

> "... a law relating to defamation, which provided that truth, spoken or written, for the public good, shall not be a defence in a libel action would impose restrictions which would be unreasonable ... the position would be no different if a law were to enact that truth should not be a defence to a charge of contempt of court if it consists in scandalising a judge.
>
> In a criminal prosecution for libel, the prosecution would fail if it were shown that specific charges were true, and it was for the public good that they should be made. But is there one law for a corrupt minister and another for a corrupt judge?"

The author then boldly says that no court in India would say that there was one law for a corrupt minister and another for a corrupt judge and says quite confidently that no court would by any process of reasoning punish for contempt the writer of an article who, in sober language, sets out specific acts of bribery and is able to successfully prove them. For this view, the author relies on a judgement of a Constitution bench of the Supreme Court itself in *B. Ramakrishna Reddy* vs. *State of Madras* 1952 SCR 425, where Justice B. K. Mukherjea said: "The article in question is a scurrilous attack on the integrity and honesty of a judicial office. Specific instances have been given where the officer is alleged to have taken bribes or behaved with impropriety to litigants who did not satisfy his dishonest demands. If the allegations were true, obviously it would be to the benefit of the public to bring these matters to light. But if they were false, they cannot but undermine the confidence of the public in the administration of justice and bring the judiciary into disrepute."

Unfortunately, these observations were read in a later case (by a bench of three judges) in *Perspective Publications Pvt. Ltd., & anr.* vs. *State of Maharashtra* (1969)[14] as not laying down affirmatively that truth and good faith could be set up as a defence in contempt proceedings. Ever since then the law in the *Perspective Publications case* is the law that is followed. Wrongly, I would submit. Particularly since years after the *Perspective Publications case,* another bench of three justices of the Supreme Court (in August 1976) set aside a full bench decision of the High Court of Punjab, which held that a *prima facie* case for contempt was made out. In that case, fifteen members of a Bar association made a complaint about observations of a high court judge made during an inspection at the District Court Bar. The judge had said nasty things about politicians, and the lawyers felt that the judge was wrong to talk politics, and they said so in the letter. The letter was addressed to the chief justice, but it was placed before a bench of the court for consideration, and on perusal of the contents, the bench said that a prima facie case of criminal contempt was made out. None of the allegations in the letter against the judge were disputed or challenged. Yet the high court proceeded on the basis that even though the letters written correctly recorded what had happened and commented adversely on the judge's conduct, the authors were guilty of contempt. The Supreme Court overruled and by so overruling, emphasised that allegations, even when true, were not capable of sustaining a charge of contempt.

Another endorsement of this view is the decision of the Privy Council (March 1999[15], in which Lord Slynn, in an appeal from the Republic of Mauritius), which, whilst upholding the constitutionality of the offence of scandalising the court under the Constitution of Mauritius, emphasised two things: First, that the scope of the offence was a narrow one (note the word "narrow"), and second, that exposure and criticism of judicial misconduct, plainly in the public interest, would not necessarily constitute contempt. That is to say, truth and good faith would trump the contempt law, which is as it should be.

Our Constitution makes freedom of speech and expression a fundamental right, and the exception to it is the law of contempt. Not any law of contempt, but reasonable restrictions in that law. The Contempt of Courts Act does not say that truth cannot be a defence and will not be a defence, and it is for the courts to interpret the meaning of the word "scandalise." If it is part of the law, as understood, that a person commits contempt if he truthfully publishes as a fact that a particular judge (God forbid, and hypothetically speaking) has accepted a bribe for giving a judgement in a party's favour, then such a law would be void as imposing unreasonable restrictions on the freedom of speech and expression. The judge who took the bribe would be false to his oath to do justice without fear or favour, and it would be absurd to say that although Article 124(4) provides for the removal of a judge for proven misbehaviour, no one can offer proof of such misbehaviour except on pain of being sent to jail for contempt of court. This is a glaring defect in our judge-made law that needs to be remedied, hopefully by the judges themselves. If not, reluctantly, then by parliament.

It is interesting to notice that when the Ontario Court of Appeal some years ago considered the offence of scandalising the court in light of the Canadian Charter of Human Rights, the majority in the court concluded that scandalising the court was no longer compatible with the fundamental freedom of speech and expression.[16]

The dictionary meaning of the word "scandalise" (and this is the expression used in Section 2(c) of the Contempt of Courts Act) is "to utter a false or malicious report of a person's conduct." There you are. Truth can never scandalise. "Sunlight is the best disinfectant" and "electric light is the most efficient policeman," which is what a great American judge (Justice Brandeis) always used to say, and it was a favourite quote of former Chief Justice M. N. Venkatachaliah.

But we still have to live with the regrettable decision of the Supreme Court in *Ravichandra Iyer* vs. *Bhattacharji*, 1995 5 SCC on page 478 (popularly known as *Bhattacharji's case*). Regrettable because the bench in that case said that even Bar associations cannot take up matters and pan resolutions with regard to allegations of corruption against sitting judges. They must take up the matter first with the chief justice and await his response for a "reasonable period." And what if the chief justice does not respond? What happens after that? Their lordships gave no answer. It is

Bhattacharji's *case* that quotes Harry Edwards, chief justice of the US Court of Appeals of the District of Columbia, who was at one-time chairman of what is known as the Judicial Council in the United States (a council for disciplining federal judges in the US—judges who are appointed for life).

I had the privilege of visiting Justice Edwards when a team of judges and lawyers (Indo-US Legal Forum) toured the United States some years ago. He is a charming person, and he told me how the Judicial Council in the US dealt with all manner of charges against all manner of judges (including his own colleagues, the federal judges) when litigants made complaints—they were investigated. He handed me a decision of his in respect of a colleague (whom I saw sitting on the bench with him) where a litigant had made certain allegations in a particular case. The allegations were investigated and dealt with in a speaking order in a judgement that was printed and circulated.

There was no hard feeling amongst the judges. The in-house procedure in the United States is both open and transparent. In *Bhattacharji*'s *case*, our courts quoted from an article by Harry Edwards in which he had said, and I quote: "Ideal of judicial independence is not compromised when judges are monitored and regulated by their own peers. This limited system of judicial self-regulation presents no constitutional dilemma as long as the removal power remains with Congress. I argue that the judiciary alone should monitor this bad behaviour through a system of self-regulation."

We have so far lacked a system of "transparent judicial self-regulation," and this must now be adopted. I was particularly happy to hear the chief justice of India say so (on the occasion of Law Day on 26 November 2001, the day the Constituent Assembly adopted the Constitution of India as Law Day):

> "Where the subordinate judiciary is concerned, the high court exercises adequate disciplinary jurisdiction, and it is very necessary that errant subordinate judges should be disciplined, after adequate inquiry. This would send out a message not

> only to other judges but to the public at large that corruption within the judiciary is not tolerated. So far as the higher judiciary is concerned, impeachment is the only legal remedy, and it is available only in the cases of what are called 'high crimes and misdemeanours.' In any case, a recent experience of the impeachment process showed how flawed it could be. The only alternative is internal, namely the in-house procedure, and I would like to see it enforced whenever the conditions to do so exist."[17]

Chief Justice S. P. Bharucha knew the importance of an in-house procedure. He was a senior judge in the Bombay High Court, where it was first initiated and tried. In June 1990, two Bar associations in the High Court of Bombay resolved that none of its members would appear before four named judges of the high court against whom there had been repeated allegations of nepotism and corruption by responsible members of the Bar, which had gone unheeded by the chief justice of Bombay, and also by the then chief justice of India. The resentment had been building up and simmering among all sections of the Bar not just for a few months, but over some period of time. In fact, when I was invited to speak at the 125th anniversary of the Bombay High Court, I had mentioned in my address about the problem of the two great C's (corruption and caste) creeping into the higher echelons of the judiciary in the state (i.e., state of Maharashtra). Chief Justice Dharmadhikari, who presided, acknowledged that the high court was faced with this very grave problem and was glad I had openly raised it, but alas, this able judge could do nothing about it as he was then only acting as chief justice.

His successor, Justice Chittatosh Mookerjee, who hailed from Calcutta and who (then) knew nothing of the problems in Bombay, was just finding his feet (He was a great judge, and judging was in his veins. His father, Justice Ramaprasad Mookerjee, and his grandfather, Sir Ashutosh Mookerjee, before him had presided over the High Court of Calcutta). So, when two representative associations of the Bombay Bar, exasperated at the lack of initiative from the judges and from the chief justice of India, took the unprecedented step of virtually declaring guilty four named sitting judges without even hearing them on the principle that the hand that holds the scales of justice must not be "seen by responsible sections of the Bar to manipulate them." Chief Justice Chittatosh Mookerjee did the right thing, viz. he carefully read the representations, made his own inquiries, and then refused to assign any work to any of the three judges named in the Bar resolutions (the fourth having resigned earlier), not in deference to the nearly unanimous wishes of the Bar, but because he himself had gone into the allegations and found them not lacking in substance. On a later visit to Bombay, a former chief justice of India reportedly upbraided the Bar associations for having taken this hasty step. Many judges of the Supreme Court had then felt likewise. But my sympathies were and are with the Bombay Bar, not because I believe in the boycott of courts by lawyers (I have long openly protested against lawyers' strikes), but because I believe the Bar was left with no choice. The higher judiciary, though repeatedly given the opportunity, *did not*, only because it *would not*, take care of its own domestic problems. If the Bombay Bar had not acted when it did, the entire high court (I believe) would have soon been swamped with ill-founded rumours by disgruntled litigants.

There is a passage in a speech by the great Lord Atkin which is purple prose. It has been forgotten by most modern judges (at least in the developing world), even after sometimes quoting from it: "The path of criticism is a public way. The wrongheaded are permitted to err therein . . . Justice is not a cloistered virtue: she must be allowed to suffer the scrutiny and respect, even though outspoken, comments of ordinary men."[18]

I recommend to our judges the Atkin approach: "Balancing" the two public interests is not difficult with this approach. Absent the Atkin approach, the dice gets loaded against free speech. The line between "destructive attacks" and trenchant criticism is always a thin one, not only in India but in other countries as well. A case in the European Court of Human Rights illustrates the difficulty of making choices. A few years ago, the European Court of Human Rights had to decide the case of *Prager and Oberschlick* vs. *Austria*. The petitioners before the European Court were Prager, a journalist living in Vienna, and Oberschlick, publisher of a periodical known as *Forum*. An article by Prager was published in *Forum* under the headline "Danger! Harsh Judges!" It contained a diatribe against judges in Austria's criminal courts. Prager said they exercised absolute power, exploited the weaknesses or peculiarities of the accused, acquitted only as a last resort, and treated lawyers for the accused "like miscreants." He described judges as "arrogant bullies," who maintained their independence as judges only to inflate inordinately their own self-importance, which enabled them to apply the law in all its cruelty and irrationality, without scruple and without anyone being able to oppose them. And so, it went on.

On 26 April 1995, the European Court of Human Rights handed down its opinion in a majority opinion—a narrow one 5:4. The majority said:

> "Of the accusations levelled by those allegations, some were extremely serious. It is, therefore, hardly surprising that their author should be expected to explain himself. By maintaining that the Viennese judges 'treat every accused at the outset as if he had already been convicted,' or in attributing to a judge a 'bullying' and 'contemptuous' attitude in the performance of his duties, the applicant had, by implication, accused the persons concerned of having, as judges, broken the law, or, at the very least, of having breached their professional obligations. He had thus not only damaged their reputation but also undermined public confidence in the integrity of the judiciary as a whole."

There were strong dissents, however, equally forcefully expressed. Judge Pettiti's views were expressive of the opinion of the minority of four justices:

"Clearly judges must be protected from defamation, but if they wish to institute proceedings, it is preferable for them to opt for the civil avenue rather than criminal proceedings. States that allow judicial proceedings to be televised accept by implication that the judge's conduct is exposed to the critical view of the public. The best way of ensuring that objective information is imparted to the public for its education is to secure, fuller, and franker cooperation between the judicial authorities and the press."

The case from Austria shows that there is a sharp divergence of opinion even amongst eminent judges as to which of the two great concepts is more necessary to be maintained and upheld in a democratic society: free expression or an independent judiciary. And Judge Pettiti's recommendation of a "fuller and franker cooperation between the judicial authorities and the press" comes not a day too late. The concern of the journalist (or media persons) is not just that courts can (and do) issue restraining orders, but that if a gag order is disobeyed, the same court will issue a contempt citation, which is enforced even if the restraining order is eventually reversed by a higher court! Most journalists (and media persons) genuinely believe in the law of the land, but do not believe that the judge, as opposed to the editor, is the one to strike a just balance between the concepts of "freedom of expression" and "fair trial."

All this is further compounded by judicial distrust of the press. In the play *Night and Day*, Tom Stoppard has one of his characters saying: "I'm with you on a free press. It's the newspapers I can't stand!" Some judges share this view but will not publicly admit it.

In fine, I would say that the current state of the law is certainly not ideal, but till altered, we must cope with it. I take the liberty of offering some guidelines to the Bar and bench.

First, to the lawyers:

1. Argue your cases competently and vigorously, and be as critical of judgements of courts as you wish. However, do remember never to use offensive and exaggerated language for not only it is bad form, but it also rebounds on you.
2. If, on rare occasions, you do have to criticise the courts, judges, and the administration of justice, *tread softly* because you tread on the feet of judges, some of whom are more easily hurt than others. We lawyers must never forget that we are also part of the administration of justice, and derogatory, irresponsible comments reflect on lawyers themselves.
3. Exercise your right to free speech and make your point, but pause in your choice of words so that people who hear or read do not get the impression that you are attributing motives or malice to the judge or to the court.

Now, to the judges:

I would respectfully recommend to them the Atkin and the Templeman approach. Courts are not fragile flowers; they do not wilt in the heat of argument nor of criticism, howsoever trenchant and caustic. I would suggest that the contempt power not be used to *discipline* either the lawyer or the press. This creates a needless conflict which (with tact) could be avoided. As for the litigant, a "benign neglect" is recommended. Treat contempt with "benign neglect" or, in other words, treat contempt with contempt!

An American judge had once said about the US Supreme Court: "The important thing we do there is *not doing*." Useful words to remember in the area of contempt jurisdiction. The law regarding scandalising the court can never be codified because the circumstances in which the courts and the administration of justice are scandalised are too diverse for an exact definition. However, I would recommend the following points:

1. Truth and good faith must be reinstated as valid defences in the power to punish for contempt (either by judicial diktat or

by law) because they are vital for the future administration of justice. The motto should be: let nothing defile the temple of justice—not the errant litigant, not the errant lawyer, nor even the errant judge.

2. In view of the vagueness of the contours of contempt jurisdiction, the power to punish for scandalising the court or the administration of justice must never be invoked by a single judge or even a bench of two judges. It must always be exercised by a bench of at least five judges, both in the high courts and in the Supreme Court, because when the judges speak in the contempt case, they speak for the court, and it is important that what they say is representative of the thinking in the court as a whole.
3. Power to commit for contempt should never be conferred on commissions or tribunals, even if they are manned by retired judges of the highest court. Judges, when they retire, love to have the full panoply of power which they enjoyed as sitting judges. The contempt of court power is too serious and fraught with too many grave consequences to be left to any ad hoc institutions, howsoever important, except established by the high courts and the Supreme Court of India.

Lastly, in this branch of the law, the watchword is to "keep your cool." Contempt law, to be justly administered, requires robust common sense and an abundant sense of humour—the ability to laugh at yourself, which prompts me to conclude with a story, reputedly a true story. It concerns Chief Justice Tate of the US Supreme Court, who once went to his former law school and jokingly told the dean (formerly his own law teacher): "Well, dean, I suppose you still teach your students that all judges are fools."

To which the dean very politely (but pointedly) responded: "No, no, chief justice. We let them find that out for themselves!"

2

The Indian Legal Profession in the Age of Globalisation[19]

In early 2017, the *Harvard Law Review* celebrated its bicentennial with a special issue in which the law school's dean wrote: "Some call this a time of crises in legal education. Others emphasise a time of innovation and renewal. Most law schools straddle theory and practice and also straddle service to the haves who pay lawyers' bills and the have-nots who often bear the weight of laws without influence to change them." She might as well have been speaking of the Indian legal system.

In this age of globalisation—the fastest of all ages over the centuries—we are obsessed with time. We don't have time for this or that. However, as Nobel laureate Rabindranath Tagore, our national poet, said in one of the verses in his great poem "Gitanjali":

> "Even the butterfly has not months but moments to live
> And yet it has time enough."

Hence, I too will adopt the butterfly approach in writing on this subject.

1. The Indian system of justice is British—adversarial, and hence unfriendly to all traces of the rustic dispute mechanisms that had originally taken root in Bharat or Hindustan.

2. The legal system under India's Constitution has everything to do with the English language. It is inextricably linked to it. Both were originally imported from abroad, but what was an English oak has become, over the years, a large, sprawling Indian banyan tree whose aerial roots have descended to the ground to become new trunks[20], some of which are alternative methods of dispute resolution like Lok Adalats and other indigenous species of ADR (alternative dispute resolution).
3. Our Constitution is founded on the rule of law, which embodies a principle of institutional morality, suggesting feasible limits on the power to restrain abuses, which occur even in the most compassionate administration of the laws. But I like that definition of the rule of law, which is the briefest, viz. the rule of law, which is also the rule of the *good* law—a law which a court can, if warranted, characterise as "abhorrent, grossly unfair, or totally unjust," a law which, in the hands of a skilled judge, can be validly invalidated under the broad parameters of Article 14 of our Constitution (the Equality Clause).
4. With regard to punishment, our criminal law is outdated and not in tune with the times. Previous attempts at reform by introducing forms of punishment like community service, compensation to victims, public censure, and disqualification from holding office were proposed but were rejected by India's parliament. I believe that these must be reintroduced.
5. We have not developed an ideal crime control model simply because under our adversarial system, we insist on the search for *proof* rather than the search for *truth*. Relentless pursuit of truth is not yet a prescribed standard for criminal trials, and criminal courts function as places where evidence gets recorded, not where the search for truth is pursued. The crafty, particularly the crafty-cum-wealthy, know how to "manipulate" police investigations and to suborn witnesses.

6. I believe that in India, the crying need of the hour, both in criminal and civil trials, is "robust judging." A good trial judge needs to have a "third ear" to hear not only what is said but to have the mental agility to comprehend what is not said as well.
7. In India, judges are too few and lawyers too many. Prof. Marc Galanter of the University of Wisconsin Law School, on his last visit to India, told us the then-favourite joke in the US. It was related as follows: "What do you say to 50,000 lawyers being dropped to the bottom of the deepest ocean?"

   The answer was: "Well, that's a good beginning."
8. Some years ago, *Oxford University Press* published a perceptive analysis of the legal profession in the US and its shortcomings. In one of the chapters, what I liked best was its unconventional heading. It read:

   "Too much law
   Too little justice
   Too much rhetoric
   Too little reform."

   This certainly sums up the current position in India.
9. This is a point with a silver lining. Over the years, the lawyer in India has shown his true mettle. He is at his best when the going is rough. Lord Atkin once said that an impartial administration of the law is like oxygen in the air. People know and care little about it till it is withdrawn.

   In India, the lawyer strives to see that the oxygen is not withdrawn, even when times are bad, as they were during the days of the Internal Emergency of June 1975. The majority of those who stood up then and were counted (I am proud to say) were the country's practicing lawyers. They and many NGOs are now crusading against varying forms of injustice and exploitation, and assisting in promoting change and development in favour of the poor and the deprived, particularly through the expedient known as PIL (public interest litigation)—an indigenous technique developed by India's judges, with the active assistance of the legal profession.

10. There are, of course, problem areas in our courts:
    i. We need more Judges, pushing more cases to a speedier resolution of the dispute at hand. What is required in many cases is not prolonged arguments nor long judgements, but solutions.
    ii. At the highest level, we do strive to see that justice gets done but not always successfully.

Let me end this chapter with my favourite story of how truly difficult the business of judging really is. Sir Owen Dixon was Australia's chief justice for more than two decades, and he sat in its high court—the court of final appellate jurisdiction. A lady sitting next to him at a dinner party was greatly enthused with the prospect of his dispensing justice. She leaned towards him and said, clapping her hands with joy, "How splendid."

Dixon's response was stern, almost unfriendly: "Madam, I have nothing to do with justice. I sit on a court of appeal where none of the facts are known. One-third of the facts are excluded by the frailty of memory, one-third by the negligence of the legal profession, and the remaining one-third by the archaic laws of evidence."

Naturally, the woman's face fell!

3

Trends in the Internationalisation of Human Rights Law

International human rights codes go back no more than three centuries, but the history of the dignity of man (and his common citizenship in society) goes back thousands of years. When Babylon was conquered by Cyrus the Great in 539 BC, the Persian king ensured the inviolability of the person of every one of its inhabitants and took care to preserve and protect their dwellings and possessions. Proud of his success, he had this good deed recorded on a clay tablet. It is exhibited in the United Nations building in New York as the earliest known "declaration of human rights."

Basic human rights norms, as we know them today, had their origin in the French and American revolutions of the late eighteenth century. They produced the concept of civil and political rights. In the early parts of the twentieth century, it was the influence of the Mexican and Russian revolutions that introduced notions of economic, social, and cultural rights. The great American and French texts of 1776, 1789, and 1791, for the first time, set forth principles that became the foundation of modern human rights law. These principles were admirably summarised by Paul Sieghart as follows:

1. *The principle of universal inherence:* Every human being has certain rights, capable of being enumerated and defined, which are not conferred on him by any ruler, nor earned or

acquired by purchase, but which inhere in him by virtue of his humanity alone.

2. *The principle of inalienability:* No human being can be deprived of any of those rights, by the act of any ruler or even by his own act (or in a democracy, even by the will of the majority of the sovereign people).
3. *The rule of law:* Where rights conflict with each other, the conflict must be resolved by the consistent, independent, and impartial application of just laws in accordance with just procedures.[21]

But the rights flowing from these basic principles found no place in international law, since the individual in whom they inhered had no recognition or protection internationally.

For centuries, one proposition remained without challenge. By reason of the doctrine of national sovereignty, the law of nations did not recognise any rights vested in *any* individual against *any* sovereign state. The traditional rule of international law, expressed in the first seven editions of Oppenheim's classic work, was that states, *only and exclusively*, were the subjects of international law. Individuals were not governed by its rules. Relations between a state and its citizens fell within "domestic jurisdiction,"[22] and sovereign governments were at liberty to treat their citizens as they liked. They were beyond the reach of international law or of legal intervention by other states.[23]

But the events leading up to the Second World War and the carnage it left behind became the catalyst for new developments. The period after the end of the Second World War produced unprecedented growth in human rights law. The entire theoretical basis of international law was transformed. It had to adapt itself to the new world order which had emerged with the adoption of the UN Charter (1945) and with the endorsement of the United Nations of the Universal Declaration of Human Rights (on 10 December 1948) by the General Assembly. The UN Charter signified the recognition, for the first time in an international treaty, of a wide generality of rights for individuals. A major achievement of its draftsmen was the emphasis on the importance of social justice and human rights as the foundations of a stable international order. The Charter imposed legal obligations not only upon member-states of the UN but upon the United Nations as a whole. Article 55(c) laid down that the United Nations "shall promote universal respect for and observance of human rights and fundamental freedoms." The individual citizen of a state was now a subject of international law. Two years after the adoption of the Universal Declaration, Prof. (later Judge) Hersch Lauterpacht wrote: "The individual has acquired a status and a stature which have transformed him from an object of international compassion into a subject of international right."[24] Lauterpacht was one of the pioneers of what came to be known as the "modern view" of international law, which was that states, though still primarily the subject of international law, were not exclusively so.[25]

The principal feature of the modern (post-1945) approach to human rights has been its unambiguous recognition of the fact that all human beings are entitled to the enjoyment not only of traditional civil and political rights but also of economic, social, and cultural rights, without which, for most people, traditional rights have little meaning. The chief claim of the Universal Declaration of Human Rights (1948) to a place in history is its recognition, in one single document, of this simple truth.

Since the adoption of the Universal Declaration of Human Rights by the nation-states of the world, the legal theory of sovereignty[26] has stood modified in two crucial aspects: *first,* as to how a state treated its own subjects had now become a legitimate concern of international law, and *second,* a superior international standard, established by common consent, could now be used for judging domestic law and also for judging the actual conduct of a sovereign state within its own territory, and in the exercise of its internal jurisdiction.

The Universal Declaration of Human Rights has been the foundation of much of the post-1945 codification of human rights, both internationally and within nation-states. It has served as a model for as many as ninety national constitutions drawn up since 1948, more than half of which make explicit reference to its provisions.

When originally adopted by the General Assembly, the Universal Declaration was not viewed as imposing any legal obligations. In the oft-cited words of Mrs Eleanor Roosevelt, chairman of the UN Commission on Human Rights (the body charged with its drafting), it was only "a declaration of basic principles of human rights and freedoms to be stamped with the approval of the General Assembly by a formal vote of its members and to serve as a common standard of achievement for all peoples of all nations."[27]

But twenty-five years later, the Universal Declaration was invoked on so many occasions, both within and outside the United Nations, that lawyers began saying that whatever the intention of its authors, the Universal Declaration of Human Rights (UDHR) had now become part of the customary law of nations and was binding on all states.[28] Despite some controversy that still persists over this issue, the pre-eminent position of the Universal Declaration amongst the nations of the world is now beyond question. At the UN World Conference of Human Rights held in Vienna in 1993, in which the governments of 171 countries participated, each one of them reaffirmed their commitment to the purposes and principles contained in the Charter of the United Nations and the UDHR, emphasising that the Declaration "is the source of inspiration and has been the basis for the United Nations in making advances in standard-setting as contained in existing international human rights instruments."[29]

Human rights instruments, since the Universal Declaration, have proliferated over the years. A compilation of international instruments concerning human rights, published by the UN Centre for Human Rights in 1993, in two volumes, contains a comprehensive catalogue of existing human rights instruments adopted at both universal and regional levels. It begins with the "International Bill of Rights," which consists of the Universal Declaration and the two international covenants—the Covenant on Economic, Social, and Cultural Rights and the Covenant on Civil and Political Rights (together with the first Optional Protocol to the latter). The compilation then goes on to chronicle:

1. International human rights treaties (variously referred to as covenants, protocols, or conventions).
2. Regional human rights treaties or instruments.
3. Declarations, principles, guidelines, standard rules, and recommendations, the last having no binding legal effect.

The value of these instruments rests on their recognition by a large number of states. They are accepted as "declaratory of broadly accepted human rights norms" within the international community.

Probably at no other time in the history of humankind have more people believed that they are *entitled* to the enjoyment of human rights than today—a tribute to the power of words and of the ideas conveyed by them.

The single most important and best-known of all human rights instruments is the ICCPR—International Covenant on Civil and Political Rights (1966). The ICCPR consists of a preamble and fifty-three articles divided into six parts. Its important feature is that it is a universal instrument which contains binding legal obligations for the states parties to it. The rights enshrined within its provisions represent the basic minimum set of civil and political rights, acknowledged as such by the ratification of 132 states (as of 1 January 1996) from all geopolitical regions of the world, rendering it less susceptible to the criticism that it is founded on Western ideals or an individualistic, alien philosophy.

Further significant features of the covenant are that it clearly protects aliens and stateless persons as well as nationals. Some of its provisions have contributed significantly to the development of customary international law. It has been adopted as a basic standard of international human rights by international, regional, and national institutions and has been used as a stimulus or model for new international instruments. In the long term, this last feature may prove to be its most enduring achievement, and the Political Covenant (together with the Covenant on Economic, Social, and Cultural Rights) may come to replace the Universal Declaration of Human Rights as the "common standard of achievement for all peoples and all nations."[30]

The status of the ICCPR in international law is also becoming increasingly important in domestic law. Its provisions are being invoked either as directly applicable superior law or as permissive guidelines for interpreting constitutional, legislative, and administrative provisions of state law. It is as persuasive authority that the clauses of the ICCPR are most frequently referred to by national courts and tribunals in many countries, e.g., in Australia, Canada, Germany, the UK, the USA, France, India, the Netherlands, New Zealand, Norway, and Yugoslavia. And national commentators now frequently compare domestic human rights law with standards established in the ICCPR, for example in Canada, Australia, India, Finland, Japan, the USA, the UK, and New Zealand.[31]

There has been a fifty-year effort at the United Nations to set universal standards. At the centre of this endeavour stands the system of human rights treaties—legally binding norms that apply to all ratifying states. The standards are largely in place, and broad legal responsibility has been assumed by states parties. At the heart of the UN's legal system for the protection of human rights are the six major human rights treaties, adopted between 1965 and 1989, each having separate monitoring or supervisory bodies. These are chronologically listed below:

1. The International Convention on the Elimination of All Forms of Racial Discrimination (CERD), 1965, which is monitored by the Committee on the Elimination of Racial Discrimination, to which states parties undertake to submit periodic reports (every two years) on legislative, judicial, administrative, or other measures they have adopted to give effect to the provisions of the convention. The convention provides that a state party may at any time declare that it recognises the competence of the committee to receive and consider communications from individuals or groups of individuals claiming to be victims of a violation by that state party of any right set forth in the convention. And where so declared, the committee is empowered to consider such communications and forward its suggestions and recommendations to the state party concerned.
2. The International Covenant on Civil and Political Rights (ICCPR), 1966, and the Optional Protocol thereto (1966). The ICCPR is monitored by the Human Rights Committee (HRC), which receives and comments on state reports regarding measures adopted to give effect to the rights recognised in the covenant. The reporting mechanism has, in turn, encouraged the initiative of a separate practice, viz. the publication of "General Comments of the Human Rights Committee."[32] The HRC also supervises and administers the Optional Protocol (1966). Where the state becomes a party to the Optional Protocol, the HRC becomes competent to receive and consider communications from individuals who claim to be victims of a violation by the state party of any of the rights set forth in the covenant. Procedures are set out as to how to deal with such complaints, and the HRC monitors the concerned state's compliance with its recommendations.[33]
3. The International Covenant on Economic, Social, and Cultural Rights (ICESCR), 1966, imposes on ratifying states obligations to submit periodic reports on the measures adopted and progress made in achieving the observance

of the rights recognised in this covenant. Since 1987, a new Committee on Economic, Social, and Cultural Rights, largely modelled on the HRC, has been set up to replace the ineffective machinery originally established under the ICESCR. It now comprises experts elected by the Economic and Social Council (ECOSOC).[34]

4. The Convention on the Elimination of All Forms of Discrimination Against Women (CEDAW), 1979, is monitored by the Committee on the Elimination of Discrimination Against Women. States parties undertake to submit for the consideration of this committee a periodic report (every four years) on the legislative, judicial, administrative, or other measures adopted to give effect to the provisions of this convention and on the progress made in this regard. Such a report may indicate factors and difficulties affecting the degree of fulfilment of obligations under this convention.
5. The Convention against Torture and Other Cruel, Inhuman, or Degrading Treatment or Punishment (CAT), 1984, obliges the state party to take effective legislative, administrative, judicial, or other measures to prevent acts of torture in any territory under its jurisdiction. No exceptional circumstances whatsoever may be invoked as a justification for torture. Each state party is to ensure that education and information regarding the prohibition against torture are fully included in the training of law enforcement personnel, civil or military, medical personnel, and all public officials involved in the custody, interrogation, or treatment of individuals subjected to any form of arrest, detention, or imprisonment. The committee which monitors this convention is known as the Committee Against Torture. The states parties are required to submit periodic reports (every four years) on the measures taken to give effect to the provisions of this convention. The convention empowers the committee to look into and independently investigate the truth of reliable information

that may appear to contain well-founded indications that torture is being systematically practiced in the territory of a state party. But such investigations are to be conducted at all stages with the cooperation of the state party. This convention also provides that a state party may at any time declare that it recognises the competence of the committee to receive and consider communications from and on behalf of individuals who claim to be victims of a violation by a state party of the provisions of this convention and where the state party so declares, there is a detailed procedure prescribed for the committee receiving, considering, and reporting on such communications.

6. The Convention on the Rights of the Child (CRC), 1989, is monitored by the Committee on the Rights of the Child. Every state party undertakes to submit to the committee periodic reports (every five years) on the measures adopted for giving effect to the rights recognised by this convention and on the progress made in the enjoyment of those rights. Such a report should indicate factors and difficulties, if any, affecting the degree of fulfilment of obligations undertaken under this convention. The committee is empowered to make suggestions and general recommendations based on information received from such reports. The treaty system of the UN is, of course, optional. Obligations are dependent upon ratification. Nevertheless, participation in the treaty system has been extensive. More than three-quarters of the world's states have ratified five of the six major human rights treaties, but only 50 per cent of them have ratified the sixth, the Torture Convention of 1984, which has the lowest number of accessions. These treaties relate to a broad range of human rights concerns: racial discrimination, economic, social, and cultural rights, civil and political rights, discrimination against women, torture, and children. They furnish a recognised source of international law.

The general importance of treaties—whether bilateral or multilateral—lies primarily in the fact that the rules established by them and the rights and obligations to which they give rise are legally binding on the parties to the treaty. For convenience, such treaties are referred to as "law-making treaties," but only for convenience. In the international community, there is no central law-making authority that makes laws for the international community as a whole in the same way that national parliaments make laws within a state. In the narrow sense, however, all treaties are "law-making" for those who are parties to them.

Human Rights Treaty Bodies—the committees supervising the six major treaties—have been, from time to time, commenting on and interpreting the treaties under their respective jurisdictions. These general comments and general recommendations help towards a proper understanding of the treaty provisions and constitute a useful source of the "law" on the subject dealt with by each of the treaties.[35]

The success or failure of these six major human rights treaties depends on three main considerations:

1. Whether they have been ratified with or without reservations, and the nature of such reservations.
2. Whether the substantive or normative quality of the rules contained in them and the procedural and enforcement mechanisms in such treaties help to promote effective implementation.
3. Their impact under domestic national law.

Making reservations to multilateral human rights treaties is a well-accepted practice in international law. It facilitates negotiations and assures states that they can eventually accept an international instrument without binding themselves to every single provision in it. It also encourages ratification because it is possible for a state to avoid assuming obligations that conflict with certain aspects of its own internal legislation.

Compared to multilateral treaties in general, human rights treaties have a very high rate of reservations. The Convention on the Elimination of All Forms of Discrimination Against Women (1965) is the most extreme case with slightly less than half of the states parties having made broad reservations. As for the Political Covenant (ICCPR, 1966), more than 50 of the 132 states parties have accompanied their instruments of ratification or accession with reservations, some of them even beyond the "permissible" limits recognised by international law.[36]

The Convention on the Rights of the Child is the one with the largest number of ratifications. As of December 1995, 170 states (out of 185 states of the UN) had ratified or acceded to the convention. The goal of universal ratification has been almost achieved. Yet this impressive support for the instrument is considerably diluted by a large number of states that have ratified with "reservations." For example, many Islamic and some Asian states have ratified the Convention on the Rights of the Child with caveats such as that the reservation "does not imply acceptance of any obligation beyond those prescribed in the written constitutions and laws" of those states. Quite obviously, such reservations do not conform to the "object and purpose" of a human rights treaty, which prescribes an overriding universal minimum standard.

But few states are prepared to challenge other states on the legitimacy of their reservations. Currently, important states like the United States of America and the United Kingdom are even resisting attempts by treaty bodies themselves to challenge reservations impermissible under international law.[37]

Reservations in multilateral human rights instruments detract from the protection of individuals, which is the purpose of all international human rights law. And that is why the widespread use of reservations in human rights treaties has been frequently criticised. They weaken the overall effectiveness of the proposed norms, which are generally expressed only as minimum standards. For this reason, human rights advocates have urged states to avoid making reservations or, if made, to reduce their scope or withdraw them altogether.

The World Conference on Human Rights, held in Vienna in June 1993, has endorsed this view:

> 5. The World Conference on Human Rights encourages states to consider limiting the extent of any reservations they lodge to international human rights instruments, to formulate any reservations as precisely and narrowly as possible, to ensure that none are incompatible with the object and purpose of the relevant treaty, and to regularly review any reservations with a view to withdrawing them.
>
> 26. The World Conference on Human Rights welcomes the progress made in the codification of human rights instruments, which is a dynamic and evolving process, and urges the universal ratification of human rights treaties. All states are encouraged to accede to these international instruments; all states are encouraged to avoid, as far as possible, resorting to reservations.

The right trend, but such proclamations at international conferences are not as yet reflected in state practice.

As for the procedural and enforcement methodologies, as already mentioned, the implementation of the six major human rights treaties is monitored by six separate committees. States parties are generally required to submit reports as to how their laws and practices adhere to the terms of the treaty, and these reports are required to be written for each treaty periodically (varying from two to five years). Once submitted, state representatives appear before the treaty body and answer questions concerning the report. The treaty body (committee) then formulates concluding observations on the state's report and about its record of compliance with treaty obligations. These concluding observations of treaty bodies are then sent to the UN General Assembly, which identifies the states that do not meet substantive treaty obligations. Its annual reports also name the states that have failed to submit periodic reports.

Generally speaking, UN treaty implementation is tardy and faulty. Forty-five per cent to eighty per cent states parties to the six treaties have defaulted on the submission of reports, with many reports being long overdue. It is estimated that an aggregate of eighty-one states—on average, sixty per cent of states parties to all the six treaties—have up to five overdue reports! About half of the states have not even submitted their initial reports (generally required to be submitted one year after ratification). All this retards the progress of universal trendsetting.

State reports are not the only means of securing obligations undertaken in human rights treaties. The right of individual petition is an optional feature of three of the six treaties: Optional Protocol to the Civil and Political Covenant (ICCPR), the Convention on Racial Discrimination (CAD), and the Convention against Torture (CAT)[38]. Where states have accepted or have ratified the optional provisions, individual victims of violations have the right to complain directly to the concerned monitoring committee. For the remaining three human rights treaties, the remedy of directly lodging individual or group complaints with the treaty body simply does not exist. There is insufficient political support for an optional protocol for the ICESCR. In the case of CEDAW (the Women's Convention), the issue is still at an embryonic stage before a working group of the Commission on the Status of Women. Even where the right of individual petition has been allowed (as in the ICCPR, CAD, and CAT), many states that have ratified these treaties have done so with express reservations refusing to permit individual or group complaints[39], which is another impediment to the development of international human rights law.

The conclusion of the ILA Committee on International Human Rights Law and Practice about recent trends in UN treaty implementation is dismal and pessimistic. This is what it said in its report presented to the 67th Conference of the International Law

Association held in Helsinki in August 1996: “The implementation crisis facing the principal human rights legal standards is now of dangerous proportions. For a great many states, ratification has become an end in itself, a means to easy accolades for empty gestures . . . The treaty requirement has been depreciated by chronic levels of non-compliance both with the substantive terms of the treaties and with existing enforcement mechanisms.”

Despite these shortcomings, there are two major bodies in the UN system that have been the main driving force of UN activity in favour of human rights. The first is the Commission on Human Rights, composed (since 1991) of fifty-three member states nominated by ECOSOC (Economic and Social Council) according to geographical groupings. Each year, ECOSOC replaces one-third of the members of the commission. A large number of other states and about a hundred NGOs participate in the work of the commission. First established in 1947, the commission has worked extensively on the implementation of the principles contained in the Universal Declaration, has thereafter set more precise standards, and has been instrumental in the drafting of international declarations and conventions. The commission has set up dozens of procedures for the supervision and implementation of human rights. Every year, the commission invites member states to cooperate with the special rapporteurs and representatives, experts, and working groups, dealing with specific problems and situations.

The fifty-three member states of the Commission on Human Rights elect every four years, twenty-three experts to the sub-commission on the Prevention of Discrimination and Protection of Minorities. The experts on this sub-commission undertake important research and international standard-setting work. Over the years, the sub-commission has engaged in a series of studies on different phenomena of human rights violations and has proposed several draft declarations and conventions to the commission. On the basis of reports and studies submitted to the Commission on Human Rights and the Sub-Commission, the secretary-general of the UN submitted a preliminary report (4 July 1995) on a set of basic policy guidelines on structural adjustment programmes and economic, social, and cultural rights. The report has stressed the importance of international financial institutions (such as the World Bank and IMF) considering the human rights implications of their work programmes: "The World Bank should be sensitive to the pronouncements of the human rights bodies of the UN and should gradually incorporate human rights criteria in its work at all stages, including in project and policy lending, preparation of policy guidelines, as well as in project and policy appraisal, monitoring, and consent."[40]

The second major body at the UN is the Human Rights Committee. It is the permanent body established under the Civil and Political Covenant (ICCPR). It is made up of eighteen independent experts who are elected to a four-year term by the party states to the covenant. It is different from the other bodies monitoring compliance of the other five human rights treaties, in that its deliberations are, to a large extent, based upon specific international standards. Implementation of the International Covenant (ICCPR) is centred on the compulsory reporting system, which dominates the agenda of the Human Rights Committee. The HRC also administers the Optional Protocol. As of January 1996, 87 of the 132 states that have ratified the ICCPR have also accepted the competence of the Human Rights Committee in respect of individual/group communications to it. The committee (HRC) hears testimony and has evidence presented to it. Generally, its deliberations are conducted in public, and compulsory reporting by party states offers a unique opportunity for participation by NGOs, the media, and the general public in the supervision process under the covenant. Whilst members of the HRC are not judges, they have the task of applying the provisions laid down in the covenant (ICCPR) and must exercise unbiased judgement. This independence has provided the committee with a vital degree of autonomy within the UN system. Christian Tomuschat (a member of the HRC for many years) says that though not an international court, the Human Rights Committee is similar to it in certain respects particularly, in regard to its obligation to be guided by exclusively legal criteria, which rightly distinguishes it from any other political body.[41] In its deliberations and conclusions, the HRC comments on the periodic reports of party states and monitors compliance with the provisions of the covenant, in the course of which it must also interpret them. Although the committee has no power to make a binding decision—its power being essentially recommendatory in nature—it does exercise a considerable influence through the publication of its views and through its reasoned conclusions. International reporting obligations, complaint procedures, and monitoring mechanisms help create a body of "case law"—a comparable institutionalised practice of interpretations. In addition, based on its vast experience over the years, the Human Rights Committee now issues "general comments," thus further contributing to the advancement of international human rights law. The HRC has so far issued twenty-five general comments. General Comment No. 24 has dealt extensively with the question of reservations, and General Comment No. 25, adopted in July 1996, emphasises that Article 25 of the ICCPR lies at the core of democratic government and requires states to adopt legislative and other measures to ensure that citizens have an effective opportunity to enjoy the rights it protects.

It is difficult to say whether the existence of the Covenant (ICCPR) and the work of the HRC is having any concrete and positive impact on human rights situations in the party states. But many state representatives who have appeared before the Human Rights Committee have consistently expressed the view that the Covenant and the work of the committee have played an important role at the national level. The machinery of the HRC has its limitations. But in an institutional setting, its mechanism is seen as a "universalist counterpart" to regional organs like the European Commission and the European Court of Human Rights. In fact, it is often preferred to the ECHR as the waiting time is shorter before the HRC (three years as compared to five years under the European Convention). And in statistical terms, the success rate for individual petitions under the Optional Protocol is considerably higher than that obtained at Strasbourg (the seat of the European Commission of Human Rights and European Court of Human Rights).[42]

Charged with giving life to the structure and mechanisms of the covenant (and the protocol) and giving meaning to the language of their provisions, the HRC has made, and continues to make, a valuable contribution towards achieving a global system of accountability in matters concerning human rights.

As for the impact of treaties in national legal systems and before national courts, back in 1950, Prof. Hersch Lauterpacht had written, with rare perception, that the preoccupation with enforcing mechanisms for international human rights norms "ought not to conceal the fact that the most effective way of giving reality to the Charter and Universal Declaration was through the normal activity of national courts and the other organs applying the law of the land."[43] National courts around the world have come to realise the real significance of these words and have given effect to them only during the last 15-20 years.

There is no uniform practice concerning the application of treaties within states. Each country has its own peculiarities regarding the promulgation or publication of treaties, legislative approval of treaty provisions, and so on. In Austria, for instance, treaties automatically bind the administration without publication, but they need to be gazetted in order to affect the rights of the public in general. And in the United States, a distinction is drawn between self-executing and non-self-executing treaties. The former does not require legislation to make it operative within the municipal field. And generally, in civil law countries, it is not at all unusual for the courts to disregard or overrule a provision of national law found to be in conflict with a rule of international law. However, in most common law countries, a clear conflict between international law and national law must be resolved in favour of the latter in view of the essentially dualist approach adopted towards the relationship between the two legal orders. In the world of common law, the impact of international treaties in domestic forums depends on two conditions: First, upon whether such treaties have been ratified and, if so, with what reservations; and second, whether by ratification, they are regarded by national courts as assimilated into national law. Generally, they are not.

Of course, courts of all states must apply national laws first and foremost. Where that law provides a sufficient set of rules to be applied to the cases at hand, there is no need for them to seek guidance from other sources of law, like international law. But on occasions, domestic courts do justify their decisions by an additional reference to international law through what is known as an "indirect application" of international law, particularly international human rights law. An illustrative case is of *Simpson* vs. *Attorney-General* (*Baigent's case*), 1994 3 NZLR 667, where despite the absence of a remedies clause in the New Zealand Bill of Rights 1985, the Court of Appeal of this country held that they had the power to grant pecuniary compensation for the contravention of rights guaranteed under its provisions. Justice Robin Cooke, then president of the Court of Appeal, relied in his judgement on the fact that the New Zealand Bill of Rights was enacted avowedly "to affirm New Zealand's commitment to the International Covenant on Civil and Political Rights." A similar view had been taken earlier, in 1993, by the Supreme Court of India (a decision mentioned in the judgement of Cooke and referred to in the concurring judgement of Hardie Boys J.). In turn, *Baigent*'s case has been cited (with approval) in a more recent decision of the Supreme Court of India,[44] thus affording an interesting example of how the Commonwealth network of human rights jurisprudence operates in practice. Lord Cooke has described such an exercise as "a valid illustration of judicial reciprocity."[45]

Sometimes, even where national law is comprehensive and sufficient, international law has been invoked. For instance, although the law of Israel permitted the trial of Adolf Eichmann for crimes against humanity, yet in view of the intense interest that the case generated around the world, Israel's court found it desirable to justify its assumption of jurisdiction on grounds of international law, offering what one cynic described as "intellectual assuagement" for the manner in which Eichmann was brought to Israel for trial![46]

In some countries (for instance, in the United Kingdom and Australia), there is a lurking fear that the provisions of human rights treaties might become incorporated "through the back door" if courts directly apply them without legislative authority from parliament. The highest courts in these countries have refused to directly apply particular provisions of these human rights instruments (universal or regional). But at the same time, they have not been averse (after referring to such provisions) to develop common law in the same direction. Thus, in Derbyshire County Council (February 1993), the House of Lords denied the right of public authorities to sue for defamation in derogation of the rights of free speech and public criticism. At the end of his speech, Lord Keith said that he had reached the conclusion "upon the common law of England without finding any need to rely upon the European convention," but added that he found it "satisfactory to be able to conclude that the common law of England is consistent with the obligations assumed by the Crown under the treaty in this particular field."[47] And in *Dietrich* (March 1992), the High Court of Australia developed, as a facet of its own human rights law, a right to free counsel in important and serious criminal cases after expressly referring to Article 14 of the International Covenant on Civil and Political Rights (ICCPR), "to which instrument Australia is a party." Then, after mentioning the approach of the Human Rights Committee to Article 14 of the covenant and to the decision of the European Court of Human Rights (construing almost identical provisions in the European Convention), the High Court concluded: "As will become clear, that approach is similar to the approach which, in our opinion, the Australian common law must now take."[48]

As Sir Robert Jennings, former judge and president of the International Court of Justice, acknowledged: "International law has much to learn from the common law."[49]

A few months after the adoption of the Charter of the United Nations (in San Francisco), the International Court of Justice (ICJ) was set up at The Hague. It began work on 18 April 1946 (when it replaced the Permanent Court of International Justice, which had functioned in the Peace Palace from 1922 till 1939). It serves as the world's highest judicial organ, but its jurisdiction is not comprehensive. It is restricted to inter-state disputes, and that too only between states that have voluntarily accepted the compulsory jurisdiction of the ICJ.

In the first fifty years of its judicial activity, it has taken seisin of seventy-three contentious cases and twenty-three requests for advisory opinions. In all, it delivered sixty judgements and gave twenty-one advisory opinions. But even in these limited numbers of judgements and opinions, the court's contribution to international human rights jurisprudence has not been significant, though it has developed to a degree "international humanitarian law." In April 1996, it celebrated the first half-century of its existence. In the foreword to the commemorative volume (*International Court of Justice*, 1946 to 1996, published by Kluwer Law International), the then-president of the court aptly described it as an institution that carries a "genetic heritage rendered vulnerable by the chromosome of state sovereignty and therefore, by its very nature, seldom spared by the crises, conclusions, and maladies which affect inter-state relations."

At the celebrations of the 50th anniversary of the ICJ (April 1996), the then-president of the UN General Assembly said that he regretted that the appeal for compulsory jurisdiction of the court in disputes between states had found little response. He then called attention to some proposals that had been put forward to extend the jurisdiction of the International Court of Justice and suggested amongst the categories of cases in which all states might be persuaded to accept the unconditional and compulsory jurisdiction of the ICJ, including cases involving human rights issues and genocide.

The role of judges (national and international) in developing human rights case law is critical to understanding and the advancement of modern international human rights jurisprudence. It lies not so much in what judges say, but in what judges do in cases that come before them. As Justice Holmes once said: "The prophesy of what the courts will do, in fact, and nothing more pretentious, is what I mean by the law."[50] There are, of course, differences in attitudes, approaches, and in emphasis. There are also changing perceptions, as there is much to be learnt, as shown by some illustrative decisions set out below:

> "In human rights cases, experience shows that national courts have been able to secure from their governments better compliance when they have not been too anxious to read directly the provisions of ratified treaties into municipal law. In other words, when they have not pressed too hard. Two cases come to mind: one from New Zealand and the other from Australia have served to highlight this fact. They typify the differences in responses to judicial attitudes in human rights cases. Governments invariably conform when requested to, even when the law declared is inconsistent with established practice."

The case from New Zealand concerned Tavita, a citizen of Western Samoa, who, on arrival in New Zealand, was granted a visitor's permit. Tavita overstayed, and a warrant for his removal was issued by the immigration authorities. He appealed to the minister, seeking cancellation of the warrant on humanitarian grounds. The minister declined the appeal. The immigration authorities then took steps to execute the removal warrant. Tavita then applied for judicial review and a reconsideration of his appeal, because during the considerable time it took for all these proceedings, he married a New Zealander, who was the mother of his daughter. He pleaded for a reconsideration of his appeal, as the minister had no occasion to consider the beneficent provisions of the Convention on the Rights of the Child and their impact on the case (the convention had been ratified by New Zealand but not incorporated into domestic law). Judicial review was declined by the High Court. On appeal, the Court of Appeal, whilst not finally deciding the point as to whether the minister in an immigration case was, as a matter of law, bound to exercise his statutory discretion in light of New Zealand's international obligations (under the Child Convention), simply adjourned the appeal (and stayed the removal order in the meanwhile) to give the minister an opportunity for reconsidering his earlier decision. The court did so after expressing its view that treaty obligations might impose implied mandatory duties on the decision-making authority.[51] In response to the court's decision, and in light of New Zealand's international obligations under the Child Convention, the minister revoked the removal order on a reconsideration of the case, granting Tavita permission to stay. He also publicly announced that the immigration policy would soon be "fine-tuned" to take into account the interim judgement of the Court of Appeal as well as New Zealand's international obligations, so as to ensure reaching a "balanced decision in all other immigration cases."

A few months after Tavita, a similar case was decided by the High Court of Australia, though in a slightly different manner and with not such a happy ending. It was also an immigration case. Teoh had entered Australia on a temporary permit and then married an Australian citizen. Three children were born of the marriage. He applied for resident status, but whilst his application was pending, he was convicted of several offences and sentenced to six years' imprisonment. Teoh's application for resident status was rejected. He appealed to the minister, referring to the impact his threatened deportation would have on his wife and family. The Australian Federal Court held that the immigration authorities had failed to give proper consideration to relevant factors mentioned in the UN Convention on the Rights of the Child (which Australia had ratified) and set aside the minister's decision, remitting the matter back to him for reconsideration. The minister appealed to the High Court of Australia, which handed down its decision on 7 April 1995, holding that Australia's accession to the Child Convention gave rise to a "legitimate expectation" in Teoh's children that his application for resident status would be treated in accordance with the terms of the convention. The response of the Australian Government was totally negative. A joint statement issued by the attorney-general and the minister of foreign affairs recorded that "an international treaty was not a reason for raising any expectation that government decision-makers would act in accordance with the treaty if the relevant provision of the treaty had not been enacted into domestic Australian law." Following the joint statement, a bill was introduced in the House of Representatives to exclude any "expectation" in relation to all decisions (including decisions on review) made after 10 May 1995, the date of the joint statement. The bill was designed to displace any legitimate expectation applicable in respect of any administrative decision arising out of Australian ratification or adherence to treaties (there were over 900 of them). The decision of the government was that Teoh should be overturned. But the bill did not get passed, only because shortly after its introduction, the House of Representatives was dissolved, and fresh elections were called.

The acute legal and political controversy over the decision has deprived Teoh of precedential value. It was and is a bold decision. However, it has been left severely alone. When Teoh's case was cited before the Court of Appeal in the United Kingdom (during arguments in *Ex-Parte Smith*), the judges "did not consider it necessary" to refer to it in their judgement.[52]

In human rights jurisprudence, the law is fast changing. Old ideas and practices are giving way to new ones. Thus, it was a widely recognised rule of international law and practice that individuals had no standing to challenge violations of international treaties in the absence of a protest by the sovereign involved. The rule was firmly established by decisions of courts in Israel, in the USA District Court: *Eichmann's case*, Vol.36, *International Law Reports* 277 (1962), and *Noriega's case* (746F Supp. 1506 at 1533 S.D. Fla.1990, a decision of a US District Court): "Rights under international common law must belong to sovereigns, not to individuals." This statement of the law has been approved in the leading textbooks; see, for instance, *Starke on International Law*, 11th Edition, 1994, page 56. But in *Prosecutor* vs. *Tadic*, the International Tribunal at The Hague[53] (trying cases of crimes against humanity in the former Yugoslavia) doubted the correctness of this view, holding that "pronouncements of this kind do not carry in the field of international law the weight they may bring to bear on national judiciaries."

Tadic had the right to contend that his trial before the international tribunal was in violation of the principles of state sovereignty enshrined in Article 2, paragraph 1 of the UN Charter ("the organisation is based on the principle of the sovereign equality of all its member"), especially since an accused before an international tribunal, where his liberty was at stake, was entitled "to a full defence." Tadic argued:

i. that the tribunal, which was set up by the UN Security Council in 1993, had been unlawfully established.
ii. that the tribunal had been improperly given primacy over national courts.
iii. that the tribunal could only adjudicate war crimes committed in the context of interstate conflicts, and it lacked authority to adjudicate offences committed in the course of a "civil war." He argued that the conflict in Bosnia-Herzegovina, where his alleged crimes occurred, was nothing more than a civil war.

The International Tribunal at The Hague (initially the Trial Chamber of three judges and later the Appeal Chamber consisting of five judges) held:

1. that "legitimate measures aimed at the restoration of peace and security," authorised under the UN Charter, included the setting up of a tribunal. Though Tadic could legitimately complain about the alleged violation of the international treaty (in this case, the UN Charter) and the tribunal could

assess the lawfulness of the actions of the Security Council, yet, on the merits, it must be held that the tribunal was in law properly established.

2. that the primacy of the tribunal did not constitute an improper intrusion on state sovereignty, which must give way in the face of offences that "do not affect the interests of one state alone but shock the conscience of mankind."
3. that the conflict was raging in Yugoslavia since 1991 and had both internal and international aspects. Hence, regardless of the type of conflict in which they were committed, the tribunal had the authority to adjudicate Tadic's alleged offences which included murder, rape, and torture.[54]

The case was then returned to the Trial Chamber for further pre-trial and trial proceedings. The Yugoslavia Tribunal at The Hague is in several ways an improvement on the Nuremberg model. Its rules of procedure incorporate positive developments over the past fifty years with respect to the rights of defendants under criminal law. The recent findings of this international tribunal (in *Tadic's case*) have considerably advanced international humanitarian law. By affirming the power and authority of the Security Council to set up in the future a Yugoslav-type tribunal, it has (hopefully) helped deter Tadic prototypes around the world. The decision of the International Tribunal (2 October 1995) has also helped to establish an oft-forgotten truism that retribution for gross human rights violations can be meted out in law.

In human rights cases, obsessive national security concerns of the state sometimes influence judicial decision-making and with strange, almost extraordinary results. An interim judgement of the Supreme Court of Israel is illustrative of this point. Muhammad Hamdan was under administrative detention and being interrogated by the General Security Service (an agency of the Ministry of Justice). An appeal was presented on his behalf to the Supreme Court in which there was a serious allegation about the use of physical force during the interrogation, and it was prayed that an interim injunction be granted restraining such action. The court agreed to the issuance of an interim injunction and prohibited the interrogating authorities "from using physical force against the appellant pending the hearing of his appeal." This was on 14 November 1996. The respondents to the appeal (the Ministry of Justice) later informed the court that they had a well-founded suspicion that the appellant was withholding extremely vital information and that an urgent need existed to continue with the interrogation of the appellant "without the needs of the interrogation being subjected to the restrictions imposed by the interim injunction." (sic)

In short, the Ministry of Justice requested the court to vacate the interim injunction. The Supreme Court of Israel, after studying the classified material presented to it and being satisfied that there was a "substantiated suspicion" that the appellant possessed extremely vital information—the immediate procurement of which would prevent an awful disaster, save human lives, and prevent very serious terrorist attacks—held that there was no justification for the continued existence of the interim injunction and the interim injunction was then annulled[55] (on 26 November 1996) with consequences that are best left to the imagination. In the interest of accuracy, however, it is necessary to state that in their judgement the judges did say: "Needless to add, the annulment of the interim injunction does not constitute permission to take, during interrogation, measures that are not in accordance with the law and which are in breach of the law." But if there was no other way in which the interrogation could be conducted, then it was obvious that annulling the injunction against torture could only have the consequence of authorising the continuation of the interrogation *with* torture!

Israel is a party to the UN Convention against Torture, having ratified it in 1991. The convention expressly provides that "no exceptional circumstances whatsoever" may be invoked as a justification for torture—a fact overlooked or ignored by Israel's highest court. This interim decision of the Israel Supreme Court may be contrasted with a much earlier judgement of the US Federal Court of Appeals (in *Filartiga* vs. *Pena-Irala*, 630F 2d. 876 [1980]).

Two Paraguayan plaintiffs brought an action against another citizen of Paraguay for the torture and death of their son and brother. Plaintiffs made their claim under the Alien Tort Statute, a federal law dating back to the Judiciary Act of 1789, which gave district courts original jurisdiction in any civil action by an alien for a tort "committed in violation of the law of nations or a treaty of the United States." Because the United States, at the time the action was commenced, had not ratified the UN Convention against Torture, the decision in the case necessarily turned upon whether the torture violated "the law of the nations," that is, customary international law. In an unreported decision, a district court ruled that the torture of a Paraguayan by a Paraguayan in Paraguay did not violate customary international law. On appeal, the US Court of Appeals reversed, holding "that an act of torture committed by a state official against one held in detention violated established norms of the international law of human rights and hence the law of nations." At the time of the act in question, the defendant was inspector general of police in Paraguay. The Court of Appeals emphasised that "official torture is now prohibited by the law of nations and that the prohibition is clear and unambiguous and admits of no distinction between treatment of aliens and citizens." Thus, federal jurisdiction over the cause of action existed under the Alien Tort Statute. On remand, "punitive damages" were awarded "to give effect to the manifest objectives of the international prohibition against torture."[56]

The *Filartiga cases* stand today as a deterrent against the recurrence of gross human rights violations and the possibility of perpetrators of such violations seeking asylum or refuge in the United States with impunity. They also stand as decisions that could be drawn upon by courts in countries other than the United States whenever similar problems arise. *Filartiga* (a series of decisions of national courts) has contributed in a meaningful way to the progressive development and application of International Human Rights Law.

The principle that human rights must be defended has become one of the commonplace clichés of our age. Though it is accepted everywhere, it is also violated everywhere. There still exists a wide gulf between the human rights documentation (in treaties, declarations, and conventions) and the arduous and sometimes unrewarding, painful work of protecting human rights on the ground. Many constitutions of the world entrust such work to the courts and the legal profession. This trust in the capacity of law to limit the powers of governments and governmental agencies has led to "occupational hazards." It has sometimes created pressures on the doctrine of separation of powers, leading even to the removal of judges (as in Malaysia in 1989) or the domination of courts by an overly powerful government (as in some other countries).

However, as a great judge once said (prior to the enactment of New Zealand's new Bill of Rights): "The working out of truly fundamental rights and duties is ultimately an inescapable judicial responsibility."[57] And later, after the Bill of Rights was brought into force, New Zealand's Court of Appeal said that defining and applying its provisions was the prime responsibility of the courts "as the ultimate guardians of personal liberty."[58] This view is gaining ground. In a case that (co-incidentally) concerned a citizen of New Zealand, the House of Lords defined the power and duty of the judiciary to be that of refusing "to countenance behaviour that threatens either basic human rights or the rule of law."[59]

"The inescapable judicial responsibility" has now emerged as a standard of almost universal application. It was endorsed when the chief justices of twenty Asian countries met in Beijing and adopted a Statement of Principles of the Independence of Judiciary in the LAWASIA region. The heads of the judiciary of countries on the continent of Asia, Australia, and New Zealand are signatories to this statement of principles. The Beijing Principles (August 1995) declare that one of the main objectives and functions of the judiciary is "to promote within the proper limits of judicial functions the observance and the attainment of Human Rights." In September 1996, the Georgetown conclusions on the effective protection of human rights through law reiterated "the principles of universal inherence" and said, "that principle transcends national political systems and is in the keeping of the independent judiciary."

Almost by universal common consent, then, the future of International Human Rights Law is now placed firmly in the hands of the judges (assisted by the legal profession). Though this is a fantastic opportunity, it is also an awesome responsibility!

4

Reforms in Legal Education on Research[60]

When people in India ask me my age, and then ask me whether I have retired from active practice, I look them in the eye and give them short shrift and sternly tell them: "Lawyers in India never retire; they only drop dead." So it is with law teachers. We should pause and take a leaf out of the book of that management guru, Peter Drucker, who died at the ripe old age of ninety-three. In life, he once described his personal experiences that had taught him "how to grow, how to change, and how to age, without remaining a prisoner of the past." This is one of life's most important lessons which each of you will have to confront—not to remain a prisoner of the past.

In his book, *The Essential Drucker: The Best of Sixty Years of Peter Drucker,* he recalled that back in the year 1949, when he first began to teach management courses at New York University, his father, then seventy-three years old, came to visit him from California. They both went to see an old friend of his father's, the famous economist Joseph Schumpeter. Schumpeter was then sixty-six years old and already world-famous and still teaching at Harvard University. The two old men had a wonderful time together, reminiscing about the old days. Suddenly, Drucker's father asked Schumpeter with a chuckle: "Joseph, do you still talk about what you want to be remembered for?" And Schumpeter broke out in loud laughter. This was because he (Schumpeter) was notorious for having said when he was only thirty years old and had already published the first of his two great books on economics: "Having been Europe's greatest lover of beautiful women and Europe's greatest horseman and *perhaps,* also one of the world's great economists, yes, yes, this question is still important to me, but I answer it differently. I want to be remembered as having been the teacher who converted half-a-dozen brilliant students into first-rate economists."

I have a junior colleague, Subhash Sharma, whose son is a brilliant student who, after graduation from Symbiosis in Noida, is now at New York University as one of its brightest students. On his short vacations, he tells me how methods of teaching law have vastly changed over the years. They are so different from how, for instance, I was taught law in the 1940s. My granddaughter, Nina Nariman, daughter of Justice Rohinton Nariman, who did her master's from Harvard, also tells me the same thing that law is not taught as it used to be. Law has to stimulate, and law has to be imbibed, and yesterday's teachers of law are today's superlative facilitators.

We all know about the Socratic method of teaching, but at NYU and as well as in Harvard, Yale, and Chicago, the teaching is not just the Socratic method. In fact, it is not teaching at all. It is guiding the students to do their own research for hours and hours and hours on end, to pause and *think,* and only then *speak*, critically analysing and commenting on everything that has been said and written on a particular topic. There has now been introduced what is known as the "role-play method"—an advanced form of the case study method. The student, after reading the material given to him or her, which is of thousands of pages, is required to be an actual stakeholder in a problem posed by the professor. The student, along with the professor, on an equal level, debates the problem, acting, reasoning, and empathising, which together have a long-lasting effect on the memory of the student and make him or her a far better practicing lawyer. The steps that are followed are:

- *First,* an introduction. Students are given their specific roles to act and speak, either as plaintiff, defendant, witness, etc., or expert in a given case, and they are expected to acquaint themselves with that role and be ready to play that role.

- *Second*, the professor makes some predetermined guidelines, and students get an opportunity to establish a network with other participating students.
- *Third*, comes the acting stage. Every class, being of a duration of two hours or more, the students play their roles in class as plaintiff, defendant, witness, expert, and judge, and communicate, negotiate, and attempt to resolve the issue under examination, contributing what they have thought about and learnt from case law. The thousands of pages that are prescribed are not only to be read but read and digested.
- *Finally*, there is the concluding stage, which is the most important stage, as there is an assessment of the extent to which each of the students has comprehended the situation that is posed by the problem and learnt not to accept everything that has been said or written without first questioning its intrinsic worth.

The essence of this so-called "teaching" is to freely and frankly promote discussion of problems and experiences in which the professor himself or herself participates. These are experiences that last a lifetime. And it is these experiences that help make one a modern successful practicing lawyer, not just in one country but anywhere around the common law world, both in civil law and criminal law. We lawyers, teachers, students, professors, and judges must stimulate the urge to think for oneself, without which our present legal system cannot long survive. And it is the ability and the resolve to transmit one's expertise to the younger generation that our profession of law gains in strength and repute.

Lastly, do remember that reforms are no longer to be gleaned from Law Commission reports. These are fat books that must remain on our shelves just to show people how learned we are in the mumbo-jumbo of the law. Reforms in legal education and research have to be stimulated by open discussions in classrooms, and not by one man or woman standing on a stage (as in my time) and spouting all he or she knows or has learnt by rote. It is the back-and-forth between the professor and student in class that helps to stimulate their mental faculties, which is so essential in the practice of law. As a practicing lawyer, you must be like a swordsman—quick on the draw! The quickest one on the draw wins.

My old senior in Bombay, Sir Jamshedji Kanga, always used to tell us that we all are "students of law" at all ages and at all times—the students, the teacher, the professor in class, the lawyer, and the judge in court. At the age of ninety-three, with seniority of sixty-five years as a practicing lawyer, he would say with the enthusiasm of a twenty-year-old, "I am still learning the law." This is not just humility; it is the sum total of a lifetime's experience in the law.

In the end, let me tell you something. I have been recently reading *The Accidental President* by A. J. Baime, which is grippingly written about Harry Truman, the former US President—accidental because he came into office by accident, due to the sudden death of the president. When he was vice-president during Franklin Delano Roosevelt's third term as president, Truman did nothing much at all as vice-president. In fact, he hardly visited the White House, where he was never invited. Suddenly, one fine day on 12 April 1945, Roosevelt died, and Truman became the inheritor of the highest, most important, and most difficult office in the world—that of the president of the United States—and that too whilst World War II was in its final stages.

When he was president till 1953, when Dwight D. Eisenhower was elected to succeed him on 20 January 1953, President Truman always kept a quotation of Abraham Lincoln in a leather portfolio on his desk and followed in practice what the quote prescribed:

> "I do the very best I know how—the very best I can; and mean to keep doing so until the end. If the end brings me out all right, what is said against me won't amount to anything. If the end

> brings me out wrong, ten angels swearing I was right would make no difference."

So do the very best you can, whether as a law student, teacher, practicing lawyer, or as a judge, till the very end. And may good luck (which we always badly need) go with you.

5

The Relevance of Ethical Values in Law[61]

I recall with anguish, what an erstwhile colleague of mine in parliament, Dr P. C. Alexander, who is no more, had said during a debate in the Rajya Sabha on the Central Vigilance Commission Bill. He spoke passionately of old times and of those working in government and the values they cherished: "When I entered the civil service way back in 1948, at the beginning of our Independence, my worry was whether my *tehsildar* would be corrupt. My sub-inspector would be corrupt, my bench clerk in my court would be corrupt. I could never imagine that my senior officers would be corrupt. I could never imagine, when I became a senior officer, that I would ever become corrupt. [Under this bill, we] have given senior officers protection. Government sanction is needed before even an inquiry can be started against them."

Dr Alexander characterised the relevant clause in the bill as "enemy number one." We both opposed the bill, but it was passed and has long since become law. I write in times that are totally different from the times Dr Alexander spoke about it in parliament. As to why they are different may be partly because I am an old-timer of yesteryear, and today's values are not the values we always cherished. However, don't for a moment think that the requisite precepts for ethical values in law are lacking, neither here nor elsewhere.

On the contrary, those ethical values in law have been set out in beautiful prose in a series of universal documents like the following: "UN Basic Principles on the Independence of the

Judiciary" adopted in November-December 1985, "UN Basic Principles on the Role of Lawyers" adopted by the United Nations Congress in September 1990, and "Restatement of Values of Judicial Life" (code of conduct) adopted at the Conference of Chief Justices in India in December 1989.

All this you will find in books, and if I were to recount the beautiful things written in these documents, I would be writing a book in itself instead of just a chapter. And I don't mean to, as all these written precepts may be a fit subject for a doctoral thesis and not for a brief chapter like this. The truth is that in a chapter for a book like this, such precepts are boring and don't amount to much. Morality in law or in the interpretation of law as a theory is terribly tiresome to listen to. Hence, here I hope to concentrate more on the practice of ethical values in law because an ounce of practice is worth more than a pound of theory, each and every time.

In the decade of the 1980s, which were for me the golden years of the Supreme Court of India, there were four judges who consciously and radically changed India's judicial history for the better. They transformed the country's highest court from what the legal scholar Prof. Upendra Baxi had once sneeringly described as the "Supreme Court of India Impoverished" into a "Supreme Court of India of Values." They were Justice Krishna Iyer, Justice P. N. Bhagwati, Justice Dhirubhai Desai, and the fourth, then the youngest, was Justice O. Chinnappa Reddy.

However, don't be under the impression that it is judges alone who are protectors of ethical values in the law. Men and women from different walks of life are the foot soldiers in the quest for ethical values in the law. Let me give you a concrete example. Many decades ago, a senior executive of a Tata company tried to help the company save on taxes. And he put up a case before the then chairman of the company, J. R. D. Tata, saying to him: "Sir, the scheme is not illegal."

JRD paused and then gave his soft-spoken response: "Not illegal, yes. But is it right?"

About paying taxes, it was left to a great English judge, Lord Denning, who had visited India on more than three occasions, when some of us had the privilege of meeting and interacting with him. He was not only a great judge but a master of his own language—English. This is how he put it: "The avoidance of tax may be lawful, but it is not yet a virtue." Beautiful, yet simply expressed!

The earthy Justice Chinnappa Reddy used to describe tax evasion as "the art of dodging tax without breaking the law." Citing from judgements of courts in England which had commended the exercise, he said: "They are like ghosts of the past that stand in the path of justice, clanking their mediaeval chains. The proper course for the judge of today is to pass through these chains undeterred. No one can now get away with a tax avoidance project with the mere statement that there is nothing illegal about it." He was strongly of the view that to expose tax dodgers for what they really were was to refuse to give judicial benediction to their practices—call it tax evasion or call it tax avoidance. His judgement, a concurring one in a bench of five judges in *McDowell's case*[62] (1985), is a gem, worthy of being read by those who go by ethical values. The remaining four judges who delivered the majority judgement (spoken through the judgement of Justice Ranganath Misra) went out of their way to endorse what Chinnappa had said about tax-dodging: "It is the obligation of every citizen to pay the taxes honestly without resorting to subterfuge. On this aspect, one of us, Justice Chinnappa Reddy, has proposed a separate and detailed opinion *with which we agree*." Mark the last four words!

So, what Chinnappa Reddy had ruled became the judgement of a bench of five judges, binding on all future judges. But the important words in the majority judgement just quoted, which proposed a separate and detailed opinion with which we agree, were overlooked and were bypassed by a later bench decision of two judges in 2004 in the *Indo-Mauritius Treaty case*. This bench of two judges could not, in law, but did take a view contrary to a bench of five, supporting the theory of what they called "tax planning," which they said was legal. This decision of a bench of two judges[63] was compounded by being quoted and affirmed ever by a later bench of three judges in the *Vodafone case*[64] (in 2012). In my humble view, this is one of the monumental judicial errors of our time.

But I come back to the story of a man, not trained to be a judge or lawyer, but who goes by ethical values in law. It is recorded in a book written by Russi Lala, *In Search of Ethical Leadership* (2005). Let me repeat the story as Russi Lala eloquently put it. It was J. R. D. Tata who started Tata Airlines back in the year 1932, not alone (as is generally believed) but at the initiation of and with the help of a qualified English friend, Neville Vincent (a fact not so well known). Tata Airlines and Neville Vincent entered into a fixed-term agreement whereby Neville would get one-third of the net profit earned by Tata Airlines because it was his innovative idea. But the investment and the services were to be provided by the Tatas.

In the first year of operation, the net profit of Tata Airlines was Rs. 60,000. Five years later, in 1937, when the contract expired, the annual net profit was ten times that amount. JRD was then a director of Tata Sons and not yet its chairman. The legal advisor of Tatas at the time, J. D. Choksi, was firmly of the view that the contract with Neville Vincent should not be renewed on its expiry on the same terms, since the profit had been much larger than the Tatas had expected. JRD was not at all happy with this decision, but he had to go along, and he told his collaborator (his friend Neville Vincent), who was terribly disappointed. JRD knew it was not fair to the man who had originated the idea of Tata Airlines and helped Jeh (as JRD was commonly known) to establish it. So, what did JRD do? He went to a senior solicitor in Bombay (a man of law by the name of Dinshaw Daji, senior-most partner of a leading firm of solicitors in Bombay, Payne & Co.). The opinion given by Daji makes me feel proud of the profession of lawyers. He wrote out his opinion in one crisp sentence: "J. D. Choksi is legally correct, morally his opinion is not." So, Jeh went and told his friend and colleague Neville and assured him on his own that the agreement would be renewed on the same terms as before.

Did he consult his co-directors? No, he did not. JRD's response to why he didn't do so was: "It was not right and fair, and this is what I just told him." Jeh was then just thirty-three years old. It was a year later that he became chairman of Tata Sons. What guided JRD was the power of his conviction, his innate ethical values, not the fine print of the law.

In England in the nineteenth century, Lord Thurlow, Lord Chancellor of England, once rhetorically asked (in a judgement often quoted): "Do you ever expect a corporation to have a conscience?" He thought not. But JRD's answer would have been yes, every time. And Jeh had a way of dealing with his shareholders as well. Once, at the annual general meeting of TOMCO (Tata Oil Mills Ltd), a shareholder got up and angrily said: "Sir, the quality of Hamam soap has deteriorated. Even the wrapping paper is not as good as before."

"Who says so?" JRD shot back.

"Sir, my wife says so."

Jeh's answer was met with peals of laughter: "In that case sir, you can do either of two things—change your soap or change your wife."

But seriously, when speaking of equality in the law, which our Constitution prescribes in Article 14, note that it is nothing but an application of ethical principles. In England, it was said by one of the judges during the course of arguments, that when counsel pressed upon him the written law and not the equity of the case, the judge's response was: "Equity is not presumed to be of an age that is past childbearing." This is the great genius of the common law, and India is still one of the many common law countries of the world, not like a country in Europe governed by civil law.

Now, I come to the eternal problem of how to decide a case in India or in any other common law country. What are the expectations of how cases in court should be decided? The answer is that there is a moral and ethical element in every positive law that can never be overlooked. There was once an English judge, Lord Ackner. He sat in England's Court of Appeal from 1986 to 1992 and had been a judge ever since the year 1967. He had the good fortune of sitting with Lord Denning in England's Court of Appeal, and he publicly acknowledged the influence of Denning's philosophy of law on him, which is nothing but ethical values in law. This is how Lord Ackner put it how best to decide a case: ". . . the need to ensure the just result and therefore, to circumvent precedent if you can do it properly . . ."

In England, there was a successful lawyer from South Africa, Johan Steyn of Dutch origin, who, when moving to England, was known to be so clever and so bright that he was quickly made a judge, and within ten years, elevated as a judge of England's Court of Appeal and then moved on to England's highest tribunal, the Judicial Committee of the House of Lords. He then became Lord Johan Steyn. In an opinion expressed in the year 1999, he expressed the view that a judge's sense of the moral answer to every question of law and a judge's instinct for edging closer to a conclusion that fits the justice of the case had always been "one of the great shaping forces of the common law."[65] This is what he said:

> "It may be objected that the House (i.e., the House of Lords) must act like a court of law and not like a court of morals. That would only be partly right. The court must apply positive law. But the judges' sense of the moral answer to a question, or the justice of the case, has been one of the great shaping forces of the common law."

But what about India? How is justice to be administered in our courts of law?

Four years after the Supreme Court of India was established, one of its first judges, Justice Vivian Bose, described in eloquent prose what the constitutional provisions meant and should mean to the justices who sat in the highest court: "We have upon us the whole armour of the Constitution and walk henceforth in its enlightened ways, wearing the breastplate of its protecting provisions and flashing the flaming sword of its inspiration." I like the phrase "flashing the flaming sword of its inspiration," which means the inspiration derived from our written Constitution. I have always believed that the "flaming sword," about which Justice Bose had written, is located in Article 142(1) of India's Constitution, a provision the likes of which are not to be found in any other written constitution of any other country in the world. It states simply:

> "142. (1) The Supreme Court, in the exercise of its jurisdiction, may pass such decree or make such order as is necessary for doing complete justice in any cause or matter pending before it . . ."

In implementing the idea of justice mentioned in the Constitution's Preamble[66], judges of the Supreme Court of India have been empowered by Article 142(1) "to pass such decree or make such order as is necessary for doing *complete justice* in any cause or matter pending before it." Justice is the supreme ethical value in all our laws. In implementing the idea of justice mentioned in the Constitution's Preamble, judges of the Supreme Court (and the judges of the Supreme Court alone) have been expressly empowered by Article 142 to pass such decree or order or make such order as it is necessary for doing *complete justice* in any cause or matter pending before it.

According to me, the best definition of this concept embodied in Article 142(1) is the title of that *New York Times* bestseller, *Justice: What's the Right Thing to Do?* by Michael J. Sandel. It encapsulates the best definition of the concept of justice embodied in Article 142(1)—"the right thing to do."

When on some rare occasion, it is found by the highest court that the enacted law, if applied, would divert the true course of justice (a rare case but it does occur from time to time), specific power is conferred on the Supreme Court, and on that court alone, to make such orders as may be necessary for doing complete justice in any cause or matter pending before it. This is the trust that the founding fathers placed in our highest court, and this is how the justices of the Supreme Court had interpreted Article 142(1) during the first forty years of the court's existence.[67] But then, successor judges of the Supreme Court of India developed "cold feet." Later, they asserted in reported judgements that nothing can be done, even by the highest court, by way of justice when enacted law stands in the way.[68] A great pity!

Lord Denning, the most celebrated English judge of the twentieth century, would have characterised these later judges of our court as he boldly characterised his own generation of judges, calling them "timorous souls." The only reason power was reserved to justices of the highest court was because it was they who were to be trusted more than any other judges in the country "for doing complete justice." They were expected, at all times, to do what was right. This was the faith that the Constitution placed in the justices of the Supreme Court—a faith unfortunately not shared or reciprocated by later justices of the court among themselves!

There are two judges, one in England and one in India, who are to be looked up to and admired not only because they were amongst the strongest proponents of *life* and *liberty* (which they were) but above all because they exercised a *humanising influence on the law* and gave it its ethical content. And what they did, they did not for large corporate bodies or for "big men" (The phrase "big men" is now commonly used).

If you watch and listen to BBC performers every day, there is a self-flattering item before the news for all to see and read. It goes: "When big men talk, they talk to the BBC." Both in England and in India, the humanising influence of the law has been (and believe me, even today is) exercised not for big men but particularly for small, insignificant men.

Let me first recount to you the case decided by the great English judge, Denning, back in the year 1974. Not only is it an enforcement of ethical values for the benefit of a very small man but by bringing justice to him, it is worth relating because it is also tragicomic! The case was about a small man, Stephen Ballog. He was a solicitor's clerk, a casual hand employed at £5 per day by solicitors for the defence in a case before the Crown Court in London (a court below the high court). The case in question had dragged on and on (as cases tend to do sometimes in England, and more often in India as well). The solicitor's clerk, Ballog, got exceedingly bored. He made a plan to liven up the legal proceedings. He knew something about a gas called nitrous oxide (N2O), which gives an exhilarating effect when inhaled. It is correctly called "laughing gas" about which he had learnt when he was at school. His education did not go much further.

During the trial, he took a half-cylinder of nitrous oxide from the hospital car park and carried it about with him in his briefcase. His plan was to put the cylinder at the inlet to the court's ventilating system so that the laughing gas would be released in the court. It would emerge from the outlets which were just in front of the row where counsel and their solicitors sat. He hoped it would enliven their speeches in court. One night, when it was dark, he got onto the roof of the courthouse, found the ventilating duct, and decided where to put the cylinder. The next morning, soon after the court sat at 11:15, he took his briefcase (with the cylinder in it) to court, waiting for the moment when he could slip up to the roof without anyone seeing him. But the moment never came. The officers of the court had watched him go up to the roof the night before. So, in the morning, they kept an eye on him and arrested him. They opened his briefcase and took out the cylinder. They charged him with stealing a bottle of nitrous oxide. He admitted it. They kept him in custody and reported the matter to Justice Melford Stevenson, the presiding judge, who had Ballog brought before him. The police inspector gave evidence. Ballog admitted it was all true. He said he meant it as a joke. But the judge thought differently. He was not amused. To him, this was no laughing matter; it was a very serious contempt of court, and he sentenced him to prison for six months.

At this sentence being pronounced, Ballog exploded and told the judge:

"You are a humourless automaton. Why don't you self-destruct?" Fortunately, for this expostulation, he was not sentenced to a further term and was taken away to serve his original sentence! The poor man languished in jail for a week and wrote a pleading letter to the judge, which was not responded to. Ultimately, the matter came before the Court of Appeal. Lord Denning, sitting in the Court of Appeal, was all sympathy for the poor wretch.

He had already suffered for seven days. "There must be some way found to get this man out." And Denning, the genius judge that he was, found a way.

"Well," he said in his judgement, "Ballog had merely prepared to commit contempt of court. He had not even *attempted* to commit it because nothing was let into the ducts; and mere preparation for committing an offence, even with intent, is not contempt. That is the law." Denning had correctly stated the law. "Besides," wrote Denning, " Ballog had apologised, and that is enough to purge his contempt, if contempt it was." The judge who had sentenced Ballog was disposed off in a few short sentences: "The judge, Melford Stevenson, acted with a firmness which became him. As it happened, he went too far. That is no reproach to him. It only shows the wisdom of having a Court of Appeal!"

We in India were fortunate to have had another judge like Denning, though his style of writing judgements was entirely different. But his heart, like Denning's, was in the right place. Justice Krishna Iyer's humanising influence on the law was first expressed in a case of little apparent public importance. But it is one of the judgements of his I like best—a case of a small-time businessman from Kerala who went by the somewhat unusual name of Jolly George Verghese. Like many others of his kind, this individual was in debt and could not afford to pay them, including a judgement debt! And so, like many other hundreds of persons at the time (and many thousands before him), the poor fellow was marched off to a civil prison. Rightly, courts in Kerala had said, relying on the provisions of Section 51 of the Code of Civil Procedure of 1908, that one of the modes of execution of a money decree (if you have no property) is the imprisonment of the debtor in a civil jail. But Jolly George Verghese was more fortunate than his other debt-ridden brethren. He appealed to the Supreme Court of India. And happily for him and for the law, the case came before a bench presided over by Justice Krishna Iyer (in the year

1980). The judgement is a treat. I advise all who are enthusiasts about ethics in law and morality in the law to read it and absorb its meaning. It is simply written, but not without fine literary flourishes, for Krishna Iyer, always a man of vast and varied reading, quotes William Shakespeare in his judgement (in this case). He writes: "Imprisonment is not to be ordered merely because, like Shylock, the creditor says, '*I crave the law, the penalty, and forfeit of my bond*'" (a famous quote from *The Merchant of Venice*). He then quoted from a book more ancient than Shakespeare—the *Old Testament*. The Bible says: "Mercy is reasonable in the time of affliction as clouds of rain in the time of drought."

What beautiful imagery! When the case first came before him, Krishna Iyer found that the enacted law gave him no choice but to uphold the judgement of the Kerala High Court. But then, like the good judge he was, he looked elsewhere and found for himself an article in the UN International Covenant on Civil and Political Rights. In Article 11 of the International Covenant on Civil and Political Rights (ICCPR), 1969, one of the major UN Covenants, and to which India had been a party, said: "No one shall be imprisoned merely on the ground of inability to fulfil a contractual obligation."

This post-Second World War provision in the United Nations Covenant was in the teeth of the pre-First World War Section 51 of the Civil Procedure Code of 1908. Krishna Iyer figured out how best he could reconcile the two in the interest of this miserable man, whose first name though Jolly, had found himself in a position that was not one bit jolly! Krishna Iyer, in his judgement, reasoned that the ICCPR, though not part of Indian law, is certainly part of international law recognised in India. He also reasoned that international law must have some influence on the interpretation of our own national law, especially when the latter British Indian law of 1908 predates India's ratification of the UN Covenant by more than sixty years.

So, by a clever process of judicial interpretation, in the light of Article 11 of the ICCPR, Justice Krishna Iyer concluded as follows:

i. That if a debtor once had the means but now, he has not the means to pay, or;
ii. even if he has the money now on which there are other legitimate and pressing claims, then;
iii. it would be violative of the spirit of Article 11, which is part of international law, to arrest and confine him in jail so as to coerce him into payment;
iv. and this is how Section 51 of the CPC post-1980 is to be understood and applied.

And so, it has been ever since. Verghese's case is a landmark case on the humanising influence of international law on a pre-First World War British Indian statute—the Civil Procedure Code of 1908. This judgement not only reflects the judge's clarity of thought but is also a tribute to judicial research (for which judges have so little time these days). It is the result of highly innovative thinking, which inheres only in a person possessed with a fertile mind.

Let me end by saying that I don't like to give advice simply because I am too haughty to accept good advice, except, of course, perhaps from my wife! But I make bold to advise all of you that if you cherish ethical values in law, then you must read a book by a great lawyer, Lord Hailsham Quintin Hogg, who was England's Lord Chancellor (from May 1979-June 1987) and England's highest-ranking judicial member during the prime ministership of Margaret Thatcher. I had the privilege of meeting him and sitting at the same table with him at a dinner given for him by the then-British high commissioner in Delhi many, many years ago. After he retired as Lord Chancellor, and at age eighty-seven, he wrote a book that is different from all other books because it is printed as written in Hailsham's own hand, *Values: Collapse and Cure.*[69] It is only seventy-seven pages and at the end of the book, he expresses the result of his convictions:

> "Forever truth is better than falsehood,
> Kindness is better than brutality,

> Virtue is better than vice,
> Beauty is better than ugliness."

But what exactly is truth, what is falsehood? What exactly, in a given context, is true kindness? What is virtue, and what is vice? These are questions to which our hypothesis is never more than provisional and always subject to revisions as we plod our way through the wilderness of life's experience.

There comes a point at which we are compelled to say that, as we approach the throne of the ineffable, words fail us. At this stage, we are compelled to say:

> "That of which we cannot speak intelligibly is something about which one is bound to keep silence. But it is the silence of worship, not of ignorance."

6

Law and Other Disciplines

What I have to say might have little to do with continuing legal education, but it has much to do with the need for lawyers to be better equipped with knowledge and experience in disciplines other than law. An outstanding example was the great and good professor, Madhava Menon, whose passing away is the greatest loss to continuing legal education in India.

Lawyers, more than their brethren in other professions, must be equipped with what (for want of a better expression) is called "significant learning," i.e., learning that is more than a mere accumulation of facts, learning that makes a difference in the individual's behaviour in society, in the course of action pursued, in attitudes, and in approaches. Knowledge of the law is not an end in itself. It is a means of equipping the inquiring mind with a liberal education. There is some stress between what society demands of lawyers and what legal education can provide. The gap is significant only because the pearly words of wisdom of legal sages of the past have been ignored.

Back in the seventeenth century, Serjeant Finch (in those days senior lawyers were known as "serjeants") picturesquely expressed the affinity of law and other disciplines: "The sparks of all sciences are rolled up in the ashes of the law." And the oft-quoted (but much-neglected) jurist of the eighteenth century, William Blackstone, said: "General academic education must be a first step to the profession of the common law, for sciences are of a sociable disposition and flourish best in the neighbourhood of each other. Nor is there any branch of learning, but it may be helped and improved by assistance drawn from other arts."[70] Of course, Blackstone thought in terms of history and philosophy, but what he said was applicable to other branches of knowledge as well.

In the nineteenth century, a great American judge, Oliver Wendell Holmes, reminded men of the law (there were unfortunately no women in the legal profession at this time): "To be master of any branch of knowledge, you must master those which lie next to it."[71] And in the 1940s, Prof. E. C. S. Wade, in an inaugural lecture at Cambridge, urged: "We should teach (and practice) law as a great human institution serving social and economic ends and in relation to the world in which we live."[72]

Sir Walter Scott was trained to become a lawyer, but his interests were in literature. He wrote many novels. In *Guy Mannering*, he showed that he had not forgotten his early impressions of what a lawyer should aspire to become. The hero in the novel visits the house of a Scottish lawyer (Counsellor Pleydell), and is shown into the lawyer's study, the walls of which are lined with a collection of the classics and other tomes on varied subjects. "These," says Pleydell, "are the tools of my trade. A lawyer without history or literature is a mechanic, a mere working mason. If he possesses some knowledge of these, he may venture to call himself an architect." If a lawyer is to be at all worthy of the society which he (or she) serves, then the yearning must be to become an "architect" in the law, not to remain a mason!

It is common ground amongst juristic thinkers of today that law is an instrument or a range of instruments through which men and women seek to achieve certain purposes in society. Judges do this all the time when interpreting statutory instruments. The modern trend is to give a purposive interpretation to the words used in legislation. "Globalisation" was the buzzword of our New Age till very recently, but judges are not deterred. They keep building a global community of law, both national and international. Networking amongst the judicial fraternity is on the rise, and judges (almost everywhere) are becoming increasingly aware of one another's decisions. The most informal level of transnational judicial contact is the knowledge of judicial decisions, foreign and international, together with a willingness to reach out and cite them. Justice Sandra Day O'Connor (the first woman judge appointed to the US Supreme Court) once chided American lawyers and judges about their insularity in ignoring foreign law and predicted that she and her fellow justices would find themselves "looking more frequently to decisions of other constitutional courts."

Notwithstanding the recent worldwide trend to look inward, the legal world has already become a global village, and the vast proliferation of national and international laws, as well as treaties and conventions on a wide range of subjects, must receive at least a nodding acquaintance from a true votary of the law. The lawyer of today must meet and contend with challenges beyond the lawyer's traditional role as an intermediary between litigants and courts of justice. Many decades ago, when the then chief justice of Australia, Sir Owen Dixon, was asked whether it was any part of the duty of a lawyer to contribute towards the progress of society, he said that it was the duty of a lawyer to keep a hand on and hold steady the *framework* and *foundations* of the law. However, that was long, long ago. The quickening pace of technological advancement and a new sense of service and duty to society have replaced the old model. In a message to the LAWASIA Conference of lawyers in New Delhi way back in 1985, the then secretary-general of the Commonwealth, Sir Shridath Ramphal, reminded us that we are "heirs to a noble tradition of intellectual inventiveness." It is a nice, well-rounded phrase of great use to the lawyer practicing law in this new millennium. It matters not where or in which part of the globe.

We live in an age where there is much economic legislation. After all, the welfare of the people is the professed objective of every civilised state. Yet there are vast expanses of uncharted ignorance amongst lawyers and judges, particularly about economics. There are now more experimental forays into economics than into law across the five continents of the world, in countries with different types of economies. Activities that were once regarded as state monopolies, like telecommunications, energy, transport, broadcasting, postal services, and the like, have now become the subject of scrutiny and regulation. Even activities such as sports, entertainment, and the media are not beyond questioning. Economics motivates laws which in turn drive the economy, and the bundle of laws that reflect societal values is now known as "sociological jurisprudence."

7

The Advocates Act, 1961[73]

The Advocates Act, 1961, was a good act when it was enacted, except that it introduced, for the first time in India, a caste system amongst practicing lawyers and recognised two distinct and separate classes of lawyers: "senior advocates" and "other advocates." This was mirrored in the practice then prevalent in England and Wales and is still current there. But that was in days gone by. Fast forward a little over sixty years. With the complete disintegration of the British Empire, we do not need to mirror our profession on British practice. Over the years, the operation in practice of two classes of advocates has created far too much heartburn and legitimate disappointment, especially amongst a large number of young and enthusiastic practicing lawyers.

Section 16(2) of the Act as enacted states that an advocate may be designated as a senior advocate if the Supreme Court or a high court is of the opinion that by virtue of *his* ability, (*his*) standing at the Bar, or (*his*) special knowledge or experience in law, *he* is deserving of such distinction. No *objective* criteria are laid down in the Act for a person qualified to be promoted to senior status. It is a purely subjective selection made by a majority of judges of a court. I doubt whether it passes the constitutional test of equality before the law.

Let me give you my own experience. I was called to the Bar in the Bombay High Court in November 1950, long before the advent of the Advocates Act of 1961. And in the mid-1950s, the complaint of us, then younger members of the Bombay Bar, was that the older members were cornering almost all the work on the original side where we practiced—especially chamber work and notices of motion, i.e., applications in suits by way of summons as well as applications for interlocutory injunctions and for other interim relief. Seeing that younger members of the Bar were disappointed, a couple of wise and far-sighted older advocates (Kantilal Desai[74] in particular) persuaded all lawyers then in active practice on the original side for twenty-five years or more to go onto an imaginary "senior list" voluntarily by choice, not compulsion. It meant that those on the "senior list" undertook no longer to appear in chamber matters or motions on the original side of the high court nor in any interlocutory applications in suits and petitions, thus giving us younger entrants in the Bar a chance to prove ourselves. And believe me, this worked. But, and this is an important "but," lawyers in practice for twenty-five years and more going on the senior list was an act of sacrifice on the part of older members of the Bar and not regarded as a badge of fame or distinction. Unfortunately, the 1961 Act reversed this healthy precedent.

Today, when I look back, I believe the voluntary system adopted by the Bombay Bar was far better than the prescription in this Act, simply because it ensured equality of opportunity amongst those practicing law with a distinct weightage in favour of the junior Bar. My considered view is that Section 16(2) of the Advocates Act offends Article 14 of the Constitution. Even if judges will not say so, there is no objective criterion. Besides, it has not been either successful or popular in practice. Over the years, there have been instances of advocates being designated "senior" in some high courts who didn't deserve that designation. But what is far more pertinent is that young lawyers of proven ability and integrity were (and still are) often overlooked for promotion to senior status even when they deserved not to be overlooked!

In my view, Section 16(2) is now an anachronism and must be deleted. Let us have only one class of advocates, like the system uniformly adopted throughout the United States of America for more than 200 years. And if, for any reason, it is felt that the distinction between senior advocate and "other advocates," as it exists, needs to be retained, then in my view, Section 16(2) needs to be reworded so that seniority in the legal profession is assessed *objectively* simply by the number of years of practice at the Bar, and not by the personal choice or opinion of a majority of judges. If one has been in practice continuously for, say, twenty-five years at the Bar, then that advocate is entitled to the designation of "senior advocate" simply because that advocate has achieved seniority in fact by continuous practice. Subjective assessment of merit must not be left to the opinion of judges, not if our profession is to be reckoned as a truly independent profession.

There is yet another problem with Section 16(2). If it remains on the statute book, we will be perpetuating a scandalous case of male chauvinism!

It looked innocent in the year 1961 because of Section 13 of the General Clauses Act of the vintage year 1898, which proclaimed, in a century of male domination, that in all central acts, words importing the masculine gender shall be taken to include females. But remember that in the year 1898, when the General Clauses Act was enacted, women were not admitted to the Bar, either in England or in India! This provision is innocent no longer—not in the year of grace 2021, not in a year in which the United States Senate voted 51-49 to approve of the appointment of Indian-American civil rights lawyer Vanita Gupta as associate attorney-general of the United States, making her the first person of Indian origin to occupy the third-highest position in the US Department of Justice. In any event, over sixty years after the enactment of the Advocates Act, 1961, I believe it is fitting that we insist that not only should gender-neutral language be used in speech, but it must also be used in statutes as well!

Next, let me offer a few home truths. The current legal system that we operate under the Advocates Act overvalues the lawyers' interests at the expense of the litigating public. When we discuss the Advocates Act and its provisions, do please remember that the practice of law is a privilege; we all must earn it to be worthy of it. And we can only earn it if we remain efficient and competent.

When one flies at great heights in jet planes, one frequently encounters patches of rough weather even when the skies are clear—the sort of weather that an airline pilot cautions passengers to expect at rare altitudes. It is called "high-altitude turbulence." Men and women who practice law in India and many parts of the common law world are passing through a similar phase—a patch of high-altitude turbulence. It is an unsettling disturbance caused by the extreme pressure of public expectation about the role of the legal profession and the disappointing response of its members and their incapacity to perform as expected of them.

This was not so when we began with our Constitution in 1950. The legal profession is the only profession or calling to be mentioned in a written Constitution. Article 22(1) of the Constitution of India proclaims: "No person who is arrested shall be detained in custody without being informed of the grounds for such arrest" and then goes on to most usefully add: "Nor shall he be denied the right to consult and to be defended by a legal practitioner of his choice." This was the confidence that the founding fathers had in members of the Indian legal profession. But let us ask ourselves: "Have we fulfilled their expectation?" I am sorry to suggest we have not. At least not in the perception of the public at large.

In this part of Asia—India, Pakistan, Bangladesh (countries that share the same common Anglo-Saxon heritage)—many people, many reasonable people, many intelligent people, go to advocates with about the same degree of hesitation as they go to public hospitals. They go only because they have to! The reason for this is that they believe that the legal profession is no longer proficient, that it lacks integrity, that it is far too costly, and it does little to serve "WE THE PEOPLE," the first three words of our Constitution.

This belief is also shared elsewhere. In a book published in the United States[75], the author Walter Olson has no kind words for lawyers. The largest number of lawyers in the world in one single country is found only in the USA. "Often greedy, nasty, and obscenely parasitical, those who run the litigation industry have helped sour social life and sap the efficiency of commerce. All this might be acceptable if America's rampant litigiousness produced more justice. But it has not. Irresponsible and ill-willed neighbours and corporations still behave just as badly. Only now they hire more lawyers to help them get away with it." And in a hard-hitting speech to the American Bar Association, a former chief justice of the United States reminded his audience of what society expects of lawyers. "The entire legal profession—lawyers, judges, and law teachers—has become so mesmerised with the stimulation of the courtroom contest that we tend to forget that we ought to be *healers of conflicts*. Doctors, in spite of astronomical costs, still retain a high degree of public confidence because they are perceived as healers. Should lawyers not be healers?" he rhetorically asked. To be effective in a developing society, especially in catering to the needs of the underprivileged, advocates need to cultivate this healing touch.

Yet another thought. The third decade of the twenty-first century has begun to make great demands on the legal system, and this calls for new approaches and innovative responses. Even for their traditional functions, lawyers continue to be needed principally because modern lawmakers just do not have the time to think or reflect, and lawmakers now only enact complicated laws rather than simple laws. And complicated law is a new challenge for us advocates—*an incentive to be better equipped than before.* Prof. Weeramantry (of Sri Lanka), a distinguished judge who sat for many years on the International Court of Justice, raised disturbing questions about the law in the wake of technological and social changes in his book, *The Slumbering Sentinels*. Its cover depicts the bench and Bar in varying postures of sleep or slumber against a backdrop of a computer readout! The passage that has relevance for all of us reads:

> "Science and technology have burgeoned in the post-war years into instruments of power, control, and manipulation . . . But we lawyers are out of our depths, our concepts out of touch, our techniques are ineffectual. Sociologists, philosophers, economists, environmentalists, ecologists, and even politicians

> have sensed some of the dangers and prepared for them. However, we lawyers have been slow to do so, hampered by outdated concepts and methods."

The transition from the role of the slumbering sentinel to that of the sentinel on the *qui vive* is difficult and arduous. But if the legal profession in India, as we know it, is to survive, we all must awaken to the realisation that those who need our help and tap our competence must not find us wanting.

Decades ago, when passing through the international airport in Copenhagen, I saw a large sign that is still there: "The earth is moving at 105,441 km per hour. So, keep up." There is no reliable information as to the speed at which the world of law is moving. But all that I can say with some degree of certainty is that at the rate at which it is moving, the vital problem for us advocates now is *keeping up.*

8

GST: Unlocking India's Potential[76]

My views on the GST (Goods and Services Tax) are structural, hence all about its constitutional aspects. However, before dealing with GST, let me place the topic in its proper perspective and setting because it was something neither thought of nor contemplated either in the Constitution of India 1950 or in the hundred-odd amendments thereafter.

Article 1 of India's Constitution declares that India is a union of states, and this characterises India as having a federal form of government. "Federal" simply because it conforms to the definition in the dictionary. In *The Oxford Dictionary*, "federal" is defined as that form of government in which two or more states constitute a political unity while remaining independent in their internal affairs, and "federalism" is the advocacy of this principle. Yes, ours is a federal republic, but with a distinct centrist bias since the message upfront in the Preamble of our Constitution is to "uphold the unity and integrity of India." The Union of India today consists of twenty-eight states and eight union territories. But this is only after some strategic manoeuvring on the part of the government of the day, by which the large erstwhile state of Jammu and Kashmir (that included Ladakh) has been cut down to size and remains divided into two separate union territories of Jammu and Kashmir and of Ladakh.

This Constitution of ours was divided into twenty-two parts, and after a spate of as many as 105 constitutional amendments, it (quite surprisingly) continues to remain divided, even today, into twenty-two separate parts! Here, I am primarily concerned with two of those parts—Chapter 1 of Part XI (Legislative Relations) and Chapter 1 of Part XII (Finance).

Chapter 1 of Part XI sets out the legislative relations between the union and the states, and the principal provision in it is Article 246, which sets out the subject matter of laws to be made by parliament and the subject matter of laws to be made by state legislatures. Parliament has exclusive power to make laws with respect to the subjects referred to in the Union List, i.e., in List 1 of the Seventh Schedule, and this power also includes the power to make laws with respect to taxes, duties, and rates that are mentioned in items 82 right through to item 92B in the Union List. The power also extends to making laws with respect to taxes on the sale or purchase of goods; "goods" not being exhaustively defined in Article 366 but inclusively defined as "including all materials, all commodities, all articles (Article 366[12])."

Article 246 doesn't end there. It then goes on to provide that every state legislature has the *exclusive* power to make laws for the state (or any part thereof) with respect to matters enumerated in the State List (i.e., List II of the Seventh Schedule). And that power also includes the power to make laws with respect to taxes, duties, and rates, but only those set out in items 46 to 63 of List II.

There is also a Concurrent List in the Constitution—List III—where parliament (and subject to parliament having exclusive power to make laws with regard to matters in the Union List), the state legislatures also have the power to make laws with regard to matters enumerated in List III in the Seventh Schedule (a common list called the Concurrent List). But, and this is a very important "but," in List III (in the common list), there are no matters at all relating to taxes, duties, or rates.

With the liberalisation of the economy in 1991, the tax regime in India experienced manifold problems. In August 1991, the Government of India appointed a committee under the chairmanship of Prof. Raja Chelliah (1922-2009), a distinguished economist who is referred to as the "Father of Tax Reforms." This committee recommended, for the first time, the introduction of "taxable services" leviable at a flat rate of five per cent from July 1994 till May 2003 (subsequently enhanced from year to year to up to fifteen per cent in June 2017). Only three types of taxable services were included, viz.:

i. To an investor by a stockbroker in connection with the sale or purchase of securities on a recognised stock exchange.
ii. To a subscriber of a telephone connection.
iii. To a policy holder by an insurer carrying on general insurance business.

And the taxable service was leviable only by the Union of India. The Finance Act 1994 also made detailed provisions (Sections 65 to 96) for the levy and collection by the Union of India of this restricted taxable service.

In the year 2003, by a constitutional amendment, Article 268A was added in the Constitution as to how service tax levied by the union was to be collected and appropriated by the states, but it has now become surplusage and 268A is now deleted under GST. Entry 92C was then inserted in the Union List in the Seventh Schedule by the Constitution 88th Amendment Act, 2003 (expressing an intention to tax a wide range of services), which never materialised because the enforcement date for "tax on services" was never notified. *India was not ready for a general service tax regime*. But in the chapter on "Finance," there were, and there still are, two very important articles which you must know. They are basic to all schemes of taxation.

First, Article 265, which says that no tax shall be levied or collected except by authority of law. In England, the principle of tax *without representation* goes back to the reign of King John in England, to the Magna Carta of the year 1215! This principle of no taxation without representation is embodied up front in Article 265. Under our Constitution, not only the levy but also the collection of tax must be under the authority of some law, and the procedure for doing this is provided for in Articles 110, 117, 123, 199, 207, and 213.

The levy cannot be by mere resolution of houses of parliament or of state legislatures, nor by executive action, nor by any administrative instruction. It can of course be imposed by subordinate legislation but only if there is express statutory authority in the statute for the charge. Again, the words "without the authority of law" in Article 265, mean without the authority of a valid law. An invalid law or an unconstitutional law or a law enacted by colourable use of legislative power will not justify the levy or collection of a tax. And also note that there can be no intendment in the levy of a tax. It has to be specifically levied by a clear statutory provision. So, in India, whilst there can be a purposeful construction of a legislative provision, there can be no purposeful interpretation of a provision imposing a tax—a very important constitutional concept.

The power to tax is an essential attribute of sovereignty, but at the same time, no pecuniary burden can be imposed by whatever name except under clear and distinct legal authority because the imposition of a tax is both a sovereign as well as a constitutional function. Before GST, i.e., before 1 July 2017, residuary powers of legislation (including on taxation) were only with parliament. The residuary powers clause in the Constitution is Article 248, which states that "parliament has exclusive power to make any law with respect to any matter not enumerated either in the State List or in the Concurrent List." And this power specifically includes the power of making any law imposing a tax not mentioned in either the Union List or the State List.

Now comes the change with GST, i.e., with the Constitution 101st Amendment Act from 8 September 2016, but effectively only from 1 July 2017. In Part XI (legislative relations between union and states) in Chapter I, Article 246A is now added, and the marginal note reads (special provision with respect to Goods and Services Tax) "goods and services tax" is now specifically defined in Article 366 (12A) as meaning any tax on the supply of goods and services. The goods and services tax now levied, i.e., GST is no longer a tax on the sale or purchase of goods. The opening words of Article 246A are important: "Notwithstanding anything which is already contained in Articles 246 and 254." Therefore, not only parliament but every legislature of a state also has the power to make laws with respect to GST—a tax that can be imposed both by the union and by the states. Except that parliament retains to itself the exclusive power to make law with respect to GST where the supply of goods and/or of services or both takes place in the course of inter-state trade or commerce.

"Services" is now defined in the constitutional definition provision (Article 366). It says that services mean anything other than goods, and "anything" means anything under the sun. To take an absurd example, both parliament and state legislatures could conceivably tax the cutting of hair on a man's head in a hair-cutting salon (it would be a service tax). And they could, if they so chose, also tax the accumulated human hair in the hair-cutting salon, which would be considered "goods" because human hair in bulk has a market. Hence, a tax on hair as goods could conceivably be imposed. Of course, neither hair cutting nor human hair when cut is taxed at present, and it likely won't be taxed in the foreseeable future. But extreme examples serve to illustrate the breadth of the GST provision, as services now could include anything other than goods.

Also note that with the provision now introduced, India still remains a federal republic. And this is because nowhere in the world is there a set theory of federalism; its concept and practice vary in different democratic political systems in different countries and even within the same political system at different times. This is why in the United States of America, the world's oldest democracy, one of the associate justices in the court, Justice Hugo Black, who served from 1937 right up to 1973, always emphasised in his judgements that whenever he wrote on federal questions, he was speaking about *our* federalism! Federalism in the US and in India are different simply because "federalism" in the Constitution of India is *our* federalism!

As for what should be covered under the new Article 246A (special provision with respect to Goods and Services Tax), this is to be determined by the Goods and Services Tax Council, set up under Article 279A in Chapter I of Part XII (Finance). How the council is to be constituted and who will be its members is also provided for in Article 279A. The IGST Act and CGST Act now provide that the union government is to act on the recommendations of the GST Council. This is to be interpreted with reference to the purpose of the enactment, which is to create a system of uniform taxation. GST was introduced because earlier, different states could provide different tax slabs and different tax exemptions. It is the GST Council as a body that has to make *recommendations*, a word deliberately used[77], and these recommendations are directed to the union and the states, i.e., to parliament and the state legislatures. The recommendations cover a wide range of topics, viz.:

a) the taxes, cesses, and surcharges levied by the union, the states, and local bodies which may be subsumed in the goods and services tax;
b) the goods and services that may be subjected to, or exempted from the goods and services tax;
c) principles of levy, apportionment of Goods and Services Tax levied on supplies in the course of inter-state trade or commerce;
d) the limit of turnover below which goods and services may be exempted from goods and services tax;
e) and above all, and very importantly, the rates including floor rates with the bands within which the goods and services tax is to be levied. The current bandwidth will keep changing on the recommendations of the council.

The GST Council is also required to make recommendations on any other matter as it may decide. In particular, the council must also recommend the date on which the GST should be levied on a certain specified set of products, viz.:

1. Petroleum crude
2. High-speed diesel

3. Motor spirit (or petrol)
4. Natural gas
5. Aviation turbine fuel

Above all, for discharging its manifold functions, the GST Council has to always be guided by "the need for a harmonised structure of goods and services tax and for the development of a harmonised national market for goods and services" (Article 279A[6]). This is the mantra that the council must follow.

As to how voting will take place in the council, it has been provided that one-half of the total number of members will constitute a quorum.

- Every decision of the Goods and Services Tax Council is to be taken at a meeting, by a majority of not less than three-fourths of the weighted votes of the members present and voting, in accordance with the principles set out.
- And the Goods and Services Tax Council must determine all other matters of procedure in the performance of its functions.
- And because every decision of the Goods and Services Tax Council is a recommendation, i.e., to say an advice not binding on either the centre or on any of the states, the Goods and Services Tax Council is empowered to, and therefore, must establish a mechanism for the adjudication of any disputes between the Government of India and one or more states or between two or more, states i.e., disputes arising out of the recommendations of the council (this is Article 279A(11).

This last provision, which is contained in Article 279A(11), would have been unconstitutional, but fortunately, through some fortuitous foresight, our founding fathers, while providing in Article 131 that the Supreme Court of India is to have the exclusive original jurisdiction in all and any disputes between the union and the states and between states inter se, had realised that conditions may change. Hence, Article 131 was made to begin with the words: "subject to the provisions of this Constitution . . ."

Hence, the provision now made in Article 279A(11) and (12) that the GST Council shall establish a mechanism for the adjudication of any disputes between the Government of India and one or more states arising out of the recommendations of the council shows clearly that such a mechanism would not trench upon the exclusive jurisdiction and powers of the Supreme Court of India under Article 131 as it opens with the words "subject to the other provisions of the Constitution."

As mentioned above, Subclause (11) of Article 279A also shows that the recommendations of the council are not by themselves binding, even though they are made through *decisions* reached by the requisite majority. Hence, the states are free to raise disputes, even though the particular recommendation was made by a majority of the council. And the reason given in a judgement of May 2022 of the Supreme Court of India is that this is the essence of "cooperative federalism."[78]

There are also some consequential matters that are provided for by the Constitution (101st) Amendment Act, 2016, in respect of the tax collected by the union and by the states under Article 246A. One of the special provisions in Article 279A is for the GST Council to recommend the date on which the GST is to be levied on certain specified items (petroleum crude, high-speed diesel, motor spirit, i.e., petrol, natural gas, and aviation turbine fuel). The other consequential matter that is provided for, in respect of the tax collected by the union and states under Article 246A, is that the taxes collected by the union under Clause (1) of Article 246A are to be distributed between the union and the states in the manner provided in Clauses (2) and (3) of Article 270. The manner of distribution is already set out in Article 270, and it is important to note that the taxes collected do not form part of the Consolidated Fund of India, and distribution has to be as per the recommendations of the Finance Commission—a body set up under our Constitution under Article 280—which provides for the setting up, from time to time, a Finance Commission whose recommendations are required to be laid before each house of parliament under Article 281 of the Constitution.

Here again, the recommendations of such a high-powered body are almost always treated with due deference by parliament and state legislatures, but they are never bound by them. Hence, as a direct consequence of GST (i.e., as a direct consequence of Article 246A):

- The taxes *subsumed* at the central level would be Central Excise Duty, Addl. Central Excise Duty, Service Tax, Central Sales Tax (levied by the centre and collected by the state), Addl. Customs Duty (or Countervailing Duty), and Special Addl. Duty of Customs;
- And the taxes *subsumed* at the state level would be State Value Added Tax/State Sales Tax, Entertainment Tax (except when levied by local bodies), Octroi, Entry Tax, Purchase Tax, Luxury Tax, and taxes on lottery, betting, and gambling.

To have the whole GST system backed by a robust IT system, parliament has set up the Goods and Services Tax Network (GSTN), which provides front-end services and will also develop back-end IT modules for states that choose the same.[79]

GST is unique because it provides for the concurrent exercise of taxing powers by the centre and the states on the same subject—an unprecedented measure. Both the centre and the states are to act in tandem based on the GST Council's recommendations. Another consequential change due to the introduction of GST is that the nature of the restriction already imposed on tax on the sale or purchase of goods under Article 286 gets changed. Before the advent of GST, Article 286 provided for tax on the sale or purchase of goods where such sale or purchase takes place outside the state. These words are now substituted, and Article 286 now reads that "no law of a state shall impose or authorise the imposition of tax on the supply of goods or of services or both where such supply takes place outside the state, or in the course of import of the goods or services or both into or export of the goods or services or both out of, territory of India." And so, with its rephrasing, Article 286(2) will now require the formulation of fresh principles by parliament as to when a supply of goods or services or both, in any of the ways now altered in Article 286(1), are to be provided for.

There is another consequential provision, viz. although parliament has power under the 1950 Constitution to increase any of the duties or taxes in Articles 269 and 270 by a surcharge for purposes of the union (i.e., taxes on the sale or purchase of goods and taxes on the consignment of goods and levy and collection of goods and services tax in the course of inter-state trade and commerce), please note that parliament does not have the power to levy a surcharge for purposes of the Union for GST levied under Article 246A. And yet parliament enacted the Goods and Services Compensation to States Act, 2017, and the validity of this tax, i.e., a cess has been upheld!

The distribution of revenues between the union and the states is now governed by a special provision. Article 269A (2), (3), (4), and (5) now provides:

2. The amount apportioned to a state under Clause (1) shall not form part of the Consolidated Fund of India.
3. Where an amount collected as tax levied under Clause (1) has been used for payment of the tax levied by a state under Article 246A, such amount shall not form part of the Consolidated Fund of India.
4. Where an amount collected as tax levied by a state under Article 246A has been used for payment of the tax levied under Clause (1), such amount shall not form part of the Consolidated Fund of the State.
5. Parliament may, by law, formulate the principles for determining the place of supply and when a supply of goods, or of services, or both takes place in the course of inter-state trade or commerce.

I have already mentioned that by the Constitution 88th Amendment Act, 2013, taxes on services levied by the Government of India were to be collected and appropriated in the manner provided for in

Article 268A. However, this being now surplusage, Article 268A has been deleted by the Constitution 101st Amendment Act. The taxes, including taxes on services, are now to be apportioned between the union and the states in the manner provided for in Article 269A. As a consequence of GST, the definition clause of Article 366 has been broadened, and in clauses 12A, 26A, and 26B of Article 366, new definitions are added. In particular, Clause 366(12A) now defines "goods and services tax" as "a tax on the supply of goods and services except on the supply of liquor for human consumption." And once the GST regime gets stabilised, it is expected that "petroleum" may also be included (petroleum products are already there)[80]. Article 366(26A) now defines "services" as anything other than goods, which ensures that no activity remains outside the taxable net. Article 366(26B) defines "state" as including union territory.

Lastly, there is a matter of supreme importance: pursuant to the power to tax under Article 246A, parliament passed the "Goods and Services Tax Compensation to States Act, 2017." If this act was not passed, or if the cess imposed by this act, when challenged, was not upheld, the entire edifice of GST would have collapsed. It was what I would call the "sweetener" for the Constitution 101st Amendment going through and being effectuated, which was conceived and pushed through by the wisdom and eloquence of the late Arun Jaitley, the then finance minister. This Act of 2017 has empowered the central government "to generate resources to compensate states for five years for any loss of revenue suffered by them on account of the implementation of goods and services tax" and therefore "imposed a cess to be levied, as recommended by the GST Council, over and above the goods and services tax on that item."

The act was challenged as unconstitutional since the cess levied under this act was in addition to the tax on goods and services (a case of deliberate double taxation). Fortunately, it has been upheld by the Supreme Court of India. And to justify the levy of cess, the Supreme Court described it as an "increment to Goods and Services Tax." And it can be said with some degree of confidence that GST would not have seen the light of day but for this incentive.

9

On Special Leave Petitions

This is a difficult subject but an important one, as one can never be precise or certain about the contours of a Special Leave Petition (SLP), which is provided for in Article 136 of the Constitution, except to say that it should be read along with Article 142, which empowers the Supreme Court of India, in the exercise of its jurisdiction, "to pass such decree or make such order as is necessary for doing complete justice in the cause or matter pending before it . . ." It's a power not given to any other court in the country.

To me, the most expansive and *comprehensive* elucidation about SLPs (special leave petitions) is to be found in two leading judgements that were reported during the first five years of the commencement of the Constitution on 26 January 1950 (Article 394).

First, the judgement in the first case *The Bharat Bank Ltd.* vs. *The Employees of the Bharat Bank Ltd.* was delivered on 20 May 1950 by a Constitution bench of the Supreme Court, which consisted of Chief Justice Harilal Kania[81] and Justices Fazl Ali, Patanjali Sastri, Mehr Chand Mahajan, and B. K. Mukherjea (along with Justice S. R. Das, the six justices had all been sitting judges in the Federal Court of India, established under the Government of India Act, 1935). Each of the justices delivered separate judgements stating that Article 136 was "very wide," and one of them, Justice Mahajan, a future chief justice of India, also elaborated on how wide it was:

> "The article occurs in Chapter IV of Part V of the Constitution: 'The Union Judiciary.' The article deals with the establishment

and constitution of the Supreme Court. Article 131 confers original jurisdiction on this court in certain disputes arising between the Government of India and the states, etc. Articles 132 and 133 deal with the appellate jurisdiction of the court in appeals from high courts within the territory of India in civil matters. By Article 134, a limited right of appeal in criminal cases has been allowed. The Judicial Committee of the Privy Council, which was the highest court of appeal for India prior to 10 October 1949, was not a court of criminal appeal in the sense in which this court has been made a court of criminal appeal under Article 134. It could only entertain appeals on the criminal side in the exercise of the prerogative of the king. Article 135 empowers this court to hear all appeals which under existing laws could be heard by the Federal Court of India. By the Abolition of Privy Council Jurisdiction Act, 1949, which came into force on 10 October 1949, all the powers that were possessed by the Judicial Committee of the Privy Council in regard to cases or matters arising in India became exercisable by the Federal Court of India, whether those powers were exercisable by reason of statutory authority or under the prerogative of the king. The powers of the Judicial Committee were conferred upon it by the Judicial Committee Act, 1844 (7 and 8 Vict., C. 69). Appeals lay to His Majesty in Council from judgements, sentences, decrees, or orders of any court of justice within any British colony or possession abroad.

Closely following Article 135, which confers all the powers of the Judicial Committee on the Supreme Court, comes Article 136. The language employed in this article is very wide and is of a comprehensive character. The powers given are of an overriding nature. The article commences with the words: 'Notwithstanding anything in this chapter.' These words indicate that the intention of the Constitution was to disregard, in extraordinary cases, the limitations contained in the previous articles on this court's power to entertain appeals. These articles dealt with the right of appeal against final decisions of high courts within the territory of India. Article 136, however, overrides that qualification and empowers this Court to grant special leave even in cases where the judgement has not been given by a high court but has been given by any court in the territory of India. In other words, it contemplates the grant of special leave in cases where a court subordinate to a high court has passed or made any order, and the situation demands that the order should be quashed or reversed even without having recourse to the usual procedure provided by law in the nature of an appeal, etc.

The word 'order' in Article 136 has not been qualified by the word 'final.' It is clear, therefore, that the power to grant special leave under this article against an order of a court could be exercised with respect to interlocutory orders also. Another new feature introduced in Article 136 is the power given to grant special leave against orders and determinations, etc., of any tribunal in the territory of India. This word did not find a place in the Judicial Committee Act, where the phrase used was 'a court of justice.' It is the introduction of this new expression in Article 136 that has led to considerable argument as to its scope.

Another expression that did not find a place in the Judicial Committee Act but has been introduced in Article 136 is the word 'determination.' A question has been raised as to the meaning to be given to these words in the article. On the one hand, it was contended that the words 'determination' and 'tribunal' were introduced in the article in order to bring within the scope of the appellate jurisdiction of this court all orders of tribunals of different varieties and descriptions. On the other hand, it was said that the words 'determination' and 'tribunal' were added in the article by way of abundant caution, and the intention was that if a tribunal exercised the judicial powers of the state and the decision was passed in the exercise of that power, this court, as the highest judicial court in the republic, would have the power, if it considered necessary in the ends of justice, to grant special leave. Clause (2) of Article 136 excludes the jurisdiction of this

> court in respect of military courts or tribunals. It is interesting to observe that in Articles 138, 139, and 140, the Constitution has conferred powers on parliament for further enlargement of the powers of this court."

In the *Bharat Bank case*, having first decided that the SLP was maintainable against the final decision of an industrial tribunal appointed under the Industrial Disputes Act, 1947, the judges held by a majority (4:1) that the case was not one in which they would admit the appeal on the merits! Thus, the petition for special leave was dismissed.

The judgement in the second notable case, *Durga Shankar Mehta* vs. *Thakur Raghuraj Singh and Ors.*, was handed down a few years later (and is reported in AIR 1954 SC 520). In it, the Supreme Court of India had been approached by way of an SLP under Article 136 of the Constitution. And the challenge was to a decision of an election tribunal in Jabalpur which was appointed under the provisions of the Representation of Peoples Act, 1951. It held that an election to a double-member legislative assembly constituency was wholly void under Section 100(1)(c) of the Representation of Peoples Act, 1951. A preliminary objection was raised to the SLP by the respondents, who contended that no special leave petition lay against the decision of such a tribunal in view of the specific provisions laid down in Article 329(b) of the Constitution—a provision that ousted the jurisdiction of *all* courts in election disputes. Stressing the supremacy of the provision contained in Article 136, the plea that there was no jurisdiction to entertain the SLP was rejected by a Constitution bench of five judges, consisting of Chief Justice Mehr Chand Mahajan[82] along with Justices B. K. Mukherjea, Bose, N. H. Bhagwati, and Venkatarama Ayyar. On this occasion, Justice B. K. Mukherjea delivered the judgement of the court (please see the enlightening footnote on this judge[83]). The judgement stated: "In the first place, Article 136 is a constitutional provision which no parliamentary legislation can limit or take away. In the second place, the provision being one which overrides ordinary laws, no presumption can arise from words and expressions declaring an adjudication of a particular tribunal to be final and conclusive, that there was an intention to exclude the exercise of the special powers." However, on the merits, the Supreme Court disagreed with the decision of the tribunal and set it aside, holding: "The result, therefore, is that in our opinion, the contention of the appellant succeeds. We allow the appeal in part and modify the order of the election tribunal to this extent that the election of respondent No. 2, Vasant Rao, only is declared to be void; the election of the appellant, however, will stand. We make no order as to costs of this appeal." So much for special leave petitions.

Having appeared in the courts for several decades, if I am asked as to when a special leave petition would be granted, I could never answer this with any degree of accuracy. The answer would be: "It all depends." One can never be sure. It all begins with the judge taking the oath (or affirmation) of the office as is set out in the Third Schedule of the Constitution. And, frankly speaking, it all ends there! The relevant part of the Third Schedule reads:

> "I ________________________ have been appointed a judge of the Supreme Court of India, do swear in the name of God --and solemnly affirm that I will bear true faith and allegiance to the Constitution of India as by law established, that I will uphold the sovereignty and integrity of India, that I will duly and faithfully and to the best of my ability, knowledge and judgement perform the duties of my office without fear or favour, affection or ill-will and that I will uphold the Constitution and the laws."

In short, upholding the Constitution and the laws is briefly what a judge of the Supreme Court of India is expected to do. As to in what manner he or she does it, that is left to the conscience and discretion of the individual judge. It can never be prescribed and hardly ever be predicted. But the oath of office that a judge takes serves, at all times, as a constant reminder: *never to cross the line!*

Here, I recall a true story related to me many years ago by a friend who was then an advocate-on-record. In May 1972, he had briefed (on behalf of his client) the distinguished and spectacular C. K. Daphtary in a special leave petition (SLP) which was to come up before Court No. 1, comprising a bench presided over by then Chief Justice S. M. Sikri. Sitting with him was to be another judge, Justice Dwivedi from Allahabad, who had just been appointed a judge of the Supreme Court of India and was to be sworn in that very morning by the chief justice. Daphtary did not attend the brief oath-taking ceremony in Court No. 1 and preferred to stand outside on the veranda, puffing away on his pipe! With the ceremony over, the advocate-on-record rushed out to inform his senior counsel that the new judge had been sworn in and that the bench would shortly reassemble for the day's work. The conversation that then ensued between the senior counsel and advocate-on-record was as follows:

CKD: "Did you attend the entire oath-taking ceremony?"
AoR: "Oh yes, sir."
CKD: "Did you hear the new judge swear and say that he would uphold the Constitution and the laws?"
AoR: "Oh yes, sir."
CKD: (With a straight face) "In that case, my dear fellow, your SLP will be dismissed. You have no case."

I suffered a somewhat similar fate in the thirty-ninth year of my law practice in the courts, when I appeared before a bench of the Supreme Court of India presided over by Justice A. P. Sen (he sat as a judge in the Supreme Court of India from 1978-1988 and was one of my favourite judges at the time). When my SLP was called, I opened my argument by saying: "My Lords, the *important* point of law in this SLP is . . ."

But before I could formulate the point of law, the response from the bench was devastating: "Mr Nariman, the only important point in this case is that you are appearing for the petitioner. SLP dismissed." Alas, I regret to inform all budding advocates that such is the fate of many (if not most) SLPs under Article 136!

Section V
ARBITRATION

1

What Next for Arbitration?[1]

What next for arbitration? Cocktails and conversation, if I may say so rightly because modern-day international commercial arbitration is too complex, far too complicated and exceedingly costly for being talked about over soft drinks. You need a couple of stiff ones before clearing your throat and talking about it.

The problem today is that life is getting more and more difficult for arbitrators in international commercial arbitration which includes international investment arbitration. The decisions of arbitral tribunals are not only in the public domain, but they are also published, talked about, and criticised. The verdicts of tribunals of arbitrations are almost like the off-the-cuff reaction of umpires on the cricket field when faced with an appeal of "How's that!" Modern cricket umpires on the field are now exposed to the cruel gaze of millions of television viewers and their frailties are found out instantly. With the help of an advanced digital computer system known as Hawk-Eye, all appeals in cricket are decided instantly, but not too sportingly, by the third umpire. There is no longer any prevarication about the question: "Would the ball have hit the wickets if it had missed the batsman's pads?" Or the inevitable other question: "Did the bat of the batsman running to the wicket cross the line before the bails were removed?" The umpire on the field is too often overruled by the third umpire who sits in the cool shade. The technological eye of the third umpire is proving more accurate than the human eye of the umpire on the field.

I foresee for the future some similar technological benchmarks with reference to which awards in arbitrations can be graded with Hawk-Eye precision for *rationality, fairness,* and *justness!* They need to be. The most critical factor in all international arbitration of course is how arbitrators shall be chosen. As the hackneyed phrase goes, "the jury is still out" on how to ensure that the best possible person is appointed as chairman of an arbitral tribunal. Egalitarianism has taken over and appears to be the order of the day.

The trend is for an increasing number of arbitrators from different countries around the world (as arbitrator or as chairman-of-tribunal) because it is hoped and expected that this would help build Third World confidence in international commercial arbitration and international investment arbitration. Fair enough! But my esteemed friend, Jan Paulsson, arbitrator emeritus, thinks otherwise. He once spoke at a gathering on "Ethics and Elitism in Arbitration." He said to his audience that it was a mistake to think that it was a good thing for the international arbitral process if the greatest number of persons possible had the opportunity to act as arbitrators, and he ventured to suggest that given the high stakes and great sensitivities involved in all types of international arbitration, there was a good case for supporting the emergence and recognition of *an elite corps of international arbitrators.*

However, his speech was not at all well-received by his audience. When sending me the text of it, Jan wrote in the margin: "Fali, have you ever been jeered at, at the end of a speech? I have and if you read the following pages, you will see why!" So, it is quite clear that general public sentiment is that we must be more democratic, more liberal in the choice of arbitrators. If so, then, as a "what next," I suggest we consider a change from the present system of challenges to arbitrators.

Under the applicable arbitral rules or ad hoc practice around the world, the current system of a challenge to the *independence* or *impartiality* of an arbitrator (or of the chairman of an arbitral tribunal)—elitist or otherwise—is loaded, far too loaded, in favour of the arbitrator challenged. My experience has been that it is just not possible to get rid of an appointed arbitrator (or chairman of the arbitral tribunal) because of some reliable information in the possession of the challenging party which it simply cannot be proved in a court of law, and therefore, cannot even be revealed!

At present, there must be some "good reason" (not suspicion) that the person already appointed is not likely to be impartial—which is an almost impossible task. But from ICSID, there comes good news. Challenges to appointed arbitrators under the ICSID regime have been far more successful in recent years than in the past. In a trilogy of cases decided by the chairman of ICSID, known as *Blue Bank*[2], *Burlington*[3], and *Caratube*[4], all decided in the last few years, challenges to the independence of appointed arbitrators have succeeded by applying not the established standard of high probability of bias but of a much lower standard of "reasonable doubt." And this was hailed in an article in the fifteenth-anniversary issue of the *Asian Dispute Review*: "It seems reasonable to surmise that the return to a lower standard (of 'reasonable doubt') as the threshold for disqualification is an institutional reaction to what are, at their core, calls for greater accountability in the investor-state arbitration system." We definitely need more calls for greater accountability both in international commercial arbitration and in investor-state arbitration!

One of the topics of discussion in this subject is on "Rise in Investment Treaty Arbitration." I would suggest a change in the title so far as India is concerned: "Towards a Fall in Investment Treaty Arbitration" is more appropriate for India because the Indian experience has been far too painful to bear repetition.

We in India have been badly bitten by investment treaties which had been signed with a flourish on the dotted line as photo-ops for India's representatives. Much rethinking about and rewriting of bilateral investment treaties is needed. I would advise avoiding BITs. They have not helped, and they will not help the Indian economy. We are better off without them. So far, there have been only invitations to financial disaster for India and the developing world.

BITs oblige governments to conduct their relations with foreign investors in a transparent fashion. If so, reciprocal if not identical, obligations lie on the foreign investor, too, one of which is the obligation to make investments in accordance with the host state's domestic law. But this never happens. As is often observed "respect for the integrity of the law of the host state is a critical part of international investment law."[5] But my experience has been that such observations are neglected and not applied to whatever case there is at hand. This is because international investment arbitration has not—not as yet—gained Third World[6] confidence though it has gained third-world recognition.

The French anthropologist Sauvy, in an article in a French magazine way back in August 1952, had coined the term Third World referring to countries that were not aligned with either the Communist Soviet block or the capitalist NATO block during the Cold War. Sauvy wrote: "This Third World ignored, exploited, despised like the third estate, also wants to be something."

The non-aligned world is dead but the term "Third World" is now used interchangeably with least developed as well as developing countries. The most constructive criticism of BITs has been from that liberal and prestigious international weekly *The Economist.* In one of its issues a few years ago, it characterised the Investor-state dispute settlement Regime (ISDS) as "The Arbitration Game." It made the following comments:

1. That multinationals have exploited woolly definitions of "expropriation" to claim compensation for changes in government policy that happen to have harmed their business.
2. That the rise in contentious arbitrations is only because companies or corporations have now learnt how to exploit arbitral clauses, even going as far as buying off firms in jurisdictions where they do not operate, only to gain access to them.

3. That the secretive nature of the arbitration process and the lack of any requirement to consider precedent allows plenty of scope for "creative adjudications."

Strong words, some of them being harsh, but as Lord Keynes famously said: "Words ought to be a little harsh because they are an assault on the thoughts of the unthinking."[7]

Is all this criticism valid? Are these onslaughts on the "thoughts of the unthinking" justified? I believe they are. But if the view is that BITs have come to stay, the next question to ask is whether the investment treaty regime can be improved. I believe it can be and my suggestions are:

1. Clauses in BITs must not be simply replicated from some model generally offered by the home state. They must be seriously negotiated at arm's length between the two states—the home state and the host state)—and when necessary, with the assistance of those competent and familiar with treaty-making.
2. The absence of a level playing field disables the developing host state from making an effective defence to investors' claims in arbitration. Even if the BIT, as signed, ensures more protection to investors in the host state without any (or hardly any) compensating safeguards for the latter, when a dispute arises, efforts must be made to establish equality in arbitration. (And this suggestion is for the particular attention of those who are called upon to arbitrate disputes.)
3. We must explode the myth about the infallibility of international arbitral tribunals; they are fallible, and we must acknowledge that they are sometimes—not often but definitely sometimes—biased and we must provide adequate safeguards against this.
4. Since an award rendered by an international investment arbitral tribunal is final and binding, and since recourse

> against it (on merits) is not presently available in courts of law (either under the New York Convention or under UNCITRAL or ICSID), there is a felt need for provision being made in the treaty (BIT) itself for an appeal or at least an agreed internal mechanism. To enable the arbitral tribunal to review its own award—at the instance of a party aggrieved, e.g., the correction of obvious and patent errors, or even for correction of errors not so patent. After all, arbitrators, like judges, are human!

❁

Now, a few words about how to conduct a transnational arbitration. In the absence of any universally recognised standard-setting body, the practical aspect of how international commercial arbitration is conducted depends very much on the composition of the arbitral tribunal. Statutes and conventions do lay down general principles (arbitrators must be quick and free of bias, respect the limits of their authority, treat both parties with equality, and give each of them equal opportunity to present their case), but rules of arbitral institutions give arbitrators a very wide discretion as to how facts are to be proved and how contracts are to be interpreted. And let's face it: parties from different cultural backgrounds often feel short-changed or unfairly treated about matters like cross-examination, discovery of documents, statements of witnesses, calling of experts, and as to how the applicable law is to be proved. As my friend Rusty Park has put it: "Parties from different cultural backgrounds (that are not Western) are sometimes made to feel they are playing American football and British Rugby at the same time, never knowing whether or when the ball can be thrown forward.[8]

So, the question is not what are the due process *sine qua nons,* but whether the arbitral tribunal is sensitive to, and prepared to accommodate, cultural differences of the parties, or even amongst members of the same tribunal. How should a mixed arbitral tribunal function when it comprises members reared in different legal disciplines and with different cultural backgrounds? The answer is that it can and must function only in a spirit of collegiality and accommodation.

About speed, over the years, American judges have discovered a good way to stop long-winded lawyers. They sit in court with a stopwatch, setting a time limit of say ten or fifteen minutes for the lawyer on each side to argue the case. I have witnessed a court proceeding in Washington where, in the midst of a heated argument, the judge interrupted to say: "Mr Murphy you have two minutes left. Would you rather take it now or wait to take it in reply to your learned friend." At this, Mr Murphy sat down mid-sentence. It is much more effective to take those precious two minutes in rejoinder to rebut the argument of the other side.

I have often wondered, if the same thing were to happen in arbitration, viz. setting of time limits by arbitrators, how would American, English, or Indian courts react to the plea that one of the parties was hustled and was therefore "unable to present his case" in conformity with due process. Of course, I have not seen any American or Indian arbitrator setting time limits, but surely this is where we must consider whether ample due process does not impede speedy arbitration even in one and the same Anglo-Saxon cultural tradition. I have not investigated how strict time limits under the modern court system in the US were introduced, but we keep learning from different cultures. And I can tell you that certain countries in the continent of Africa would not be surprised if such strict time limits were pre-set by arbitrators for being observed by the parties.

Amongst certain tribal communities in the continent of Africa, when there are disputes between two groups, they all go before the chief who sits on a throne covered with a lion's skin. He listens to the spokesperson from each side. But the rule is that the spokesperson can speak only as long as he can say what he wants to on one leg; the moment that leg comes down, his time is over. In fact, there is a story, probably apocryphal, about one smart guy from a tribe who had the benefit of a school and college education. He tried to be too smart. The rule said that he must argue and present his case whilst standing only on one foot, but the rule did not say on which foot. So, this wise guy said what he had to say on his left foot, and when his left foot got tired, he put it down and began arguing on the right foot and so on. But retribution is swift in African customary law. Infractions of unwritten rules are looked upon far more seriously than transgression of written arbitral rules. It is said that the wise guy paid for being too smart with an award of 20 lashes!

Quite seriously, this is not entirely the case when "legal cultures collide." So, how does one comport oneself in other places and at "other times, other manners" as the famous Irish novelist Oliver Goldsmith used to say? In the matter of the impartiality and independence of arbitrators in international commercial arbitration, we have now the IBA guidelines with three of the principal colours of the rainbow. But cultural approaches in different parts of the world make it impossible to prescribe a worldwide standard. There is, for instance, a rule in the arbitration law of the People's Republic of China, which is not found in the arbitration laws of other countries. It stipulates that an arbitrator must recuse himself or withdraw from an arbitration not only where he or she is a close relative of the party or has a personal interest in the case, but also where "the arbitrator has privately met with the other party or his agent or even accepted an invitation for entertainment (including dinner)." This is as per Article 34(4) of the Arbitration Law of the People's Republic of China 1994. This only goes to show how important appearances are amongst some people and in some societies! And apart from the rules, *your* arbitrator and *my* arbitrator having a convivial meal together is definitely not viewed with great favour in this part of the world. Surely one of them (the one who didn't pay the bill) must have been bought over.

Whatever the varied cultural differences in different parts of the world, the majority of international arbitrations are conducted in English. Arbitral awards are also written mainly in English. English is the language, of this century or at least for another twenty-five or fifty years. Hence, to all arbitrators, I would recommend that they be proficient in the language they know because of their familiarity with the varied shades of meaning of words, and they must always mind their language!

There is much misunderstanding in arbitration when cultures clash. I recall a case concerning a senior colleague of mine from ICCA years ago, the famous Swedish Judge Nils Manguard. He was extremely soft-spoken and a man of great rectitude. But he got into serious trouble when he was sitting as a judge in the Iran-US Tribunal. On one occasion, the Iranians protested bitterly over what they considered to be very prejudicial remarks of Judge Manguard. It appears that during the hearing of a case before the Iran-US Tribunal, the judge was heard to say (quite softly) that he was shocked to hear about the execution of judges in Iran. This led to howls of protest from the Iranian advocates and complete confusion was written on the face of the judge, who said (again softly) that he had been misunderstood and that he was only complaining about the execution of judgements (in Iran), not the execution of judges. But no one would listen to him and the matter ballooned into a diplomatic incident. The dispute became so serious that everyone concerned lost their sense of balance and humour, and this dispute (as to what Judge Manguard really said) had to be referred to the arbitration of a judge from the Netherlands. Unfortunately, that gentleman too had no sense of humour. Instead of bringing both parties to their senses and getting the minor misunderstanding amicably settled, he solemnly proceeded with the arbitral proceeding and produced a fifty-page award in which he concluded that Iran had not proved its case.

The moral of this story is that an arbitrator must speak up and make himself understood to the parties whose main language is not English. And don't do the converse, as some of my English friends do. Don't show off in French if you are English speaking. Don't forget the story of the former British Prime Minister Tony Blair, who, during an official visit to Paris, decided to flatter his host, the then French prime minister. He meant to say how much he admired Lionel Robert Jospin in many ways. But after he had spoken, his audience was simply appalled because what he actually said, in French, was that he desired Jospin in so many different positions. The moral of this story is always to stick with the language of communication you are used to. Don't experiment and never show off in a lingo whose idioms you don't entirely comprehend.

The expression "due process" does not mean the same thing as fairness even on the two sides of the Atlantic. Standards of fairness vary in different legal climes. In his 2002 Freshfields Lecture, my friend Prof. William (Rusty) Park, professor of law at Boston University, recalled a conversation with his former law student, working in a large New York firm, who was about to file a request in his first ICC arbitration in Paris. With complete sincerity, a student asked Rusty Park if it was true that the ICC Rules did not provide what the student described as "even the most basic guarantee of pre-trial fairness." By this oblique reference, he meant the right to full US-style discovery. "How can we prove our claim," he asked, "without knowing what documents the other side has?"

Prof. Park's wry but pertinent comment was: "My dear fellow, your counterpart on the continent of Europe would have quite different expectations, anticipating that no claimant would commence arbitration without first having evidence." Good advice from an experienced arbitrator: Never commence an arbitration, not even an ICC arbitration, unless you first have evidence to substantiate your claim. Unless of course, your client is like the one in the story from India about Sir Dinshah Mulla, privy councillor and India's foremost jurist in the 1930s. A solicitor wanted advice on whether his client should file a suit. So, he marched off with his client to consult with Mulla, gave the facts, and Mulla shook his head and said, "No, no, no."

"But what if we put it this way?" the solicitor persisted.

Again, the shake of the head: "No, no, no. There is no case."

But the solicitor would not give up: "Sir Dinshah suppose we say this . . ."

Now Sir Dinshah Mulla was firm, but he wasn't stupid. He could see that the solicitor desperately wanted his client to file a suit. So, he said: "Tell me, Pochkhanawalla, is your client a sporting chap?"

The client, who was present, chipped in, "Yes sir I am a sporting chap."

"Then fire away," said Mulla. The client fired away and filed the suit which was ultimately dismissed with costs. As a result, he was down Rs. 30,000, which was a very large sum of money in those days!

So don't let your client get into the "sporting chap" syndrome when he suggests an international arbitration. Give good legal advice and before taking the first step, negotiate. And only when negotiations fail, embark on the risky and costly experiment of arbitrating.

V. V. (Johnny) Veeder, a district judge of the US District Court, once put the following question at a session: "What is more important to an arbitration than the impartiality of the arbitrator?" Let me suggest that in some places that are not in the Western world, what is considered more important even than impartiality and independence *is the state of the arbitrator's mind.* My friend and one-time colleague on the ICC Court, Toshio Sawada, once showed me a specially tailored arbitration clause that he had come across in Japan, and since it was in the local language, he also helpfully translated it for me. He assured me that the clauses, given below, are not a product of his imagination. They were actually negotiated and agreed to in a construction contract executed by a Japanese party with a German engineering firm many years ago, and they provided for contingencies that no arbitration clause has ever provided for. When cultures collide, we must live and learn. Let me give you some of the clauses for your enlightenment:

1. Should either party come to feel that the arbitrator is insane for reasons it comes to know after the commencement of the arbitration, it may consult with the other party, and should both parties agree that the arbitrator is likely to be insane, they shall serve a notice of doubt on the arbitrator.

"Causes giving rise to a notice of doubt" must be extreme and not be limited to continuously making senseless remarks, absentmindedness, and queer conduct such as dancing alone in public without cause, and the parties may serve a notice of doubt only once during the arbitration.

2. On such notice of doubt being served, the arbitrator may not refuse medical examination by a psychiatry specialist at one of the hospitals listed in Appendix 1 appended to and made a part hereof.
3. If in the opinion of the psychiatry specialist, the examination would require more than four weeks or if the specialist is unable to conclude that the arbitrator is positively insane, then the arbitrator shall be deemed to be not insane. The medical examination shall be at the parties' cost and shall be conducted on the condition that the result will be made known only to the arbitrator and the parties.
4. If the arbitrator is found insane, he shall resign, in which event, he shall not be entitled to the fee for the services he will have rendered, but each party shall pay to the arbitrator a get-well fee of 100,000 yen and one-half of the disbursements covering the amount the arbitrator will have expended in connection with the arbitration. If the arbitrator is found not insane as the result of the examination, the parties shall jointly provide him with a letter of apology and each party shall pay a so-sorry fee of 1,000,000 yen to the arbitrator which he may treat as damages for tax purposes. The arbitrator, however, may not count the time spent for the medical examination as time spent for arbitration.
5. While the provisions of these clauses are not intended to permit the parties to take the arbitrator to the hospital by dint of force, it does not bar the parties from initiating the judicial proceeding for removal of the arbitrator. Such proceedings may be resorted to only where the arbitrator refuses to subject himself to the medical examination or where the

> parties are not satisfied with the findings of the psychiatrist that the arbitrator is not insane. If the parties initiate judicial proceedings and fail to remove the arbitrator, each party shall pay a nuisance fee of 2,000,000 yen to the arbitrator. During such proceedings, the arbitration may proceed, but the arbitrator may not render an award. If rendered, such an award may not be enforced.

William Shakespeare was right (as he always is) when he said: "There are more things in heaven and earth, Horatio, than are dreamt of in your philosophy." With such detailed sanity clauses in place, international arbitrators face the prospect of being compensated with a get-well fee or a so-sorry fee or a nuisance fee, even when they do not perform their arbitral function. Despite all this, the future of arbitration is bright, perhaps only because the future of litigation is not. An English judge, who did not wish to be quoted, once famously said: "Litigation is an activity that has not markedly contributed to the happiness of mankind." If arbitration is not to suffer the same fate, I would suggest that arbitrators around the world raise their sights and adopt a culture-conscious transnational outlook.

At a conference I attended in Geneva some years ago, in response to the question of how to conduct a trans-cultural international arbitration, the given answer was: "Like you make an omelette." The ingredients differ in different parts of the world; breaking the eggs is the only common factor. The same goes for differing procedural expectations.

A countryman of mine found during a trip to London that he had a severe toothache. So, he went off to a Harley Street specialist. The doctor took one look at the offending tooth and told him: "I can relieve you of your pain by extracting your tooth. It will take me just 3 minutes, but it will cost you 300 pounds."

"300 pounds for 3 minutes," said my Indian colleague, doubling up with more pain.

"Well," said the dentist, "I could also do it slowly."

Hence, let me end with a plea to the world's international arbitrators: Never use due process as an excuse. Whatever the provocation for God's sake, *don't do it slowly!*

Now let me apprise you about the ethics in arbitration.[9] I have a book in my library, *The Doubter's Companion: A Dictionary of Aggressive Common Sense*. It has two pages on ethics. I have provided the opening and concluding paragraphs of the book below.

As per the opening paragraph: Ethics "is a matter of obviously practical concern described glowingly in universal terms by those who intend to ignore it." The concluding paragraph says: "Ethics being a matter of practicality needs to be included in our systems so that citizens can treat them as they normally would as a standard aspect of everyday life."

My own experience in the school of hard knocks, which we call life, is that ethical goals are good only to assuage the conscience of those who have a conscience. They have no effect on people who have none. That is why corporate codes of ethics have been tried so often and have failed. And I predict that the same fate awaits the fifth, sixth, and seventh Schedules added by Parliament in the Arbitration and Conciliation Amendment Act, 2015 because ethics is not only good but essential.

But codes of ethics, by whatever name they are called, are neither good nor essential. The problem today is that life is getting more and more difficult for arbitrators in international commercial arbitration which includes international investment arbitration. The decisions of arbitral tribunals are not only in the public domain, but they are also published, talked about, and criticised. The leading US Supreme Court case, *Commonwealth Coatings Corp.* vs. *Continental Casualty Co.*, 393 U.S. 145 (1968), was decided way back in 1968. In this decision, Justice Hugo Black, writing for the majority, suggested that the test of arbitrator impartiality should be at least as strong as what judicial ethics requires of judges (or even greater since arbitrators decide fact and law, usually without right of appeal). Justice Byron White whilst concurring with the result suggested that arbitrators should be held to a different standard from judges because as he put it "they are men of affairs, not apart from, but of the marketplace, and may be chosen particularly because of their interests in the business world (and not because they are Article III judges)."

On the facts presented in the case *Commonwealth Coatings*, Justice Abe Fortas, dissented and said he would not have overturned the arbitration award at all (where it was discovered after the fact that the arbitrator had had substantial business dealings with one of the parties) because the arbitral award by the tribunal of three was unanimous and there was no showing of "actual bias." (Fortas took a different approach from Justice Black and Justice White.) These three articulations of arbitrator *conflicts of interest* remain with us today, with Justice White's formulation of a "different" arbitral standard (from judicial conflicts of interests) being the most dominant (on a "party-consent" theory of arbitral choice).

2

Reviving the Spirit of Arbitration: Lessons from the Past, Directions for the Future

Let me tell you at the start that at my age, when I am pushing ninety-two, it is like searching for something in particular in a crammed drawer and not finding it. Very occasionally, something else falls out at the back of the drawer and engages your attention. It was in this chatty way that, back in the year 2010, I recalled some episodes from my life, making comments along the way on men and matters. This was in my autobiography *Before Memory Fades*, now in its twenty-seventh reprint. However, now in 2021, my sense of recall has considerably dimmed. Yet, certain events from the distant past I do recall quite vividly, and one of them is that we still have a long way to go in international arbitration.

Way back in 1983, in Paris, at the sixtieth-anniversary celebrations of the ICC Court of International Arbitration, I was an eye-witness to a clash between a distinguished proponent and an equally distinguished opponent of international arbitration. During one of the sessions, Judge Howard Holtzmann (arbitrator emeritus from the United States), confident that he was expressing a widely accepted view, stressed the idea of the judge and arbitrator being "partners in a system of international justice." But Judge Keba Mbaye (then president of the Supreme Court of Senegal, later a judge of the International Court of Justice, and also its president) refuted him. He said that the notion that there is a system of international justice will not be shared by some countries notably those in Africa, Asia, and Latin America who still see arbitration as a "foreign" judicial institution imposed upon them. Mbaye recalled the hostility of African courts to arbitrators manned by foreign tribunals and added: "As everybody knows, arbitration is seldom freely agreed to by the developing countries. It is often included in contracts of adhesion, the signature of which is essential to the survival of these countries."[10] He also complained (at the time, a valid complaint) that developing countries were rarely the venue of international arbitration, and, even more rarely, produced arbitrators.

Keba Mbaye was a jurist with a vision. At the Paris Conference, he expressed the hope that international arbitration would gradually gain Third World acceptance and ultimately secure Third World confidence. His hope has been fulfilled, at least in part. There is now Third World acceptance of international arbitration. However, international investment arbitration has not as yet gained Third World[11] confidence. There are critics from the First World as well as others whose criticisms are documented and are in the public domain. Besides this, most cases that stood at one time, it seems have been wiped out due to a fading memory. But I do remember some of these cases which had an impact:

1. *Yukos Capital* vs. *Rosneft* and its sequel. It is a case that has set the cat among the pigeons in international arbitration. Four awards aggregating to 13 billion roubles in favour of Yukos Capital by the International Court of Commercial Arbitration of the Russian Federation were set aside by the courts in Moscow but their enforcement in the Netherlands, which had been initially denied, has been upheld, and even the suspension of these awards, pending final decision, has been tentatively denied (following the advocate-general's opinion). It is expected that the highest court in the Netherlands will ultimately enforce these awards.
2. Decision of the Supreme Court of the UK of 2020 in *Halliburton Company vs. Chubb Bermuda Insurance Ltd*,

2020, UK SC page 48, confirming the decision of the Court of Appeal to the effect that arbitrators have a legal duty to disclose all such matters which might lead to a conclusion that there is a real possibility that they are biased. This has become a leading case around the world on the arbitrators duty of disclosure.

3. Indian Supreme Court decision in August 2021, in *Amazon Holdings* vs. *Future Retail Investment* (2J) which has inferentially expanded the scope of the Indian Arbitration and Conciliation Act, 1996 by holding that an award delivered by an emergency arbitrator under the Arbitration Rules of the Singapore International Arbitration Centre (SIAC Rules) could be assimilated as an interim measure of protection under Section 17(1) of the Arbitration and Conciliation Act, 1996 and so acted upon by an Indian court.
4. *GE Energy Power Conversion France* vs. *Outokumpu Stainless USA* of October 2020, reported in 140 SC 1637, in which the US Supreme Court has unanimously held the New York Convention permits non-signatories to International Commercial Arbitration Agreements to compel recourse to arbitration on the basis of domestic law.

I have often been asked for my tips for aspiring arbitration lawyers. My first tip which I recommend strongly is: speak well! Arbitration advocates' bread and butter may be their written submissions, but we do have to speak as well and distinctly. Bruce Lee once said that he was not afraid of a man who practised a thousand different types of punches just once, but he did fear the man who practised a single type of punch a thousand times. The reason for me saying this is simple: if you want to build up your arbitration practice, then begin with practice. As the saying goes, practice makes perfect. The more exposure you have in terms of the volume of work with arbitration, the faster you will learn the procedure and the greater your scope for learning the myriad of questions of law that may come up in an arbitration scenario.

Moreover, keep your eyes open and learn general skills. Do not shy away from seeking out and asking questions from the luminaries in the legal field who not only have a good grasp on arbitration law and practice but on other fields of law as well. Arbitration is a very client-oriented and competitive industry. It is not just about your client's instructions to you, but also about what the client really wants in terms of the big picture and their wider strategy. Try and anticipate their needs because it helps not having to ask them questions at every turn. When in doubt, ask yourself WWTCD? (What would the client do?) That is the "know yourself" part. Knowing your enemy is not just helpful but vital. Anticipate their arguments, their actions, whether strategic or tactical. What are their motives? What are the reasons they have pressed for such and such claim? Why have they filed this misc. application?

Hence, the first important thing you do upon becoming an advocate, whether in court or before an arbitral tribunal, is to improve your knowledge of and proficiency in the English language. This you must do by reading and absorbing the great pieces of writing in English literature. This is not in order to make you anglicised. Far from it. It is to give you an opportunity to establish yourself and be successful in the legal profession because the law in India is, and will remain, English in origin.

Now my suggestions.[12] My earnest plea to all who administer international commercial arbitration is that they strive towards an arbitral regime that rekindles the spirit of arbitration, best encapsulated in that very evocative phrase *"l'esprit de l'arbitrage."* I was ignorant of what that phrase connoted. Some years back, I turned to my friend Michel Gaudet, honorary president of the ICC Court of International Arbitration, for enlightenment. Michel Gaudet[13] was the living embodiment of all that is good and wise in arbitration. He explained: "The dominant feature of arbitration is mutual understanding so as to be able to solve the conflict that has occurred. The aim of arbitration is not to draw from the applicable law a decision against the parties involved but to clarify, together with the parties, what should be done in a given situation to achieve justice with cooperation. (This is what I expect from arbitration, whether commercial or diplomatic, national or international.) Achieving this process requires all along that all participants are inspired by '*l'esprit de l'arbitrage*.'" Simply, but most effectively put!

Now for some regrets. There is just far too much law in international commercial arbitration and far too much disputation about law. The acronym ICA has become almost indistinguishable from litigation, which it was once intended to supplant. The legal baggage with which international commercial arbitration is weighed down has continued to increase over the years. And the mills of this arbitration have been working full-time with learned articles in arbitration journals, magazines, newsletters, and particularly in books which have grown both in weight and in size. The ICCA Yearbook 1976 made its appearance with a slim volume of 250 pages. It has expanded in the past four successive years to 1,100 pages per volume!

The 1999 edition of Fouchard Gaillard and Goldman's *International Commercial Arbitration* is most informative but also very bulky, with 1,280 printed pages bound in hard covers. It is richly annotated with the ratio of hundreds of court decisions around the world and splattered with extracts from and references to scores of international arbitral awards. All of this is (of course) most rewarding for us lawyer-arbitrators. But I wonder whether it is the function of private arbitral awards to develop international jurisprudence. The private nature of arbitration, I would submit, is inconsistent with any law-making function. All that should matter at the end of the day is that the arbitral tribunal in each case has reached a result that commends itself as just. ICA has lost that lightness of touch that had characterised its early manifestations.

Reasoned decisions—whether majority, concurring, or dissenting—are now increasingly long and turgid and much too full of legal learning. If private awards were intended for the parties alone (as they are), they ought to be brief, with the conclusions and main reasons being presented in a simple format. But unfortunately, some of us "players" in international arbitration have been "muddying the waters" and I do not exclude myself from this criticism. We are increasingly tempted to address a much wider audience, expecting to create something that will form part of a body of "legal opinion," and we are driven to a more and more elaborate composition.[14]

Far too often these days, an award will quote or cite from other awards rendered in what is stated to be a similar fact-situation, ignoring the wise caution offered by England's Lord Chancellor (way back in 1901) in the case of *Quinn* vs. *Leatham* (a leading case familiar to us all). He advised that every decision must be read as applicable to the facts proved and not as an exposition of the whole law on the subject; that every case in which expressions of law are to be found must be read as qualified and conditioned by its own peculiar facts.

Cedric Barclay was a doyen amongst English commercial arbitrators. He was particularly renowned as a maritime arbitrator. I had the privilege of knowing him personally and occasionally working with him. In his lifetime, he made some trenchant comments on the disquieting features of modern international commercial arbitration. For instance, his remarks, made way back in 1981, are even more relevant today than when he expressed them:

> "Arbitrators do not have to imitate the courts. Commercial justice can be dispensed without the turn of phrase and the logic, which is expected from the Court of Appeal. The AAA and the Commonwealth Associations have survived without giving of reasons. The short and concise decisions, which we have given hitherto, were much superior to the essays in jurisprudence which the ICC and others deem appropriate. Our function is to decide, not to teach. It is a fallacy that the publication of awards will teach others something. More often, it leads to confusion and equivocation. Look at this bundle of 1,500 reasoned awards. How many have we learnt from? It is not the motivation which one abhors, but the endless expositions and padding which we find infiltrating our system. Brevity is the essence of wit; justice needs no adornment."[15]

In this twenty-first century, Cedric Barclay's distilled wisdom has fallen on deaf ears. What we find in the first twenty years of the new millennium is a tidal wave of "arbitral law" which has become too precedent-bound in practice (even though arbitral awards are not judgements of courts). The spirit, the ethos, has gone out of international commercial arbitration. It has been transformed into what the late Sir Michael Kerr once characterised as "international disputology."[16]

Twenty years ago, Howard Holtzman, former judge of the Iran-US Claims Tribunal (and later international arbitrator; he was also editor of the authoritative *Guide to the UNCITRAL Model Law*), offered the following advice to the community of lawyers practising international commercial arbitration: "We must avert the fate of the dinosaur."[17] And Michael Mustill (formerly a judge in the House of Lords, and later also subsequently arbitrator emeritus) spoke in the same vein but said in his own inimitable style: "Nobody has yet discovered why the dinosaurs became extinct, but it is a reasonable summarise that their bulk was a significant factor, and it would be a pity if arbitration went the same way. This is unlikely to happen but it is at least worth asking whether a course of slimming might be in order."

The danger is that ICA, as a forum of dispute resolution, has become so overburdened by its own weight and size that it is being supplanted by other speedier, more fruitful, and more rewarding methods. The alacrity with which over fifty-odd sovereign states around the world have signed on to the most recent convention (the Singapore Convention 2020) on mediated settlements is a pointer that perhaps all may not be too well with ICA. Users of international commercial arbitration are neither organised nor vocal (as are NGOs in the field of human rights) and therefore, they do not intrude upon that growing sense of complacency that appears to have overtaken us international arbitrators about our own work and performance, which is somewhat, reminiscent of what was once said at a Lord Mayor's banquet, way back in the year 1936, by England's then Chief Justice Lord Hewart. Somewhat pompously, he informed his audience that: "His Majesty's judges are supremely satisfied with the almost universal admiration in which they are held." Substitute "international arbitrators" for "His Majesty's judges" and you will get the current view of arbitrators on arbitrators!

Lord David Pannick, who has written a controversial but delightfully entertaining book, *Judges*[18], after quoting England's chief justice of 1936, says that it is difficult to believe that the universal admiration is at all reflected in the true feelings of many of the customers of Lord Hewart's own court! I suggest that if a study was undertaken about the "true feelings" of the customers of International Arbitral Tribunals around the world, the results may not be too flattering.

One more observation. International commercial arbitration is by no means the exclusive preserve of lawyers. In fact, the world of commercial arbitration is not premised on its participants possessing any legal qualifications. It is only in four (or five) out of the 164 or 165 New York Convention countries that there is an express legal requirement that an arbitrator must be a qualified lawyer.[19] The New York Convention of 1958, the Washington Convention of 1965, and the UNCITRAL Model Law of 1985 are all silent on arbitrators' qualifications. The only requirement is that the person appointed (as arbitrator) should be independent and impartial.

International commercial arbitration could certainly be helped along by lawyers. It has been so far (and very efficiently too), but it could benefit from inputs from others as well. Dr Robert Briner, former president of the ICC Court in Paris (when he was with us), recalled a construction case between an African country and a contractor from Continental Europe, in which the chairman was a former judge of the English Court of Appeal and his co-arbitrator was an English engineer. English counsel estimated that the examination and cross-examination of witnesses would last at least four weeks. However, this mixed tribunal was able to reduce the hearing schedule to twelve days, and it was the engineer-arbitrator who was able to successfully nudge parties to settle the entire case even before the hearing actually commenced.[20]

My submission is that the spirit of international commercial arbitration could be (and should be) revived in two ways (both cumulative): *First*, the "non-lawyer arbitrator" should be a much more frequent member of an arbitral panel (particularly in disputes requiring scientific expertise or some special type of technical knowledge). *Second*, every arbitral tribunal in international commercial arbitration should keep asking itself in every single arbitral proceeding as to what justice demands in the fact situation before it. Then it should inquire whether there is anything in the applicable law that would militate against the tribunal arriving at a just decision.

Lord Ackner (member of the judicial committee of the House of Lords) sat quite frequently with dear old Lord Denning and publicly acknowledged the influence of Denning's philosophy of law on him. He said that in every case that came before him, he put foremost, "The need to ensure the just result and therefore, to circumvent precedent if you can do it properly." He then set out what he thought was the right approach: "The right approach, I am sure, is—what does common sense indicate as the right result? Then, what are the relevant principles? And then what is the situation so far as precedent is concerned?"[21] (in that order).

3

In the Conscience of Every Arbitration, There Is a Mediator Who Is Asleep: How Do You Wake Him Up?[22]

Arbitration is no longer national; it is global. And GAR, like the BBC's music television programme, is the Top of the Pops! Over the years, it has witnessed as well as contributed to the progress and prosperity of international commercial arbitration. And international arbitration has now moved into fields that were once considered taboo.

I recall many years ago an old friend, Paul Gelinas, a former president of the International Law Commission of the ICC, intervening at one of the working sessions of the ICC court in Paris. He said: "In the conscience of every arbitration, there is a conciliator who is asleep, and we must wake him up." Well, thanks to the Singapore Convention (September 2020), the waking up has been done. Signed by as many as fifty-five nations (as of now), the international arbitrator is now expected to wear an additional hat: that of *settlement facilitator*. And in India, there is an encouraging sign. In December 2021, a comprehensive Mediation Bill No: XLIII of 2021 was introduced by the Government of India in the Rajya Sabha, with the statement of objects and reasons stating: "Mediation results in amicable resolution of disputes in civil, commercial, family, and matrimonial matters and fosters a collaborative approach, reduces the burden on the courts, and preserves relationships amongst disputants."

There is a growing body of opinion around the world that arbitration, both domestic and international, and even arbitration that is well conducted by competent arbitrators, is not necessarily the most successful way of resolving disputes, especially commercial disputes. Other ways have to be explored. Skilled mediators are now able to achieve results satisfactory to both parties, far beyond the power of lawyers, and even beyond the reach of courts. This is the way *sensible* people (and *responsible* corporations) resolve business disputes. And this is precisely why an enabling new chapter (Part III on Conciliation) was added to India's Arbitration and Conciliation Act, 1996, the only chapter in the Act that has so far not seen much activity.

I believe that there must be a constant attempt by arbitrators to invoke and apply Section 30 of the 1996 Act[23] simply because it encourages parties, at the very start, to get into a mediation-friendly frame of mind. Section (S.30) provides that with the agreement of the parties, the arbitral tribunal may "use mediation, conciliation, or other procedures at any time during the arbitral proceedings to encourage settlement." And the best way to "encourage settlement" is to initiate it. We all know that suits and legal proceedings in court get compromised, more often than not, simply because the presiding officer (the judge), who after familiarising himself (or herself) with what the case is all about, *suggests* and later *nudges* parties to an amicable adjustment of the entire case.

Twenty-five years ago, experienced arbitrators were inclined to be dismissive of ADR, taking the rather lofty view that whilst it would no doubt work well enough in family disputes, it was quite unsuited to disputes of a commercial character. That view has now proved to be misplaced. ADR is growing. Yes, it is expensive, but it is far quicker and much cheaper than litigation. Besides, attempts at ADR are generally successful, ending in some form of agreement. ADR is not constrained by strict legal rights or rules; it facilitates even non-legal forms of relief, such as the offer of a *substitute contract* to the aggrieved party (unthinkable in a traditional arbitral proceeding) or the *resuscitation of an agreement already terminated* (almost impossible to justify on strict legal principle).

The traditional purpose of arbitration always was that of accommodation, of compromise, of a third person giving a helping hand to parties to reach a just solution to the differences between them. But unfortunately, all this had been jettisoned in modern-day arbitrations (including commercial arbitrations) in the mistaken belief that mediation and conciliation was someone else's job, not the arbitrator's.

At the Millennium Conference of the Chartered Institute of Arbitrators in London (19 November 1999), the late Lord Mustill complained that we have now lost the culture of compromise! He was right. As a consequence, arbitration has lost its best ally. The use of different terminology ("arbitrator," "conciliator," "mediator") is suggestive of different and separate tasks to be performed, which is misleading. An arbitrator is an arbitrator is an arbitrator, whose function is not merely to adjudicate the dispute but also to help resolve it amicably with the cooperation of the parties. In my view, arbitration must never be considered as excluding from its purview, at any stage, the *settlement* of the dispute (which can only be effectuated by negotiation and mediation).

More than twenty-five years ago, in the United Kingdom, the pressure on parties to actively consider ADR was extended to all cases in the high court, following a Practice Direction issued by Lord Taylor, the then-Lord Chief Justice.[24] It required a solicitor in a high court action to sign and lodge with the court a checklist (with answers) that had the following three questions:

1. Have you or counsel discussed with your client(s) the possibility of attempting to resolve this dispute (or particular issues) by ADR?
2. Might some form of ADR procedure assist to resolve or narrow the issues in this case?

3. Have you or your client(s) explored with the other parties the possibility of resolving this dispute (or particular issues) by ADR?

One can find this Practice Direction reproduced in Vol.1 of 1995 *All England Reports.*

This Practice Direction was followed six months later by another Practice Direction, this time of the Court of QBD (Queen's Bench Division), in which the court "hoped that it might be possible to identify cases which might be susceptible to settlement by mediation" and requested that any party to an appeal who considered that mediation might be appropriate should notify the Registrar of Civil Appeals of that fact. Whilst the Practice Directions in the UK were careful to highlight the voluntary nature of the submission to an ADR process, the mandatory requirement of a checklist, recognises the professional duty of a lawyer to give thought to the suitability of ADR as a means of resolving the dispute. The willingness of the English courts to put their weight behind the active consideration of ADR processes at all stages of a dispute, up to and including the appellate stage, is now regarded (in the UK) as one of the more "welcome" developments in legal reform.

All this needs to be emulated by lawyers as well as by judges. But in India, it is not because arbitration in India has been, and continues to be, regarded in the way in which S.28 of the Indian Contract Act of 1872 said it should be regarded as an *exception* to litigation and not as an *alternative* to it. This has stuck in the Indian psyche. And alternative dispute resolution (ADR) is not yet ingrained in the Indian psyche. It is a new graft, like a transplanted heart or a newly implanted kidney. The legal system looks for an opening to reject it!

In some situations, solutions that are more imaginative could better meet the requirements of justice and the expectations of the parties as well. Consider the simplistic example of a dispute over an orange, an example offered by a highly competent and dedicated arbitration lawyer from Switzerland[25], Richard Hill, who has written in the *Arbitration International* about two persons who have a legitimate claim to an orange but neither of whom is willing to accept half of the orange. If the claim is to be resolved in accordance with a judicial paradigm (i.e., by arbitration), one of them will get some portion (possibly none) of the orange, and the other will get the remaining portion. But then, a mediator is called in who asks each person *what they intend to do with the orange*. The first person answers that she intends to use the rind to make perfume, while the second says that she intends to use the pulp to make orange juice. The mediation process yields a solution that is fair and better satisfies the expectations and interests of the parties than a solution based on an adversarial process!

Thus, the same subject matter of disputation between two parties can be dealt with in two different ways, not necessarily exclusive: *First,* by attempting to resolve a dispute in such a way that the parties involved win as much as possible and lose as little as possible through the intervention of a third party steeped in the techniques of mediation. *Second,* (failing this) the dispute would be left to be resolved by each party presenting its case before a disinterested third party with an expectation of a binding decision on the merits of the case: *a win-all, lose-all, final determination*!

However, the downside to all this of course is that a regime that permits arbitrators to act as settlement facilitators[26] is full of "occupational hazards." How far can one go? It is difficult to say. The uncertainty of decisions rendered by courts of law in criminal cases had once prompted an English judge to say that he did not know of any procedure under which someone could be told with precision just how far he could go before he may incur some civil or criminal liability, but what he could say with a degree of greater certainty was that: "Those who skate on thin ice can hardly expect to find a sign which will denote the precise spot where they may fall in."[27]

There are problems and pitfalls when (as the saying goes) the cobbler does not stick to his last. In other words, when the arbitrator steps outside his ordinary business of arbitrating and permits his attention to be diverted towards bringing parties to the negotiating table, it is difficult to recommend how best this should be done. If the arbitrator is old-fashioned ("a timorous soul"—Lord Denning's favourite description of judges who do not dare!), he may only suggest that the dispute could be more appropriately settled with the intervention of a third party and adjourn the arbitral proceedings for a brief period to enable parties to approach someone else as conciliator or mediator. But if requested by the parties to himself facilitate a settlement, he must move with circumspection, conscious that if the talks fail to produce an accord, it may be difficult for him to steer parties back to arbitration.

At the heart of the settlement-facilitation process is the caucus—a private discussion between the facilitator and each of the disputants. Discussions move to and fro, from one disputant to the other, with the facilitator exploring the perception, the prejudices, and the objectives of each party, in a free-ranging examination of the merits and the demerits of the dispute. Such discussions take place under a solemn commitment not to divulge any confidences and information without the specific authority of the parties. "Caucusing" enables the facilitator to comprehend the whole range of elements involved in the dispute and helps guide the parties towards an agreed resolution. But the dust raised by "caucusing" quite often undermines the confidence of one or other of the parties in the arbitrator who undertakes the dual task.

Way back in September 1998, at the seventy-fifth anniversary celebration of the ICC Court in Geneva, one of the subjects discussed was: Whether the same person could or should act as arbitrator and mediator. Different opinions were expressed and there were many learned speeches about Article 19 of the 1980 UNCITRAL Rules of Conciliation[28] and about changes in perceptions since then reflected in the then newly enacted arbitration laws of Hong Kong and India. But the comment that most appropriately described the role of the arbitrator as a settlement-facilitator came from the floor. Axel Baum, a well-known international arbitrator, said that an arbitrator and mediator were like two porcupines: “You know those seemingly useless of God’s creations that are full of sharp quills . . . that they can release when under attack. And do you know how porcupines make love?” But Axel Baum would not tell us how porcupines make love. He stopped short by saying: very carefully!

4

The Evolution of International Investment Law: Challenges and Opportunities

(The following is an inaugural address by Mr Fali S. Nariman delivered on 13.06.2022 [virtually] at the Conference of the Permanent Court of Arbitration [PCA] and the Ministry of External Affairs for a three-day training programme on Investment Arbitration, held from 13th June to 15th June 2022.)

Mr Justice Chandrachud, senior judge, Supreme Court of India; Mr Dammu Ravi, secretary, Ministry of External Affairs; my colleagues in India; ladies and gentlemen listening in, both here and abroad.

In contemplation and in intent, this three-day session is essentially a training programme and a joint initiative of:

1. The Permanent Court of Arbitration at the Hague (a body founded more than 125 years ago and still going strong), along with
2. The Ministry of External Affairs, Government of India (a body that traces its authority and origin to the Constitution of India, 1950).

And the topic is: International investment law—part of a much broader topic, viz., public international law.

Public international law, along with International Investment Law, consists mainly of treaties entered into between nation-states; treaties that lay down rules of conduct between sovereign nation-states. They are principally governed by what is now known as the Vienna Convention on the Law of Treaties, which consists of 89 articles drafted by the International Law Commission of the United Nations and approved at an International Conference held in Vienna in May 1969.

We are fortunate to have with us—virtually, of course—a most distinguished group of international lawyers to enlighten us on the subject of International Investment Law. And I am deeply conscious of an observation made many years ago by that master of the English language, Winston Churchill. He gave some preciously sound advice. In a speech at the Guildhall, this is what he said: "I advise you never, never talk about a topic to a group whose speciality is that topic."

Fortunately, this brief intervention of mine is not addressed to any of our distinguished experts; it is only for the benefit of the participants (the listeners). And there are nearly 200 of them: 80 of whom are officials in the Ministry of External Affairs, Government of India, located in Delhi, as well as different parts of India, and as for the rest, they are spread around the world—government officials in over 89 Indian embassies abroad!

What prompts me to deviate a bit from the distilled wisdom of Winston Churchill is not a sense of presumptuousness, but something that I experienced in Canada many years ago when my wife and I attended the seventy-second Biennial Conference of the International Law Association held in Toronto. At this conference, a former governor-general of Canada, Mrs Adrienne Clarkson, gave the keynote address and after she spoke, someone in the audience asked her for her views on international law. And her response was a one-liner. "International law has not achieved much but it is good that it is there."

As to the first part of Adrienne Clarkson's quip—"International law has not achieved much"—I would respectfully disagree.

In this globalised, interdependent world, the five principal Human Rights Treaties of the United Nations have influenced much law-making within nation-states around the world. When the European Union was still a distant dream, Lord Denning, sitting as Master of the Rolls in England's Court of Appeal, spoke about what he called "The European Treaty" with a piece of imagery only a Denning could conjure up. He said that, for England, the European Treaty was: "Like an incoming tide . . . It flows into the estuaries and up the rivers. It cannot be held back." So, it is with international law—it has influenced many post-Second World War constitutions. Article 51 of India's Constitution expressly stipulates that it is the fundamental duty of the state to foster respect for international law and treaty obligations. And it was the most enlightened of India's Judges, Justice Krishna Iyer, who in a celebrated judgment of the Supreme Court, almost compelled us citizens of India to live up to this ideal.

In India, in domestic law (or municipal law), the Civil Procedure Code of 1908 provides that where a court decree is for the payment of money, one of the modes of execution of that decree is by way of arrest or detention of the debtor in prison. One such debtor from Kerala, with the rather rollicking name of "Jolly George Varghese," owed his bank over seven hundred thousand rupees. Since he had no money to repay, the bank had him arrested under the relevant provision of the Civil Procedure Code and also detained him in civil prison. Courts in Kerala, including the high court, refused to give him any relief and it was only when he came to the Supreme Court that Justice Krishna Iyer carved out a constitutional niche for him. And this is how he did it.

India was, and is a party, to the UN International Covenant on Civil and Political Rights (ICCPR of 1966), one of the five UN treaties on human rights. Article 11 of this treaty provided: "No one shall be imprisoned merely on the ground of his inability to fulfil a contractual obligation." Invoking Article 21 of India's Constitution, which states "no person shall be deprived of his life or personal liberty except according to procedure established by law," the court—speaking through Justice Krishna Iyer—said that since international law laid down in Article 11 of the ICCPR 1966 said that a debtor could not be confined to prison simply because he was unable to pay his debts, it was not a *fair* procedure to deprive Jolly George Verghese of his personal liberty just because he did not have the means to discharge his contractual liability. Jolly George Verghese's constitutional right to personal liberty under Article 21 was solemnly upheld only because of the operation of international law.

Ever since this decision of the year 1980, international law in India has secured an undisturbed place for itself, almost equal to domestic law. As Justice Chandrachud mentioned in his opening address a few minutes ago, in recent times, domestic law and international law have become increasingly blurred. But as Lord Denning had said, the mixing of flows cannot be held back.

As to the second part of Governor-General Adrienne Clarkson's quip: "but it is good that it is there," it is self-evident, although as expressed, it does sound a bit patronising.

I prefer the optimism of the original editors of the International Law Reports, each of whom later became judges of the Permanent Court of International Justice (PCIJ)—the World War II predecessor of the precent International Court of Justice (the ICJ). They were Judge Arnold McNair and Judge Hersch Lauterpacht.

Way back in the year 1929, in the first volume of the International Law Reports, these judges recorded that there is more international law in existence than the world dreams of. And with an eye to the future, they also said: "It is more international law that this world needs." I believe they were right.

As to how investment treaties between state and state are to be enforced, I am afraid there is no globally enforceable treaty on foreign investment. Disputes can be and are often resolved inter-state—i.e., between states—by resort to arbitration, but as to whether an award made in such an arbitration can be enforced, and if so, by what means, is—as we common law lawyers put it—something on which the jury is still out. But hopefully, it is something on which our experts will enlighten us.

Sovereign states are viewed as independent autonomous entities, interacting within the state system. They are seen to behave like a collection of billiard balls moving over the billiard table and colliding with one another. The billiard ball model of world politics has two implications: *first,* that there is a clear distinction between domestic politics, which is concerned with the state's role in maintaining order and carrying out regulations within its borders; and *second,* that international politics is concerned with relations between and amongst states.

Sovereignty is the hard shell of the billiard ball that divides the outside from the inside. But over the years, relations amongst states in the modern world have come to be characterised by growing interdependence and interconnectedness. And the billiard ball model needs correction if the nation-states of the world are not to descend into international anarchy.

In the foreword to a book published by Kluwer in 1966, commemorating the fiftieth anniversary of the International Court of Justice, its then President (Judge Bedjaoi from the Middle East) wrote about the ICJ's genetic infirmity. He said that the court—the ICJ—carried with it *"a genetic heritage rendered vulnerable by the chromosomes of state sovereignty."* However—and this is significant—Judge Bedjaoi also paid tribute to the foresight and wisdom of the framers of the New York Convention for having recognized, way back in the year 1958, the primary importance of sovereign national courts, to whom its main provisions are addressed. The framers of the NYC saw long before anyone else had that the genetic heritage of national courts could never be ignored and that without the aid and assistance of local municipal courts, transnational arbitral awards could never be effectively enforced.

Before I conclude, I suggest that it will be useful for all you listeners and participants in this training programme to keep before you the 1969 Vienna Convention on the Law of Treaties. As I said before, it consists of 85 articles drafted by the International Law

Commission and approved at the conference held in Vienna in May 1969. It is easily available; it can be downloaded on the internet, and I recommend that you do so for a better understanding of the comments of our distinguished and honoured experts.

5

Challenge and Enforcement of Awards[29]

Let me begin this chapter with a story that reflects an almost eternal problem about modern commercial arbitration (domestic and foreign). It is one that my good friend, Arbitrator William Park ("Rusty Park") of Boston, USA, loves to tell. "There is a sign in the window of a shoe repair shop in downtown Boston run by a Greek immigrant who is fed up with customer complaints. So, he puts up a triangular sign outside his shop:

Δ

FAST SERVICE
(top of triangle)

LOW PRICE (at one end)	HIGH QUALITY (at the other end)

Underneath the triangle is the instruction in capital letters: "Pick any two." Rusty Park's message to the arbitration community is: Fast service, low price, and high quality—all three together are just unattainable in modern-day commercial arbitration! And this, despite the provisions of that most successful of UN instruments, the New York Convention, 1958, reproduced in Part II of our 1996 Act. And (also) despite the beneficent provisions of the UNCITRAL

Model Law of 1985 (now adopted or adapted by more than eighty countries around the world, including India) and reflected in Part I of our 1996 Act.

The Arbitration and Conciliation Act, 1996, has been amended a bit too frequently in 2015, 2019, and 2020. With the rest of the arbitration world left complaining that Indian arbitration law is a work in progress, I may add, a work in *slow* progress.

A study was conducted not so long ago by the Global Centre for Dispute Resolution (which is affiliated with the AAA [American Arbitration Association]) in order to ascertain what was *the* most important element in all commercial arbitration. After getting the views of as many legal practitioners as possible, as well as of as many parties to commercial arbitration as possible, on both sides (petitioners and respondents), the conclusion of this study was that between seventy-five to ninety per cent of those interviewed (and there were thousands) ultimately rated a just and fair result as the most important element in commercial arbitration above all other considerations like speed, cost, and finality. Of course, speed has already been taken care of by what, in my view, is the most useful amendment of all to our 1996 Act, though at the time when it was introduced, it was the most criticised by judges and lawyers. It provides that the award shall be made by the arbitral tribunal within a period of twelve months from the date of completion of pleadings before the tribunal, with power to the parties by consent to extend this period, but not beyond six months. As I mentioned above, it was widely criticised by lawyers and mostly by arbitrators themselves, and yet it is today the most progressive amendment that has ensured timely awards. And do you know who suggested the amendment? Not a lawyer, nor a judge. It was the present prime minister, Narendra Modi!

The *Times of India,* in its edition of Saturday, 28 August 2021, carried a report under the headline:

> "SC (Supreme Court) mulls young lawyers as arbitrators to cut costs.

> The spiralling cost of arbitration, once touted and vigorously promoted as the preferred alternative dispute resolution mechanism, on Friday (27 August 2021) forced the Supreme Court to seriously mull engaging young and competent lawyers as arbitrators instead of retired high court and apex court judges.
>
> Justice D. Y. Chandrachud informed the counsel appearing in the case that, 'The Bombay High Court has already devised a way for speedy completion of arbitration proceedings by appointing young, competent, and knowledgeable lawyers as arbitrators. They take it as an honour to be chosen by the high court. They conduct the arbitration proceedings smoothly and charge meagre fees.'
>
> Last week, Chief Justice N. V. Ramana opened the process for establishing an international arbitration centre at Hyderabad and had said it would be both an answer and assurance for international investors who had apprehensions about India's costly and time-consuming litigation process."

Note the emphasis on the present "costly and time-consuming litigation process" as well as the hope that young, competent, and knowledgeable lawyers will set it right. Fair-mindedness and proficiency on the part of arbitrators are the most sought-after qualities in all arbitrations. Of course, it is always difficult to draw arbitrary lines in the sand about completely independent arbitrators because if arbitrators are to be completely sanitised from all possible external influences on their decision-making, then, "only the most naive and incompetent would be available!"

I recall that the late Sir Michael Kerr, founder of the LCIA (and its first president), once told a senior colleague of his who had just been informed about his nomination as a party-appointed arbitrator: "My boy, steer a middle course between too much and too little independence." In commercial arbitrations, there is much tension between finality and fairness. Freeing awards from judicial challenge promotes finality, but embracing fairness calls for some measure (but not too much!) of court supervision. In all arbitrations, there are two sides: the winning side that looks for finality, and the losing side that invariably suggests judicial scrutiny of doubtful decision-making! So, arbitrators must constantly have sensitivity to these two overriding and competing concerns in all arbitrations—that of the "winners" and that of the "losers."

It is the prospect of judicial review in some limited form or the other that makes arbitrators far more responsible and accountable than they would otherwise be. The aim of all commercial arbitration is to ensure a fair and just result, but I regret to say that I am old enough to have seen and known of arbitral awards that are neither fair nor just. Sometimes they have to be read to be believed. But of course, no one will admit this because such awards are never *mine*, they are never *yours*, they are always *someone else's!*

I recall that in 1983, at a celebration of the 60th anniversary of the ICC Court of International Arbitration held in Paris, the great Professor Pierre Lalive, a grandfather amongst international arbitrators, described such awards as "lawless awards." Even if their number is not large, I venture to suggest that we should speak and write more about them, and much more frequently. Only then is there hope for improvement in the quality of awards in commercial arbitration. As with cricket umpires, national and international, life is getting more and more difficult for arbitrators, both national and foreign. Their decisions are not only in the public domain, but they are most widely published in a plethora of journals, most frequently talked about, sometimes applauded, more often criticised, somewhat like the off-the-cuff verdicts of cricket umpires when faced with an appeal of "How's that!"

However, nowadays, decisions of modern-day cricket umpires on the field are also exposed to the cruel gaze of the third umpire (who sits in the pavilion) and who, with the help of an advanced digital computer system known as Hawk-Eye (a system based on technology used in brain surgery), corrects the mistaken decisions of the umpire standing in the sun and ultimately comes to the right decision. In cricket at least, things have vastly improved as the Hawk-Eye system now claims definitively and accurately to answer the question: "Would the ball have hit the wickets if it had missed the batsman's pads?" My hope is that by the end of the present decade, we will have a somewhat similar technological benchmark with reference to which awards, both domestic and foreign, can be graded with Hawk-Eye precision for *rationality, fairness,* and *justness!*

As to how arbitrators or the chairman of an arbitral tribunal must be chosen, it has become critical and crucial, though in the prevailing climate of egalitarianism, it is difficult to determine how this can be best ensured. For instance, in foreign arbitrations, the modern trend is for an increasing number of arbitrators from different countries around the world to be chosen (as an arbitrator or as a chairman of a tribunal) since it is hoped and expected that this would help build Third World confidence in commercial as well as in investment arbitration! But whether the chosen persons are appointed from the First World or the Third World or partly from one and partly from the other, they must also possess an extraordinarily high degree of proficiency, knowledge, and competence, apart from possessing that all-important overarching quality of high integrity.

This brings me to the current system of challenges to arbitrators (under the Model Law), which is reflected in our 1996 Act. In my view, the arbitral rules and ad hoc practices to determine the independence or impartiality of an arbitrator are too heavily loaded in favour of the arbitrator challenged. It has been the experience of many, including mine, that it is just not possible to get rid of an appointed arbitrator or chairman of an arbitral tribunal despite there being reliable information in the possession of the challenging party (which only for want of proof), i.e., proof that will be acceptable in a court of law, invariably prevents such information from being even stated, much less revealed! At present, under Section 12 of the Act, there has to be "justifiable doubts" as to an arbitrator's independence or impartiality, if he or she is to be challenged, not just "reasonable doubt"—an almost impossible burden. And the dice are loaded.

Who decides as to the justifiable doubt? Section 13 gives the answer—the arbitral tribunal itself! This is in accordance with the UNCITRAL Model Law, which was prescribed most reluctantly, only to enable the award to be made in a reasonable time. But now that we have Section 29A inserted in the Act—award within twelve months, extendible only to eighteen months and no longer—it is time parliament took a fresh look at Section 13 and deleted the provision that the arbitral tribunal be made the initial arbiter in an application challenging the independence of an appointed arbitrator.

Elsewhere, however, there is good news, as the winds of change are blowing in the right direction. Recent challenges to appointed arbitrators under the ICSID regime (i.e., under the Washington Convention, 1965)[30] have been far more successful in the recent few years than at any time in the past. This is simply because in recently decided cases by the chairman of ICSID[31], challenges to the independence of arbitrators have succeeded only because of not applying the Model Law standard of "justifiable doubt," but of a much lower standard of "reasonable doubt."

The return to a lower standard of "reasonable doubt" as the threshold for disqualification is an institutional reaction to what, at its core, is a call for greater accountability in the entire arbitration system (domestic and foreign). And I welcome it. We definitely need more calls for greater accountability of arbitrators both in commercial arbitration (domestic and foreign) as well as in investor-state arbitration. And it was this that prompted the Law Commission of India, in its 246th report of August 2014, to propose the addition of a new subsection (2A) to Section 34: "Application for setting aside arbitral awards." It has since been made a part of the Arbitration and Conciliation Act, 1996. The English Arbitration Act, Section 69 of the 1996 Act, has gone even further. In England, legal errors (not just patent illegality) can also be corrected. Section 34(2A) now states that "arbitral awards arising out of arbitrations (other than 'international commercial arbitrations') may also be set aside by the court if it finds that the award is vitiated by patent illegality appearing on the face of the award."

However, since errors apparent on the face of the award under our old law (the 1940 Act) and under old English law (the old 1933 English Act) had resulted in good and just awards being set aside also for accidental mishaps, the Law Commission of India had taken care to recommend (which is again part of our law [subsection 2A of Section 34]) that the award shall not be set aside merely on the grounds of erroneous application of the law or by reappreciating evidence. This new provision of Section 34(2A) has been noted in a series of judgements handed down by the Supreme Court of India in the years 2015, 2019[32], and subsequent years. They are too numerous to be mentioned here.

However, whilst a patent illegality, i.e., illegality apparent on the face of the award, may be set aside in all domestic commercial arbitrations, it does not follow that the court can, therefore, modify the award. Here again, the Supreme Court has now corrected itself. Earlier, it had upheld courts modifying an arbitral award[33] (in an application for setting aside), but no longer. An award under Section 34, now (after 2019-2020), can either be set aside in its entirety or remanded, but only in the circumstances mentioned under Section 34[34]; it can no longer be modified by the court. Also, please do remember that even if there is a patent illegality in an award, under Section 34, a court is not obliged to set it aside. It may, which means it also may not. And why or when will it not set it aside, even if there is a patent illegality on the face of it? And the answer is only in the overriding interests of justice!

In the case of "foreign awards," however, under the New York Convention (covered by Part II of the 1996 Act), patent illegality of a foreign award cannot be raised as a ground to resist enforcement because this ground is absent in the New York Convention, 1958. It is, therefore, omitted in Section 48 of the 1996 Act in Part II, giving effect to the New York Convention, 1958, in India. Do remember that the whole purpose of the New York Convention, 1958, was to deal with the under-enforcement of awards that had resulted from the "double exequatur" (double execution) requirement of the earlier convention (the Geneva Convention, 1927), which called for judicial recognition of an arbitral award, both at the arbitral situs (at the or seat of arbitration) well as in the enforcement forum. The International Chamber of Commerce (ICC) had proposed a new treaty that aspired to make "arbitration completely independent of national laws." But later, the Economic and Social Council of the UN (ECOSOC) rejected this broad notion of so-called "international awards" in favour of making foreign awards more transportable from one country to another (and this is what has been achieved by the New York Convention, 1958).

This middle course taken (in the New York Convention) was one that has reduced but has not (deliberately) eliminated the role of the arbitral situs! Confirmation at the seat of arbitration is now no longer necessary. But at the same time, enforcement of foreign awards that have been vacated at the situs (or seat of arbitration) may now be refused under Section 48, which, therefore, advisedly and deliberately leaves uncertain, and at the discretion of the enforcement forum, the fate of annulled foreign awards.

How then should conscientious arbitrators avoid making awards that do not bear on their face the stamp of "patent illegality"? I would say in the same manner in which Lord Denning used to approach legal problems and difficulties that came before him. That great English judge, who had visited our country on three separate occasions,[35] believed that there is a moral element in every positive law that must never be overlooked. A colleague, Lord Ackner, who frequently sat with Lord Denning in England's Court of Appeal, had publicly acknowledged the influence of Denning's philosophy of law on him. In a public address, he once informed his audience that Denning put foremost: ". . . the need to ensure the just result and therefore, to circumvent precedent if you can do it properly . . ." And then he set out what Denning had described as the only correct approach: "The right approach, I am sure is: What does common sense indicate as the right result? Then, what are the relevant legal principles? And then what is the situation so far as precedent is concerned (and only in that order)?[36]"

Arbitrators, like judges, are decision-makers, and I believe that moral dimensions of decision-making must find more and more adherents in India, whether in the courtrooms or in arbitration centres or wherever young, competent, and enthusiastic arbitrators sit and make their arbitral awards.

Annexure I

In matters relating to the arbitrability of a dispute in India, there is a discernible trend in our courts to narrow the range of disputes that are capable of being submitted to arbitration.[37] The extent of "non-judicial intervention" mandated by Section 5 of the Act now has to be read along with Section 2(3) of the Act (also in Part I), which states: "This part shall not affect any other law for the time being forced by virtue of which certain dispute may not be submitted to arbitration." And the interpretation given by the Supreme Court of India to Section 2(3) has limited the concept of arbitrability rather than extended it. In the decisions of our courts, the range of non-arbitrable disputes has been extended to include:

i. disputes relating to rights and liabilities which give rise to or arise out of criminal offences;[38]
ii. matrimonial disputes[39] relating to divorce, judicial separation, restitution of conjugal rights, child custody;
iii. matters concerning guardianship;[40]
iv. matters relating to insolvency and winding up of companies;[41]
v. testamentary matters (grant of probate, letters of administration, and succession certificate);[42]
vi. certain disputes under the Consumer Protection Act, 1986;[43]
vii. in eviction or tenancy matters governed by special statutes where the tenant enjoys statutory protection against eviction and only the special courts are conferred jurisdiction to order eviction or to decide disputes between landlord or tenant;[44]

viii. and lastly, while dealing with the issue of arbitrability regarding allegations of fraud, in one questionable decision, the Supreme Court of India has ruled that there is a distinction between "*serious* allegations of fraud" and "*mere* allegations of fraud" and courts would have to deal with the question of whether allegations are "*serious* allegations" or "*mere* allegations," with the latter alone is to be decided by the arbitral tribunal; *serious* allegations of fraud (according to this decision) are not arbitrable.[45]

Annexure II

Detailed list of cases of domestic awards in Part I of the Act set aside and not set aside.

Up to date, in applications for setting aside arbitral awards under Part I of the Act, the following decisions have been handed down by courts in India under Section 34 of the 1996 Act on the grounds mentioned in Section 34(2) and 34(2A):

i. There are only five cases[46] in which domestic awards, under the 1996 Act, have been set aside by the Supreme Court of India: See also the case of *National Highway Authority of India* vs. *Progressive Construction Ltd*: 2021 (2) SCALE 503, judgement dated 12 February 2021, where the Supreme Court of India upheld the high court single judge's order, which had substantially set aside and arbitral award of 27 April 2016 by the arbitral tribunal (presumably under Section 34[2A]), since it had "drawn incorrect inferences from documents on record" and had "not considered vital and relevant evidence in reaching its conclusions," and appointed arbitrators to determine the disputes between the parties.
ii. There are twenty-five cases[47] in which domestic awards, under the 1996 Act, had been initially set aside by high courts, but their decisions were reversed by the Supreme Court of India. As a consequence, the domestic awards, though challenged under Section 34, were ultimately not set aside.

iii. There are sixteen cases[48] where recourse was taken to courts against domestic awards (for them to be set aside), but each such recourse was unsuccessful. None of the domestic awards that had been challenged in courts were set aside.

Annexure III

Article 34 of the UNCITRAL Model Law, 1985, sets out the standards against which courts of the Model Law state (India is one of the eighty Model Law states) are to judge the arbitral award, which is the final product of the arbitral proceedings.

The primary issue before the secretariat was whether the grounds for setting aside an award should be limited to those grounds on which recognition and enforcement of an award may be refused under the New York Convention, 1958. The secretariat had urged that they should be so refused. The Working Group (which included reps. from India) agreed, and the UNCITRAL Commission revisited this question but ultimately the Working Group decided to adopt the New York Convention grounds because it would help prevent a foreign award from falling victim to "local particularities of law." According to the Working Group's report: "That solution would facilitate international commercial arbitration by enhancing predictability and expeditiousness and would go a long way towards establishing a harmonised system of limited recourse against awards and their enforcement. It was (further) stated in support that the reasons set forth in Article V of the New York Convention provided sufficient safeguards, and that some of the grounds suggested as additions to the list were likely to fall under the public policy reason."

Lessons on advocacy are invariably imbibed from the great and successful, and I offer to every young practicing lawyer *encouragement,* not with pompous and pretentious advice, but with examples worthy of emulation.

First, from England, where the profession of law in India initially originated. Mr Quintin Hogg, much later, Lord Hailsham of St Marylebone, Lord Chancellor of England and Wales, and editor-in-chief of the fourth edition of *Halsbury's Laws of England* , has recorded in his memoirs that one of the most useful lessons in advocacy that he had learnt was when he was a totally inexperienced pupil at the Bar, from Wilfrid Greene, then Master of the Rolls (as the president of England's Court of Appeal is known). Quintin Hogg had the good fortune to sit next to him one night at a dinner, when the master suddenly shot at him the question:

> Greene: "Suppose you were instructed in a case where you had two points to argue, both of them bad, but one worse than the other, which would you argue first?"
>
> Hogg: "I suppose sir, I would argue the less bad of the two."
>
> Greene: (forcefully) "Quite wrong. You must argue the worse and put your very best work into it. Eventually, the judges will drive you into a corner, and you will have to admit defeat. You will then say, 'My Lords, there is another point I am instructed to argue. But I am not quite sure how to put it.' And you will then put the better of the two arguments—*but not quite as well as it could or should be put.* And after a little while, one of the old gentlemen on the bench will interrupt you and will say, 'But surely Mr Hogg, you might put it in this way.' And he (the judge) will put it exactly as you really ought to have put it in the first place. It is then, only then, that you will be at least halfway to winning your case!"

It was from this dinner dialogue that young Quintin Hogg first learnt that it is an illusion to believe that great cases are won or lost because of their inherent strength or weakness. Because nine times out of ten, advocacy contributes much to the success (or failure) of a case in court!

The *second* instance I offer is indigenous—purely Indian—and nearer home, of a case in India's Supreme Court, somewhere in the mid-1960s, in Court No. 1 before a bench presided over by Chief Justice P. B. Gajendragadkar (he was the seventh chief justice of India). Sitting with him was a judge who hailed from Calcutta, Justice R. S. Bachawat. The arguing counsel was Viswanatha Sastri, who was one of the five greatest lawyers of the twentieth century. He was arguing a civil appeal before their lordships in his inimitable "soft-but-sure" manner, when Justice Bachawat (a judge who always had the latest law on his fingertips) observed that the proposition that Sastri was then canvassing for was directly contrary to what the Privy Council had held in a reported case, and Justice Bachawat gave Sastri the reference to the Privy Council judgement!

For a few moments, there was complete silence in the court, and after a while came Viswanatha Sastri's reply, not a defiant one, but a reply expressed with humility, though with supreme confidence: "Yes, my Lord, and I believe (if my recollection is right) that this is the only decision of the Privy Council that has been adversely commented on in *Halsbury's Laws of England*, which you will find, I think, in volume such and such of Halsbury." Now there are, and always have been, more than fifty volumes of every edition of *Halsbury's Laws of England* (the fourth edition consisted of 56 volumes, and the fifth edition of 103 volumes!).

This back and forth from bench to Bar and Bar to bench impressed the erudite and scholarly chief justice (the presiding judge), who then said: "Let us suspend the proceedings for a while and send for the decision of the Privy Council, mentioned by my brother Bachawat, and send for the volume of *Halsbury* mentioned by Mr Sastri."

The books were sent for and when they were brought in, sure enough, there was the judgement of the Privy Council, as Justice Bachawat had recalled off the cuff, but equally surely, there was also that passage in that particular volume of *Halsbury's Laws of England* which had commented adversely on the opinion of the Privy Council, and which, on the spur of the moment, Viswanatha Sastri had adverted to!

This is a classic example of how well-prepared and well-stocked every practicing lawyer must be on every day of his life in the court. Difficult . . . often very difficult, but one must try. Because good luck (and loads of it) invariably follows upon a hard and strenuous work ethic!

6

Inter-state Dispute Settlement[49]

A few years ago, I was at a meeting in Washington of the American Society of International Law. One of the speakers at this meeting was the dean of the prestigious Yale Law School, who told his audience a story about the *unsigning* of the Kyoto Protocol 1997, which was a protocol to an international treaty about global warming (the Kyoto Protocol was the one that US President Bill Clinton signed, and which his successor, US President George Bush, unsigned!). And the dean quite blandly told his listeners that, in international law, it was a settled practice that a sovereign government could sign treaties and conventions, and, if it had second thoughts about them, it could proceed to unsign them as well!

Someone in the audience could not believe what he had heard and promptly asked him: "What then, sir, is international law?"

Without batting an eyelid, the dean shot back, saying: "International law is like that Tina Turner song: 'What's law got to do with it?'" So, when we talk about international law as between two or more nation-states, the first thing to remember is that "law" is quite often a dispensable element, especially when one or more of the great powers are involved. International law, as you all know, is mainly about treaties, which are its principal subject matter. And as for treaties, the former president of France, Charles de Gaulle, once famously said, "Treaties are like roses and little girls. They last whilst they last."

Of course, there is greater predictability with respect to a few aspects of international law that deal with stable interests like diplomatic privileges, jurisdiction, extradition of criminals, maritime law, and the like. However, the vast majority of cases in international law revolve around what I call "political considerations." Such cases are subservient not to law as we lawyers know it, but to *shifting political interests.*

The problems in world order arise because of the inclination of sovereign nation-states to interpret treaties and international conventions as they choose to interpret them. And even when the International Court of Justice (ICJ) propounds the correct applicable law as between parties to a convention and renders a decision on it, there is no authority that can enforce that decision. A most revealing case in point is the ICJ judgement of July 2016, between the Philippines and the Republic of China as to the use of waters in the South China Sea (under the 1982 Convention on the Law of the Sea) and about the lawfulness and otherwise of certain actions by the People's Republic of China.

Another older example (not a very laudable one) was the termination by our own, the Government of India, way back in the year 1955, of its acceptance and adherence to the Optional Protocol to the ICJ statute. This was done the moment Portugal raised claims (in the same year) to the right of passage over Indian territory of Portuguese civilians and goods between Goa and Daman (two enclaves within India that were then subject to the sovereignty of the state of Portugal). India then reissued her declaration to the Optional Protocol of the ICJ with a new reservation, which excluded disputes with regard to matters that were "essentially within the domestic jurisdiction of India as determined by the Indian Government"—language borrowed from the innovative declaration of the USA to the same Optional Protocol way back in the year 1946! The sequel to this was that India's preliminary objections to the jurisdiction of the ICJ got short shrift from the court. However, on merits, India got the better of Portugal!

Amongst nation-states of the world, international law is really nothing more than the distilled practice of civilised nations, which is why some academics prefer to call it "international relations." When the subject of *international relations* matured into *international law*, it didn't stay there but went downhill again, as in the case of the *laws of war* when it relapsed into international relations, as if law had little to do with it!

The laws of war have witnessed a cataclysmic change since the middle of the last century. In August 1945, the devastation in Hiroshima and Nagasaki was flashed on the conscience of the world. Dr Robert Oppenheimer, the Princeton scientist who was incharge of the development of the atom bomb, himself witnessed a test of the first nuclear explosion a month before the real event, in a desert in New Mexico. He was not only a great scientist but was also well-read, and his well-stocked mind reminded him of a passage from the Bhagavad Gita, the ancient Hindu scripture, in which the following passage occurs: "If the radiance of a thousand suns were to burst at once into the sky, that would be like the splendour of the Mighty One!" And then, during the trial run in Mexico, when the enormous mushroom cloud darkened the sky, he remembered an even more ominous line from the same Bhagavad Gita: "I am become Death, the destroyer of worlds." It is this second recollection that kept haunting him.

Oppenheimer had misgivings about what he had achieved, and after the atom bomb that he had invented was actually used to devastating effect, bringing the Second World War to an abrupt end, Oppenheimer became a pacifist, devoting the rest of his life to the study of the ethics of science in society! As the saying goes, "Out of evil, sometimes comes good." And it was this realisation of the destructive qualities of uranium and plutonium that hastened the conclave of victorious nations in September 1945, at which the Charter of the United Nations was forged.

Wars, as the world knew them for centuries, were by common consent of nations abolished by the UN Charter. But since world peace kept eluding humankind, and continues to elude us, in its place came the less alarming phrase "armed conflicts." For centuries before September 1945, one proposition in international law remained without challenge, and it was that the law of nations did not recognise any rights vested in any individual against any sovereign state. But the UN Charter of 1945 altered all this. Article 55(c) required all member nations of the UN "to promote universal respect for and observance of human rights and fundamental freedoms." As a result, at one bound, the individual citizen of every state became a subject of international law.

Two years after the adoption of the Universal Declaration, Prof. Hersch Lauterpacht, one of the great exponents of international law and a judge of the International Court of Justice, wrote: "The individual has acquired a status and a stature which have transformed him from an object of international compassion into a subject of international right." Lauterpacht was one of the pioneers of what came to be known as the "modern view" of international law, which was that states, though still primarily the subject of international law, were not exclusively so.

Post-1945 to the present day, during umpteen armed conflicts in various parts of the world, the emphasis has been on the humanitarian aspects of international law, such as the *law* relating to refugees, the *law* relating to displaced persons, the *law* as to how civilians are to be treated in times of armed conflict—the emphasis being on the Geneva Convention of 1949 and its two protocols. Here again, the word "law" is a misnomer. The more appropriate expression is "settled practice."

Sixty years after the establishment of the UN, the world witnessed a new concern, or rather the same old concern in a new garb! In October 2006, there were headlines in newspapers around the world, a typical one of which read: "Defying the World, North Korea's Isolated Dictator Blasts into the Nuclear Club." Apparently, he claimed it to be in the interest of North Korea's national security. The build-up of military and nuclear arsenals all around the world is professedly in the interest of national security. But national security beyond a point is a *will-o'-the-wisp*—an illusion that remains even today, despite the warnings of contemporary historians. One of them, Sir Herbert Butterfield, the most distinguished philosopher and professor of history at Cambridge, had written: "This universe was always unsafe and those who demand a watertight security are always a danger in any period of history . . . I wonder if it could not be formulated as a law that no state can ever achieve the security it desires without so tipping the balance so that it becomes a menace to its neighbours."

The International Court of Justice had the occasion to formulate just such a law, but it failed us. Over thirty years ago, the International Court of Justice was requested for its advisory opinion on a resolution of 15 November 1994, adopted by the UN General Assembly, and the opinion sought from the world court was: "Is the threat or use of nuclear weapons in any circumstance permitted under international law?" In other words, whether use of nuclear weapons could be reconciled with the basic principles of humanitarian law? Representatives of twenty-two nation-states of the world from A to Z—from Australia to Zimbabwe—appeared before the world court and made written as well as oral submissions. In the end, the majority of twelve judges out of the fifteen said that humanitarian law had to be read as subject to an exception, and the exception was that it permitted a state to use nuclear weapons in self-defence when its survival was at stake, even where such use would otherwise be a breach of humanitarian law. Alarming, but true.

Only three judges out of the fifteen disagreed: Judge Weeramantry of Sri Lanka, Judge Shahabuddin of Guyana, and Judge Koroma of Sierra Leone. All three were from the developing world. According to them, "the concept of the humanitarian laws of war was not a recent invention nor the product of any one culture. It was deeply rooted in many ancient cultures: Buddhist, Hindu, Chinese, Christian, Islamic, and traditional African. Each of these cultures had given expression to a variety of limitations on the extent to which any means can be used for the purposes of fighting one's enemy. And that the problem under consideration was a universal problem, and the world court being a universal court, its composition (as required by its statute) should reflect the world's principal *cultural* traditions." According to them, of special relevance in connection with nuclear weapons was the ancient South Asian tradition regarding the prohibition of the use of *hyper-destructive weapons* as they used to be called in the ancient texts.

Two celebrated Indian epics were referred to in their judgement/opinion: the Ramayana and the Mahabharata, "which are not only well-known, but the stories from these epics have been regularly reenacted through the length and breadth of South and Southeast Asia as part of the living cultural tradition of the region."[50] The Ramayana, for instance, told the epic story of a war between Rama, prince of Ayodhya in India, and Ravana, the ruler of Sri Lanka. During this epic struggle, described in this classic in the minutest detail, a weapon of war became available to Rama's half-brother, Lakshmana, which could "destroy the entire race of the enemy, including those who could not bear arms." Even though Ravana was fighting an unjust war with an unrighteous objective, Rama had warned Lakshmana that the weapon should not be used in the war as such destruction *en masse* was forbidden by the ancient laws of war. These laws of war, which Rama spoke of, were themselves ancient even in his time.

The judges also referred to the Mahabharata, the story of an epic struggle between the Kauravas and Pandavas and quoted from it to emphasise the embargo on the use of "hyper-destructive" weapons. Equipped with the necessary array of principles and cultural traditions with which to respond to the question addressed to them by the UN, Judge Weeramantry of Sri Lanka (and his two colleagues) felt that international law could have contributed significantly towards rolling back the shadow of the nuclear-free age. But it was not to be. Three members in a court of fifteen, however strident and far-seeing in their views, did not constitute a majority. Their dissent could only be addressed to "the brooding spirit of the future."

The only portion of the opinion that was unanimous was the one which affirmed the "obligation of all states to pursue in good faith and bring to a conclusion negotiations leading to disarmament in all its aspects." However, even this observation of the court, though unanimous, did not penetrate into the policy-making circles of the states belonging to the once exclusive nuclear club. Over the years, whilst everything about the North Korean blast is negative, there is only one positive aspect, viz. that all the nations of the world—nuclear and non-nuclear—if they are to survive, must join together to establish a regime of a nuclear-free world for one reason and one reason only, illustrated in a true story:

After the end of the Second World War, Dr Oppenheimer, who had invented the atom bomb, was called to testify before the US Senate Armed Services Committee, which asked him if there "is there any defence against a nuclear weapon?" The inventor of the atom bomb promptly replied: "Yes, peace." He knew, not only as a world-famous scientist but also as a citizen of the world, that even after decades of enormous scientific progress, there was no defence against a nuclear bomb except peace. That is why in the Preamble to the Constitution of UNESCO—one of the agencies of the United Nations—there is a sentence which could be addressed appropriately to all of humanity: "Wars begin in the minds of men, and it is in the minds of men (and women) that the defences of peace must be constructed."

Acknowledgements

I am deeply grateful for the incredible support and encouragement I have received. I want to acknowledge a few people who made this special book possible.

First, after the passing of my mentor, Mr Fali Nariman, my great thanks go to his generous and divine son, Hon'ble Mr Justice Rohinton Nariman, and his ever-supportive and charming wife, Mrs Sanaya Nariman. I also want to profoundly thank Mr Fali Nariman's benevolent daughter, Anaheeta F. Nariman, who has always been generous, open-hearted, and encouraging throughout.

My thanks extend to the two wonderful granddaughters of my mentor, Ms Nina Nariman (and her husband, Rohan Alva) and Ms Khursheed Nariman.

I also thank the diligent staff of the late Mr Fali S. Nariman, especially Mr Vinod Kumar, who helped me immensely even in his poor health, along with the great support of Mr Narender Kumar and Mr Lakhvinder. I also extend my gratitude to the dedicated secretary, Mr Vinod K. Anand, who maintained the balance of the office for decades.

Thanks also to other staff members—Vijay Upadhyay (court clerk), Ram Kumar, Haroon, Jitender, Ms Lalita, and Kaviraj—for taking care of the house and office.

I am especially grateful to our wonderful publisher, Hay House, particularly Mr Ashok Chopra, its chief executive, and his energetic team. They worked tirelessly to edit and publish this book in record time.

My heartfelt thanks to my loving wife, Sadhana, my wonderful son, Moksh, and his charming wife, Astha, for taking care of me from time to time. I am also grateful to my dear friend Lance Gooden from Texas.

In the end, I hope this book will inspire and guide the young generation around the globe.

—Subhash Sharma
Advocate

References

Section I : Nation

1. Written on 27 July 2013.

2. Nehru, Jawaharlal, *The Discovery of India* (first published 1946), Third Impression, pp. 61-62.

3. *The Times Book of Quotations*, 2000, p. 193.

4. 322 to 185 BCE (before the Christian era).

5. *Parliamentary Debates*, Vol. XII-XIII, Part II, Col. 9617, 29 May 1951.

6. Ralph Bunche (African American) was an academic and diplomat who received the 1950 Nobel Peace Prize.

7. Dhavan, Rajeev, *The Supreme Court of India: A Socio-Legal Critique of Its Juristic Techniques*, Bombay, N. M. Tripathi, 1977. Dhavan (a Supreme Court advocate and a human rights activist) suggests that this is India's version of the "happy mean," a broad margin of tolerance, which is in keeping with the pattern of the common law.

8. Galanter, Marc, *Competing Equalities: Law and the Backward Classes in India,* Los Angeles: University of California Press, 1984, p. 539.

9. "A Real Partnership," *Yes Minister*, TV Series I, Episode 5, 1986.

10. Written on 9 October 2021.

11. Associate justice of the US Supreme Court who served from 1916 to 1939 before retiring as a judge.

12. Urofsky, Melvin I., *Louis D. Brandeis: A Life*, New York: Schocken Books, Penguin Random House, 2012, pp. 432-433.

13. India's "Constituent Assembly" received statutory recognition in the British Parliament's Indian Independence Act, 1947. It was described there as the "Constituent Assembly (Legislative)." Members of the Constituent Assembly wore two hats—in the morning, it was the pro-tem legislative body for British India, while in the afternoon, it attended to drafting the Constitution. On and from 26 November 1949, having completed its task of framing the Constitution of India, the Constituent Assembly became India's full-time "Provisional Parliament," which later passed the Constitution First Amendment Act, 1951. The first general elections under India's Constitution were held in 1952, after which India's elected parliament took over.

14. Singh, Tripurdaman, *Sixteen Stormy Days,* London: Bloomsbury Publishing, 2024.

15. Another well-researched book (published in 1999) is Prof. Granville Austin's *The Working of a Democratic Constitution.*

16. By the Indian Independence Act, 1947.

17. *Constituent Assembly Debates,* 25 November 1949, Book No. 5, V ols. X-XII, p. 975.

18. The 105th Amendment of the Constitution of India (18 August 2021) restored the power of state governments and union territories to identify and specify socially and educationally backward classes (SEBCs) for preferential treatment in educational institutions and in public employment, a power which, by judicial decisions, had been reserved only for the Government of India.

19. The PREAMBLE reads: "WE, THE PEOPLE OF INDIA, having solemnly resolved to constitute India into a [SOVEREIGN DEMOCRATIC REPUBLIC] and to secure to all its citizens:

    JUSTICE, social, economic and political;

    LIBERTY of thought, expression, belief, faith and worship;

    EQUALITY of status and of opportunity; and to promote among them all

    FRATERNITY assuring the dignity of the individual and the [unity and integrity of the Nation];

    IN OUR CONSTITUENT ASSEMBLY this twenty-sixth day of

November, 1949, do HEREBY ADOPT, ENACT AND GIVE TO OURSELVES THIS CONSTITUTION."

(The words "SOCIALIST" and "SECULAR" were added in capital letters by the Constitutional Amendment of 1976).

20. In January 1950, India consisted of six states (corresponding to six provinces under the Government of India Act, 1935). With the subsequent division of states on a linguistic basis and for various other reasons, the number of states in India is now twenty-eight with eight union territories. The executive in each state consists of the governor (appointed by the Government of India) and a council of ministers with the chief minister at the head to aid and advise the governor in the exercise of his functions, along with state legislatures and a high court in each state.

21. Each state is to be divided into territorial constituencies in such a manner that the ratio between the population of each constituency and the number of seats allotted to it is (so far as practicable) the same for all states (Article 81[2][b]). At present, there is a freeze on the inter-state delimitation of seats based on the 1971 census, which will be lifted only after the relevant figures for the first census taken after the year 2026 have been published (proviso to Article 81[3]). The new parliament house has a Lok Sabha Chamber (i.e., chamber of the House of the People) that can seat 772 members on the expectation that the members of parliamentary constituencies will increase on the lifting of the freeze after the year 2026.

22. Articles 162, 245, and 246 read with the Seventh Schedule to the Constitution.

23. *Rai Sahib Ram Jawaya Kapur and Ors.* vs. *State of Punjab,* 1955 (2) SCR 225 (a bench decision of five judges).

24. See *Shankari Prasad* vs. *Union of India*—AIR 1951 SC 458 (bench of five judges); *Sajjan Singh* vs. *State of Rajasthan*—AIR 1965 SC 845 (bench of five judges); and when the judges thought they had found it in *Golaknath* vs. *State of Punjab*—AIR 1967 SC 764 (bench of eleven judges), where by majority (6:5) the court held that a constitutional amendment was governed by the restrictions imposed in the Fundamental Rights Chapter. The majority decision in *Golaknath* was later overruled and

held not to be good law; in a decision of a bench of thirteen judges in *Kesavananda Bharati* vs. *State of Kerala*—AIR 1973 SC 1461 (7:6), where "the doctrine of basic structure" was first invoked.

25. AIR 1973 SC 1461.

26. The few other cases in which the basic structure doctrine has been invoked since then include:

    1. *Minerva Mills* vs. *Union of India*—AIR 1980 SC 1789 (bench of five judges);
    2. *P. Sambhamurthi and Anr.* vs. *State of Andhra Pradesh*—1987 (1) SCC 362 (bench of five judges);
    3. *L. Chandra Kumar* vs. *Union of India*—AIR 1997 SC 1125 (bench of seven judges);
    4. and *Supreme Court Advocates-on-Record* vs. *Union of India*—2016 (5) SCC 1 (bench of five judges).

27. 1981 (Supp.) SCC 87.

28. (1993) 4 SCC 441 and (1998) 7 SCC 739 (the latter a unanimous decision of a bench of nine judges).

29. *Constituent Assembly Debates,* 25 November 1949, Book No. 5, Vols. X-XII, p. 979.

30. "However good a Constitution may be, it may turn out to be bad because those who are called upon to work it happen to be a bad lot, and however bad a Constitution may be, it may turn out to be good if those, who are called upon to work it happen to be a good lot."

31. Written on 15 March 2013.

32. Desai, Lord Meghnad, *Divided by Democracy*, New Delhi: Lotus Books, 2005.

33. Dworkin, *Oxford Journal of Legal Studies.*

34. Nehru, Jawaharlal, *The Discovery of India*, first published in 1946, Third Impression, pp. 61-62.

35. Selected as one of the hundred best novels in English literature.

36. *The Times Book of Quotations*, 2000, p. 193.

37. Written on 23 March 2019.

Section II: Judiciary

1. Written on 12 January 2013.

2. Murlidhar, S., *Law, Poverty, and Legal Aid*, New York: LexisNexis Butterworths, 2004.

3. Written on 1 May 2013.

4. Dershowitz, Alan M., *Reversal of Fortune: Inside the Von Bülow Case*, New York: Random House, 1986.

5. The high court was established by Royal Charter pursuant to the Indian High Courts Act, 1861, passed by the British Parliament. The Crown was empowered to establish high courts of judicature at Calcutta, Madras, and Bombay. Prior to this, there was the Mayor's Court, the Recorder's Court, and the Supreme Court of Judicature at Bombay, established by the statute of 1823.

6. Vachha, P. B., *Famous Judges, Lawyers, and Cases of Bombay: A Judicial History of Bombay*, Bombay: N. M. Tripathi, 1962.

7. Ibid., pp. 270-271.

8. It was republished and released in April 2011 by Vachha's son, Russi Vachha, himself a lawyer of standing who left the profession to become one of the chief executives of Mackinnon Mackenzie & Company. The book is worth reading, with an excellent foreword by Soli Sorabjee.

9. Since then, trial by jury was abolished throughout the state.

10. Gajendragadkar, P. B., *To the Best of My Memory*, Bombay: Bhartiya Vidya Bhawan, 1983, p. 43.

11. Article 124(4) read with Article 217(b).

12. 1941 (3) All. E.R. 338.

13. AIR 1976 SC 1207.

14. 1980 (1) AER 80—*IRC* vs. *Rossminster.*

15. Sardar Swaran Singh was one of the longest-serving union cabinet ministers. In 1952, he became a cabinet minister during the prime ministership of Jawaharlal Nehru and remained in successive governments as cabinet minister till 1975 when he resigned.

16. *Kenchava* vs. *Girimallappa*, AIR 1924 Privy Council 209.

17. He travelled to India in 1862 and served in official positions. He was president of the Commission on Indian Law in 1879.

18. There is a beautiful and well-preserved marble statue of a seated Justice Muthuswamy Iyer within the court premises of the High Court of Madras.

19. Illustrious son of the equally illustrious social reformer of the nineteenth century, Sir Syed Ahmed Khan. Syed Mahmood was born in 1850 and served as a judge in the High Court of Allahabad from 1887 to 1893, then the only Indian amongst the judges of the high court.

20. Ronald Dworkin, "Hard Cases," *Harvard Law Review*, Vol. 88 No. 6 (April 1975), pp. 1057-1109; a reproduction of an inaugural lecture by Ronald Dworkin given at Oxford in June of 1971.

21. This question is raised as a result of my two books in *The Arbitration Series: HARMONY Amidst DISHARMONY,* New Delhi, Hay House Publishers, 2020 (in two volumes—Volume I: "The Indian Framework" and Volume II: "The International Framework").

22. "Clause 7 provides for the settlement of disputes outside the court. The provisions of Clause 7 are based on the recommendations made by the Law Commission of India and the Malimath Committee. It was suggested by the Law Commission of India that the court may require the attendance of any party to the suit or proceedings to appear in person with a view to arriving at an amicable settlement of disputes between the parties and making an attempt to settle the dispute between the parties amicably. The Malimath Committee recommended making it obligatory for the court to refer the dispute, after issues are framed, for settlement either by way of arbitration, mediation, or judicial settlement through Lok Adalat. It is only when the parties fail to get their disputes settled through any of the alternative dispute resolution methods that

the suit could proceed further. In view of the above, Clause 7 seeks to insert a new section 89 in the Code in order to provide for alternative dispute resolution."

23. 2003 (1) SCC 144.

24. Civil Procedure Alternative Dispute Resolution and Mediation Rules, 2003.

25. 2005 (6) SCC 344 (3J)—*Salem Advocates Bar Association* vs. *UOI.*

26. A statutory presumption under British India's Evidence Act of 1872, which continued under India's Constitution.

27. The 45th Amendment Bill, 1978 (introduced after the revocation of the Internal Emergency of June 1975), contained provisions for the repeal of Articles 323A and 323B, but they were not passed.

28. Felix Frankfurter was also the most controversial justice of his time. Though he denied having any party affiliation and served under both Democratic and Republican administrations, his politics were openly progressive. Justice Louis Brandeis, whom Professor Frankfurter aided with research and other services, called Frankfurter "the most useful lawyer in America." Despite, or perhaps because of the accolade, Professor Frankfurter was feared by conservatives and corporate spokesmen as a dangerous radical.

29. Which is the official language of the Supreme Court of India.

30. What legal reformers at the time called "sociological jurisprudence," Justice Louis Brandeis (1916-1939, judge in the US Supreme Court) had developed a reputation as a lawyer "who knew more about his client's business than they did," a "master of facts and a courtroom advocate feared by his opponents."

Section III: Constitution

1. Written on 29 October 2005.

2. *Liyanage* vs. *Reginam,* 1966 (1) All E.R. 650, p. 658.

3. AIR 1951 SC 458.

4. AIR 1965 SC 845.

5. AIR 1967 SC 1643.

6. AIR 1973 SC 1461.

7. Article 19(1)(f) and Article 31 of the Constitution (the Property Clauses) were deleted from the Fundamental Rights Chapter by the Constitution 44th Amendment Act, 1978. Article 300A, inserted by the 44th Amendment, now provides that no person shall be deprived of his property save by authority of law.

8. AIR 1975 SC 2299.

9. AIR 1980 SC 1789.

10. 6th Edition, Volume O, pp. 210-211.

11. Bagehot, Walter, *The English Constitution,* republished in 1991 by the Fontana Press, UK, p. 113.

12. *Memoirs of Giani Zail Singh: The Seventh President of India,* Har-Anand Publications, New Delhi, 1997, p. 279.

13. Austin, Granville, *Working a Democratic Constitution,* UK: Oxford University Press, 1999, pp. 513-514.

14. Rodney Brazier has suggested that the monarch (a constitutional head of state) can legitimately, if extraordinarily, intervene in the legislative process. For example, if a Government Bill designed to achieve a permanent subversion of the democratic basis of the Constitution, it could be vetoed. Brazier, Rodney, *Constitutional Practice*, 1994, 2nd Edition, pp. 189-192.

15. Interview with Karan Thapar on 1 October 2023.

Section IV: Law

1. 1 December 2001.

2. 1995 (2) SCC 584.

3. *Supreme Court Bar Association* vs. *Union of India,* 1998 (4) SCC 409.

4. *P. N. Duda* vs. *P. Shiv Shankar*, AIR 1988 SC 1208, p. 1213.

5. *S. Mulgaokar's case*, AIR 1978 SC 727.

6. *Conscientious Group* vs. *Mohammed Yunus and Ors.*, AIR 1987 SC 1451.

7. *Mohd. Zahir Khan* vs. *Vijai Singh & Ors.*, 1992 Supp (2) SCC 72.

8. *Borric & Lowe, Law of Contempt*, 3rd Edition, p. 331.

9. *R.* vs. *Almon*, 1765 Wilmot 243.

10. *Smt. Archana Guha* vs. *Sri Rajnit Guha Neogi @ Runu Guha Neogi*, 1989 (1) Calcutta High Court Notes (CHN) 252.

11. The decision of the Calcutta High Court helps underscore another important point: the contempt jurisdiction is not to be used merely because proceedings in a court of law are erroneously reported. For this, resort should be had to the registrar communicating to the press, pointing out what the correct facts are. It is only if the misreporting has persisted that invocation of the contempt jurisdiction may perhaps be justified, not otherwise.

12. *R.* vs. *Metropolitan Police Commissioner*, 1968 (2) AER 319, p. 320.

13. *Attorney General* vs. *Guardian Newspaper*, 1987 (3) AER 316 (HL).

14. 1969 2 SCR 779.

15. *Gilbert Ahnee* vs. *Director of Public Prosecutor*, 1999 (2) W.L.R. 1305 = 1999 (2) AC 294.

16. *R.* vs. *Kopyto*, 1987 (47) DLR 4th Series.

17. The issue of judicial accountability had been discussed at the conference of chief justices held in 1990, and on the basis of the broad consensus emerging out of the deliberations, the then-chief justice of India summed up the position in the following words:

    "The chief justices of the high court have the competence to receive complaints against the conduct of the judges of his court, and when he receives any, he would look into it for finding out if it deserves to be closely looked into. Where he is satisfied that the matter requires to be examined, he shall have facts ascertained in such manner as he considers appropriate keeping the nature of allegations in view, and if he is of the opinion that the matter is such that it should be reported to the chief justice of India, he shall do so. The chief justice of India shall act in a similar manner in regard to complaints relating to conduct of judges of the Supreme Court and in regard to conduct of chief justices of the high courts.

On the basis of the facts ascertained, the chief justice of the high court or the Supreme Court, as the case may be, shall take such appropriate action as may be considered proper, keeping the interests of the judiciary as the paramount consideration."

My comment on this is that there has to be more transparency, more accountability, and something to show that the in-house procedure is in fact in operation and is being used.

18. *Andre Paul* vs. *Attorney-General* (1936), AC 322.

19. 15 December 2017.

20. The banyan is a species of fig (Ficus benghalensis) that assumes a remarkable form as a tree. Native to tropical Asia, it can reach a height of up to 100 feet with an extensive lateral spread, thanks to its aerial roots that grow downwards and form new trunks.

21. Sieghart, Paul, *The International Law of Human Rights*, UK: Oxford University Press, 1983, p. 8. This is one of the earliest comprehensive works on the subject.

22. With one possible exception, which arose from the duty of states to observe a certain minimum standard of justice in their treatment of aliens and their liability to compensate not the injured alien but the state of which he was a national, for any failure to observe this standard. In the theory of the law, the right to protection belonged not to the alien but to his state. The customary rules of international law governing the treatment of aliens constituted an impressive body of law, the effect of which was to protect the rights of at least one class of individuals.

23. The only exception then existing went by the name of "humanitarian intervention." If a government committed atrocities against its citizens, which shocked the conscience of mankind, then, it was said, other powers had the right to intervene. There were a number of such interventions in the nineteenth century, mainly to protect religious

minorities, but in practice it was force, not law, that determined the occasion of its exercise.

24. Sir Hersch Lauterpacht, *International Law and Human Rights*, 1950, pp. 4 and 159.

25. This is what he wrote when editing the first volume of the 8th Edition of Oppenheim's International Law (1955). In the subsequent 9th Edition (1992), editors Sir Robert Jennings and Sir Arthur Watts restated the "modern view": "It is no longer possible, as a matter of positive law, to regard states as the only subjects of international law, and there is an increasing disposition to treat individuals within a limited sphere as subjects of international law" (*Oppenheim,* Vol. I, 9th Edition, pp. 848-849).

26. Austin's legal theory of sovereignty centred around the "habit" of obedience: "The generality of the given society must be in the habit of obedience to a determinate and common superior. Whilst that determinate person or determinate body of persons must not be habitually obedient to a determinate person or body. It is the union of that positive with this negative mark which renders that certain superior sovereign or supreme . . ."

27. In 1948, Mrs Eleanor Roosevelt had expressed the hope that the UDHR might well become "The International Magna Carta." Towards fulfilment of that expectation, 10 December is celebrated all over the world as Human Rights Day.

28. A view expressed by several distinguished commentators over the years, notably by: (i) Prof. John Humphrey, who drew up the first draft of the Universal Declaration for the Human Rights Committee; (ii) Sir Humphrey Waldock, a judge of the International Court of Justice in the 1970s; and (iii) Mr Philip Alston. A contrary view was forcefully propounded and persistently adhered to by Hersch Lauterpacht, first as professor and later as a judge of the International Court of Justice. Whilst always maintaining that the UN Charter was a "legal" document, "and that its language (was) the language of International Law" (see article written in 1948 in Vol. 64 LQR, page 97 at pages 101-102), he steadfastly held the view that the language of the Universal Declaration of Human Rights, the circumstances and reasons for its adoption and, above all, the expressed intentions of the states who voted for its adoption in

the General Assembly, showed clearly that the declaration was not "a legal document imposing legal obligations" (see *International Law and Human Rights,* 1950, p. 408).

29. Vienna Declaration and Programme of Action adopted by the World Conference on Human Rights on 25 June 1993.

30. McGoldrick, Dominic, *The Human Rights Committee* (Oxford Monographs in International Law), UK: Clarendon Paperbacks, 1994, p. 498.

31. Elkind, J. B., *"Application of the International Covenant on Civil and Political Rights in New Zealand,"* Vol. 75 AJIL (1981), pp. 169-172. Elkind, J. B. and Shaw, A., *A Standard for Justice*, 1986.

32. These have been useful in setting the pattern for an objective approach to important problems faced by the HRC in the course of its deliberations, including discussions during presentation of periodic reports by state parties. So far, the HRC has issued twenty-five general comments, the more recent have concerned freedom of thought, conscience, and religion, the rights of minorities, the question of reservations, and the right of citizens to participate in public affairs.

33. As of 31 July 1995, an aggregate of 645 communications had been registered with the Human Rights Committee, of which 131 were during the period 1992 to 1995. Since New Zealand's accession to the Optional Protocol (1966) on 26 August 1989, it has been possible for individual complaints to be filed with the HRC, complaining that New Zealand has violated rights affirmed in the covenant. The important precondition, of course, is that the person must have exhausted all domestic remedies. In an interesting article in the *New Zealand Law Review* (1996, Part III), "Human Rights and the Bill of Rights" by Professor P. T. Rishworth, the author supplies a range of figures about complaints declared admitted by the HRC and pending before it—145 from Jamaica (the highest as of April 1996), 4 from New Zealand (the lowest), 14 from Australia, and 80 from Canada.

34. The expert committee has contributed to speeding up implementation. It has published a series of general comments in order to guide member-states on their reporting obligations. Monitoring reports of party states, the committee performs a useful interpretative function

as well, correcting erroneous impressions about the covenant. Thus, when considering the report of New Zealand, the committee members expressed disappointment over the statement of a minister (in 1992) that the "health, education, and welfare services were privileges, not rights." The Government of New Zealand, in its response, then expressed its commitment to implement these rights in a serious way (see *Human Rights Monitor*, December 1993, p. 14).

35. A compilation of general comments and general recommendations adopted respectively by all the human rights treaty bodies has been published (see UN Publication HRI/GEN/1/REV. II, 29 March 1996). When setting out and interpreting relevant provisions in the human rights treaties, national courts frequently overlook these general comments and general recommendations.

36. In the absence of a provision to the contrary, it would now appear that reservations to multilateral treaties are permissible only to the extent that they do not conflict with "the object and purpose of the treaty" (see decision of the International Court of Justice in its Advisory Opinion on Reservations to the Convention on Prevention and Punishment of the Crime of Genocide, 1951). It is this criterion that has been adopted by the Human Rights Committee in its General Comment No. 24 on issues relating to reservations made upon ratification to the ICCPR and the Optional Protocol thereto. In this Comment No. 24, the HRC has clarified that an absence of a prohibition on reservations does not mean that any reservation is permitted and has further declared that reservations that offend "peremptory norms" would not be compatible with the object and purport of the Covenant. Thus, for instance, a state may not reserve the right *not* to present a report and have it considered by the HRC. So also, the committee's role under Article 40 or under the two Optional Protocols necessarily entails interpreting the provisions of the covenant and a development of its jurisprudence. Hence, a reservation that rejects the committee's competence to interpret the requirements of any provisions of the covenant would be contrary to the object and purpose of the treaty.

37. See 1995 Annual Report of the Human Rights Committee, A/50/40, pp. 131-139.

38. The CAD and CAT have built-in provisions in the main treaty itself, conferring rights of individual petition. A draft Optional Protocol to the Convention against Torture (CAT) is being studied by a working group, which provides for a system of preventative visits to places of detention in party states.

39. The percentages of state parties to the respective treaties that do not allow such complaints are 35 per cent in the case of ICCPR, 85 per cent in the case of the Racial Discrimination Convention, and 60 per cent in the case of the Convention against Torture (these statistics are as of 1 December 1995).

40. See Final Report of Special Rapporteur Daniel Turk, para 233, incorporated in the *Report of the secretary-general*, UN Document E./CM/4/1995/10, dated 4 July 1995.

41. Quoted in the Oxford Monograph on International Law, titled *The Human Rights Committee* by Dominic McGoldrick, Clarendon Press, Oxford, p. 54.

42. The figures are taken from an article in *Human Rights Quarterly,* Vol. 19 No. 1, February 1997, pp. 78-112, at p. 111.

43. *International Law on Human Rights*, 1950.

44. *D. K. Basu* vs. *State of West Bengal*, judgment dated 18 December 1996, reported 1996 (9) Scale 298.

45. Lord Cooke of Thorndon, "Dream of an International Common Law," an article in the book *Courts of Final Jurisdiction*, pp. 138-145.

46. In the *Eichmann case* (1961), the Jerusalem District Court held in a decision affirmed on appeal that it had jurisdiction for crimes against humanity and other crimes, notwithstanding that Adolf Eichmann had been forcibly abducted to Israel from Argentina. See 1961 Vol. 36, *International Law Reports 5*, and 1962 Vol. 36, *International Law Reports 277.*

47. *Derbyshire County Council* vs. *Times Newspapers & Anr.,* 1993 (1) All ER 1011, at p. 1021.

48. *Dietrich* vs. *R.*, 109 ALR 385, p. 393 (1992).

49. In an article in *International and Comparative Law Quarterly,* Vol. 45, Part I (January 1996), p. 9.

50. Holmes, Oliver Wendell, *Collected Papers,* 1920, pp. 172-173.

51. *Tavita* vs. *Minister of Immigration*, (1994) NZLR 257; interim judgment, dated 17 December 1993 of the Court of Appeal, delivered by Cooke P.

52. This was Lord Lester's comment in an article in *Public Law* (Summer 1996), p. 187 footnote (4). The decision in *Ex. parte Smith* is reported in 1996 All ER 257 CA.

53. The full title of the tribunal is "The International Tribunal for the Prosecution of Persons Responsible for Serious Violations of International Humanitarian Law Committed in the Territory of Former Yugoslavia in 1991."

54. *Prosecutor* vs. *Tadic,* a decision dated 2 October 1995 of the Appeals Chamber, which consisted of Judge President Cassese and Judges Li, Deschenes, Abi-Saab, and Sidhwa.

55. *Muhammad Hamdan* vs. *The General Security Service,* requested by the attorney-general, ministry of justice, unreported judgment dated 26 November 1996, Supreme Court of Israel sitting as the High Court of Justice.

56. *Filartiga* vs. *Pena-Irala*, 575 F. Supp. 60 (EDNY) (1984).

57. R. Cooke, "Fundamentals," an article in 1988 NZLJ 158.

58. *R.* vs. *Butcher,* 1992 (2) NZLR 257, 267 (Cooke P.).

59. *Bennett* vs. *Horseferry Road Magistrates' Court,* and Article 1993 (3) ALL ER 138 HL (Lord Griffiths).

60. Written on 13 April 2019.

61. Written on 27 April 2019.

62. *McDowell & Co.* vs. *CTO*, 1985 (3) SCC 230.

63. *Union of India* vs. *Azadi Bachao Andolan*, 2004 (10) SCC 1.

64. 2012 (6) SCC 613.

65. Lord Steyn in *McFarlane* vs. *Tayside Health Board*, 1999 (3) WLR at page 1319 = 1999 (4) All ER 961 at page 977.

66. WE, THE PEOPLE OF INDIA, having solemnly resolved to constitute India into a SOVEREIGN SOCIALIST SECULAR DEMOCRATIC REPUBLIC and to secure to all its citizens:

    JUSTICE, social, economic and political;
    LIBERTY of thought, expression, belief, faith and worship;
    EQUALITY of status and of opportunity; and to promote among . . .

67. *UCC* vs. *UOI*, 1991 (4) SCC 584 (five judges).

68. *V. C. Mishra*—1998 (4) SCC 409 (five judges); *Nidhi Kaim* vs. *State of M.P.*—2017 (4) SCC 1 (bench of three judges).

69. The book is published by HarperCollins Publishers in the year 1994, when Hailsham was eighty-seven years old. He died at age of ninety-three.

70. Blackstone, William, 1765, "Introduction on the Study of Law," *Commentaries on the Laws of England*, Vol. I.

71. "Law as a Profession" (1886) 20, *American Law Review*, pp. 741-742.

72. "The Aims of Legal Education," Vol. 9, *Cambridge Law Journal* (1945-1947), p. 286 at 288.

73. 24 April 2021.

74. Much later, he became a judge of the High Court of Bombay and retired as chief justice of the High Court of Gujarat.

75. Olson, Walter, *Litigation Explosion*.

76. Written on 16 July 2022.

77. The dictionary meaning is: "to mention or introduce (a thing) with approbation or commendation (to a person), in order to induce acceptance or trial."

78. In a judgment of a bench of three judges dated 19 May 2022, in *Union of India* vs. *Mohit Minerals*, it was unanimously held that the recommendations of the GST Council are not binding either on the

union or on the states for the reasons therein given. The Union of India had pleaded that the recommendations by majority were binding, but the court disagreed. However, while exercising the rule-making power under the provisions of the Central General Sales Tax Act and the Integrated General Sales Tax Act, the governments (central and states) would be bound by the recommendations of the GST Council. But this binding principle does not mean that the legislative power of parliament or of state legislatures is bound.

79. As was held by the Kerala High Court in *Sheen Golden Jewels India Pvt. Ltd.* vs. *STO* (2019) in its judgment dated 11 January 2019.

80. Report of Select Committee on Constitution 122nd Amendment Bill, 2014, presented to Rajya Sabha on 22 July 2015.

81. The first chief justice of India, who prematurely passed away in office in November 1951, was succeeded by Justice Patanjali Sastri (CJI from November 1951 to January 1954).

82. Chief Justice of India from January 1954 to December 1954.

83. Justice B. K. Mukherjea was appointed Chief Justice of India on 23 December 1954, upon the retirement of his predecessor in office, Justice Mehr Chand Mahajan. But he (Mukherjea) may have been chief justice much longer if he had responded to Prime Minister Jawaharlal Nehru's call that he (Mukherjea) take on the office of CJI after the retirement at age sixty-five of the then-chief justice of India, Patanjali Sastri, in January 1954. Mukherjea (to his credit) had declined the offer of Prime Minister Nehru, since in order of seniority (as was the practice), it was Mehr Chand Mahajan's turn to be appointed CJI. When Nehru pressed him, Mukherjea said he would sooner resign than usurp the highest office before his turn! Mehr Chand Mahajan was then appointed CJI (on the retirement of Justice Patanjali Sastri) on 4 January 1954, and it was only after Mehr Chand Mahajan retired at age sixty-five in December 1954 that Justice B. K. Mukherjea assumed the office of CJI. He was a judge long before my time, but amongst the first judges of the Supreme Court. He was (in the reckoning of all whom I have spoken to), perhaps the greatest.

Section V: Arbitration

1. Written on 15 September 2017.

2. *Blue Bank International & Trusts (Barbados)* vs. *Bolivarian Republic of Venezuela.*

3. *Burlington Resources Inc.* vs. *Republic of Ecuador.*

4. *Caratube International Oil C LLP* vs. *Republic of Kazakhstan.*

5. *Fraport AG Frankfurt Airport Services Worldwide* vs. *Republic of Philippines* (ICSID Case No. ARB/03/25) Award dated 16 August 2007, para 402.

6. Due to the complex history of evolving meanings and contexts, there is no clear or agreed-upon definition of the Third World.

7. *New Statesman* and *Nation* (dated 15 July 1993).

8. Park, William, "Arbitration's Discontent: Of Elephants and Pornography," published in *Arbitration International*, Vol. 17 (3) 2001, p. 265.

9. Written on 1 September 2018.

10. Mueller, Sam and Mujs, Wim (Eds.), "The Flame Rekindled" in *New Hopes for International Arbitration*, Netherlands: Martinus Nijhoff, 1994, p. 134.

11. Due to the complex history of evolving meanings and contexts, there is no clear or agreed-upon definition of the Third World. The French anthropologist Sauvy, in an article in a French magazine in August 1952, coined the term "Third World" referring to countries that were not aligned with either the Communist Soviet bloc or the capitalist NATO bloc during the Cold War. Sauvy wrote: "This Third World, ignored, exploited, and despised like the third estate, also wants to be something." The term "Third World" is now used interchangeably with "least developed" as well as "developing countries."

12. Written on 5 December 2020.

13. Davis, Benjamin G., (Ed.), "Improving International Arbitration," Liber Amicorum Michel Gaudet, Paris: International Chamber of Commerce Publishing S.a., Paris, 1998.

14. See, for instance, the article by Marcel Fontaine: "Drafting the Award: A Perspective from a Civil Law Jurist" in the *ICC International Court of Arbitration Bulletin*, May 1994, Vol. 5, No. 1, pp. 30-37.

15. Cited in *Arbitration International*, Vol. 5, No. 2, 1989, pp. 102-136 on p. 105.

16. Concord and Conflict in International Arbitration in *Arbitration International*, Vol. 13, No. 2, pp. 121-123 (1997).

17. Lecture of Howard M. Holtzmann: "What an Arbitrator Can Do to Overcome Delays in Arbitration," reproduced in "Justice for a Generation" (1985), p. 336.

18. Pannick, David, *Judges*, UK: Oxford University Press, 1987.

19. China, Peru, Colombia, and Ukraine are the only four New York Convention countries that have prescribed legal qualifications for arbitrators.

20. Dr Robert Briner, chairman, ICC International Court of Arbitration, "Domestic Arbitration: Practice in Continental Europe and its Lessons for Arbitration in England" in *Arbitration International*, 1997, Vol. 13, No. 2, pp. 155-158 (based on the Bernstein Lecture 1996).

21. Sturgess, Garry, and Chubb, Philip, *Judging the World: Law and Politics in the World's Leading Courts,* New York: Butterworths, p. 269.

22. Written on 3 March 2022.

23. Section 30 reads as follows:

    1. It is not incompatible with an arbitration agreement for an arbitral tribunal to encourage settlement of the dispute and, with the agreement of the parties, the arbitral tribunal may use mediation, conciliation, or other procedures at any time during the arbitral proceedings to encourage settlement.

    2. If, during arbitral proceedings, the parties settle the dispute, the arbitral tribunal shall terminate the proceedings and, if requested by the parties and not objected to by the arbitral tribunal, record the settlement in the form of an arbitral award on agreed terms.

3. An arbitral award on agreed terms shall be made in accordance with Section 31 and shall state that it is an arbitral award.
4. An arbitral award on agreed terms shall have the same status and effect as any other arbitral award on the substance of the dispute.

24. See 1994 (1) WLR 14 (Cresswell J). See also 1994 1 WLR 1024.

25. See "The Theoretical Basis of Mediation and Other Forms of ADR: Why They Work" by Richard Hill, published in *Arbitration International*, Vol. 14, No. 2 (1998), p. 181.

26. As in Hong Kong and India.

27. *Reg.* vs. *Knuller (Publishing Printing and Promotions) Ltd.*, 1973 A.C. 435 at 463-464 (Lord Morris).

28. Article 19 provides that "The parties and the conciliator undertake that the conciliator will not act as an arbitrator or as a representative or counsel of a party in any arbitral or judicial proceedings in respect of a dispute that is the subject of the conciliation proceedings. The parties also undertake that they will not present the conciliator as a witness in any such proceedings."

29. Written on 28 August 2021.

30. Convention on the Settlement of Investment Disputes Between States and Nationals of Other States, International Centre for Settlement of Investment Disputes, Washington, 1965.

31. *Blue Bank International & Trusts (Barbados)* vs. *Bolivarian Republic of Venezuela* (*Blue Bank*), ICSID Case No. ARB/12/20, *Burlington Resources Inc.* vs. *Republic of Ecuador* (*Burlington*), ICSID Case No. ARB/08/5, and in *Caratube International Oil C. LLP* vs. *Republic of Kazakhstan* (*Caratube*), ICSID Case No. ARB/13/13.

32. Paragraph 42.3 in *Associate Builders* vs. *Delhi Development Authority*, 2015 (3) SCC 49, affirmed in *Ssangyong Engineering and . . .* vs. *National Highways Authority of India*, 2019 (15) SCC 131. In *Patel Engineering Ltd.* vs. *North Eastern Electric Power*, 2020 (7) SCC 167, the Supreme Court of India upheld an order of the high court which had correctly applied the test of patent illegality as laid down by the Supreme Court of India in the 2015 case of Associate Builders.

33. *Satyanaryana Construction Co.* vs. *Union of India,* 2011 (15) SCC 101 (under Section 34): The high court judgment reported in 2005 (2) *Arbitration Law Review* 496, modifying the award, was upheld by the Supreme Court. In *ONGC* vs. *Western Geco International,* 2014 (9) SCC 363, the award was modified by the Supreme Court itself.

34. Judgement dated 20 July 2021, in *Project Director National Highways* vs. *M. Hakeem*: 2021 (8) SCALE 391. It is also clear from a subsequent decision of 28 July 2021, *PSA SICAL Terminal Pvt. Ltd.* vs. *The Board of Trustees of V.O. Chidambranar Port Trust Tuticorin and Ors.*, 2021 (8) SCALE 579, that in an application under Section 34, the court is not expected to act as an appellate court or to reappreciate evidence, and no judicial interference on account of interfering with the merits of the award is permissible. But a finding based on no evidence at all or an award which ignores vital evidence in arriving at its decision could be described as perverse and therefore liable to be set aside.

35. Once during the Internal Emergency of 1975-1977, he delivered a series of lectures throughout India titled "The Law is (Always) Above You."

36. Sturgess, Garry, and Chubb, Philip, *Judging the World: Law and Politics in the World's Leading Courts*, New York: Butterworths, p. 269.

37. Very recently, UNCITRAL proposed a solution to reach a consensus on a list of non-arbitrable issues (A/CN.9/460 paragraph 33). This has been adopted by the German Arbitration Law, 1998 (Section 1030), as well as by the Tunisian Arbitration Code, 1993 (Article 7), reproduced on page 40 of Dr Peter Binder's 2019 publication of his 4th Edition of *International Commercial Arbitration and Mediation in UNCITRAL Model Law Jurisdictions*, published by Wolters Kluwer, Netherlands (the book was registered in the US Library of Congress only in the second half of 2019).

38. *A. Ayyasamy* vs. *A. Paramasivam & Others,* 2016(10) SCC 386, 403, 409 (fraud); *Abdul Kadir S. Bubere* vs. *Madhav Oak*—AIR 1962 SC 406; *N. Radhakrishnan* vs. *Maestro Engineer,* 2010 (1) SCC 72; *Narasimha Raju* vs. *Gurumurthy Raju*—AIR 1963 SC 607.

39. *Malka* vs. *Sardar*—AIR 1929 Lahore 394.

40. *Mahadeo Prasad* vs. *Biswanath Prasad*—ILR 30 Allahabad 137; *Sami Chetty* vs. *Adai Kalam Chetty*—AIR 1924 Madras 484.

41. *Ladha Singh* vs. *Bhag Singh*—34 IC 549.

42. *Mohamohini vs. Dayachand,* ILR 31 Cal. 357; *Khela* vs. *Chet Ra.* AIR 1952 Punjab 67; (Question of Genuineness of a Will, see *Charanjilal Shrilal* vs. *Jasjit Singh,* 1993 (2) SCC 507, paragraphs 18, 20, "Construction of a Will Can be Arbitrated").

43. See *Emaar MGF Land Limited* vs. *Aftab Singh*: a recent decision of a bench of two judges of the Supreme Court of India (10 December 2018) holding that the remedy provided by the Arbitration Act, 1996, is barred by implication. However, it was also clarified that where a person entitled to seek an additional special remedy provided by the statute (the Consumer Protection Act) does not opt for the additional special remedy and is a party to an arbitration agreement, there is no prohibition for disputes being proceeded with in arbitration.

44. In *Himangi Enterprises* vs. *Kamaljeet Singh Ahluwalia*, 2017 (10) SCC 706 (two judges), it was held that matters relating to tenancy or leave-and-licence agreements were not arbitrable (see also two earlier decisions: *Vishwanath Sood* vs. *Union of India*, 1989 (1) SCC 657, and *Prabartak Commercial Corpn.* vs. *Chief Administrator*, 1991 (1) SCC 498). The correctness of the decision in *Himangi Enterprises* (2017) has been questioned in a later case, reported in 2019 2 Arb. L.R. 121 (SC). In the last-mentioned case (*Vidya Drolia* vs. *Durga Trading Corporation* 2019), it has been stated that the decision of the bench of two judges in *Himangi Enterprises* that the mere fact that an exemption from the Rent Act is available cannot mean that the matter becomes non-arbitrable. *Vidya Drolia* was a case under the Transfer of Property Act, 1882, an act silent on arbitrability, and the court said that the judgment in *Himangi Enterprises* will "require a relook by a bench of three Hon'ble Judges of this Court."

45. *A. Ayyasamy* vs. *P. Paramasivam* 2016, (10) SCC 386, paras 17, 18, 22, 23, and 24. Also see *Ameetalchand* vs. *Rishabh Enterprises*, (2018) 15 SCC 678, but these decisions are contrary to the law declared earlier, e.g., the case of *World Sport Group Mauritius Ltd.*, AIR 2014 SC 968, p. 975.

46. *Oil and Natural Gas Corporation Ltd.* vs. *SAW Pipes Ltd.*, (2003) 5 SCC 705 (Sections 34[2][a][v] and 34[2][b]); *Security Printing and Minting Corporation of India Limited and Ors.* vs. *Gandhi Industrial Corporation*,

(2007) 13 SCC 236 (34[2][b][ii]); *ONGC Ltd.* vs. *Garware Shipping Corpn. Ltd.*, (2007) 13 SCC 434 (Section 34) (judgment does not refer to the particular clause of Section 34); *Delhi Development Authority* vs. *R. S. Sharma and Co., New Delhi*, (2008) 13 SCC 80 (Section 34[2]).

47. *Narayan Prasad Lohia* vs. *Nikunj Kumar Lohia and Ors.*, (2002) 3 SCC 572 (Section 34[2][a][v]); *Tata Hydro Electric Power Supply Co. Ltd. and Ors.* vs. *Union of India*, (2003) 4 SCC 172 (Section 34) (judgment does not refer to the particular clause of Section 34 while reversing the decision of the high court); *M. Anasuya Devi* vs. *M. Manik Reddy*, 2003 (8) SCC 565 (Section 34) (high court judgment set aside and case remitted to); *Hindustan Zinc Ltd.* vs. *Friends Coal Carbonisation*, (2006) 4 SCC 445 (Section 34[2][b]) (trial court judgment restored); *McDermott International Inc.* vs. *Burn Standard Co. Ltd.*, 2006 (11) SCC 181=2006 (2) Arb. LR 498; *Venture Global Engineering* vs. *Satyam Computer Services Ltd.*, 2008 (4) SCC 190 and 2010 (8) SCC 660 Section 341(2) (International Commercial Award [London]). The Supreme Court set aside the high court and the trial court orders and remitted award for reconsideration; *Bharat Drilling and Foundation Treatment Pvt. Ltd.* vs. *State of Jharkhand*, 2009 (16) SCC 705 (Section 34[2]); *State of Goa* vs. *Praveen Enterprises*, AIR 2011 SC 3814) (Section 34: Judgment does not refer to the particular clause of Section 34 part of the award which had been set aside by the high court, was upheld by the Supreme Court; *J. G. Engineers Pvt. Ltd.* vs. *Union of India (UOI) and Ors.*, 2011 (5) SCC 758=AIR 2011 SC 2477) (Sections 34[2][a][iv] and 34[2][b][ii]); *Leela Hotels Ltd.* vs. *Housing and Urban Development Corporation Ltd.*, AIR 2012 SC 903 (Section 34) (judgment does not refer to the particular clause of Section 34); *Associate Builders* vs. *Delhi Development Authority* (2015) 3 SCC 49 (Section 32[2][b][ii] and 34[2][a][iii]; *Sri Chittaranjan Maity* vs. *Union of India*, AIR 2017 SC 4588; appeal partly allowed (Sections 11[6], 34, and 31) (the Supreme Court of India partially allowed the appeal to the extent of the interest being made payable); *Sutlej Construction Limited* vs. *Union Territory of Chandigarh*, 2018 1 SCC 718 (Section 34); *Ssangyong Engineering and Construction Co. Ltd.* vs. *National Highways Authority of India* (*NHAI*) (2019 SCC Online SC 677) 2019 (8) Scale 41 (Section 34[2][a][i][iv]) (majority award, which was also upheld by the high court, was set aside, and minority award was directed by the Supreme Court as the award to be executed; *Parsa Kente Collieries Ltd.* vs. *Rajasthan Rajya Vidyut Utpadan Nigam Ltd.*, 2019 (8) Scale 434 (Sections 34(2) and 37).

48. *Olympus Superstructures Pvt. Ltd.* vs. *Meena Vijay Khetan and Ors.*, (1999) 5 SCC 651 (Section 34[2][b][i]); *Satyanarayana Construction Co.* vs. *Union of India* (2011) 15 SCC 101 (Section 34) (the high court judgment, reported in 2005 [2] Arb. LR 496 modifying the award and the same was upheld by the Supreme Court); *Shipping Corporation of India Ltd.* vs. *Mare Shipping Inc.* AIR 2011 SC 2608 (Section 34); *P. R. Shah, Shares, and Stockbroker (P) Ltd.* vs. *B. H. H. Securities (P) Ltd. and Ors.* AIR 2012 SC 1866 (Section 34); *ONGC* vs. *Western Geco International* 2014 (9) SCC 363 (Section 34[2][b][ii]); *Navodaya Mass Entertainment Ltd.* vs. *J. M. Combines* (2015) 5 SCC 698 (Section 34); *Swan Gold Mining Ltd.* vs. *Hindustan Copper Ltd.* (2015) 5 SCC 739—(Section 34[2][b][ii]); *State of Orissa* vs. *Samantary Construction* 2015 SCC Online SC 856 (Section 34[2][b][ii]) (upheld partially by the Supreme Court to the extent of the amount of the award) 2007 (2) Arb. LR 309 (Orissa); *State of West Bengal* vs. *Associated Contractors* AIR 2015 SC 260 (Section 34); *Harsha Constructions* vs. *Union of India* AIR 2015 SC 270—Section 34(2)(a)(iv) (the Supreme Court partially upheld the award); *National Highways Authority of India* vs. *JSC Centrodorstroy* (2016) 12 SCC 592 (Section 34); *Union of India* vs. *Susaka Pvt. Ltd. And Ors.* AIR 2017 SC 5721. (Section 34 and 31[7][a] and [b]; *Maharashtra State Electricity Distribution Company Ltd.* Vs. *Datar Switchgear Limited and Ors.* AIR 2018 SC 529 (Section 34[2][a][iv]; *MMTC Ltd.* vs. *Vedanta Ltd.* AIR 2019 SC 1168 (Sections 34[b][2][ii] and 37).

49. Written on 6 February 2021.

50. Dissenting opinion of Judge Weeramantry of Sri Lanka.

ALSO AVAILABLE

In this captivating volume, Fali S. Nariman invites readers into the fascinating world of law, life, and everything in between. With a masterful blend of wit, wisdom, and keen insight, he paints a vivid portrait of the legal craft, interwoven with pivotal moments and memorable milestones from the legal fraternity.

The first part of the book presents a collection of vignettes and anecdotes on the judiciary, arbitration, and the practice of law, alongside Nariman's personal reflections that illuminate the spirit of the legal profession. It also offers glimpses of the towering figures he encountered throughout his distinguished career and the enduring lessons drawn from decades of legal experience.

The second part brims with sharp and profound ruminations on a wide range of themes—from federalism, democracy, and human rights to freedom of the press, corruption, and corporate governance—highlighting the dynamic interplay between life and law. For anyone intrigued by the law's rich tapestry, this book offers both inspiration and timeless wisdom from one of India's most celebrated legal minds.

'The gateways to wisdom and knowledge are always open.'

Louise Hay